The Development of the English
School System

Studies in Teaching and Learning
General Editor
Denis Lawton, B.A., Ph.D.
Professor of Education and Director,
University of London Institute of Education

In the series:

The Development and Structure of the English School System

Keith Evans

HODDER AND STOUGHTON
LONDON SYDNEY AUCKLAND TORONTO

British Library Cataloguing in Publication Data
Evan, Keith
   The development and structure of the English school system.——
   (Studies in teaching and learning)
   1. Schools——England——History——19th century
   2. Schools——England——History——20th century
   I. Title   II. Series
   371'.00942   LA631

ISBN 0 340 35905 6

First published 1985

Printed and bound in Great Britain for
Hodder and Stoughton Educational,
a division of Hodder and Stoughton Ltd,
Mill Road, Dunton Green, Sevenoaks, Kent,
by Page Bros (Norwich) Ltd, Norwich, Norfolk.

Typeset in 10 on 11 pt Plantin (Compugraphic)
by Colset Pte. Ltd., Singapore

Contents

Studies in Teaching and Learning

The purpose of this series of short books on education is to make available readable, up-to-date views on educational issues and controversies. Its aim will be to provide teachers and students (and perhaps parents and governors) with a series of books which will introduce those educational topics which any intelligent and professional educationist ought to be familiar with. One of the criticisms levelled against 'teacher-education' is that there is so little agreement about what ground should be covered in courses at various levels; one assumption behind this series of texts is that there is a common core of knowledge and skills that all teachers need to be aware of, and the series is designed to map out this territory.

Although the major intention of the series is to provide general coverage, each volume will consist of more than a review of the relevant literature; the individual authors will be encouraged to give their own personal interpretation of the field and the way it is developing.

Preface

This book has grown out of its more wide-ranging Unibook forbear on *The Development and Structure of the English Educational System* (1975). But to economise on space and to provide a more functional focus for teacher training students, the present work concentrates on the development and structure of the statutory system of schooling in England and Wales. The chronological canvas embraces the nineteenth and twentieth centuries, but the post-war years are given extra weighting, and a special effort is made to deal with the last decade. Throughout, educational development is considered within the wider societal context, and the opening chapter provides a thematic analysis of those factors which bear most closely upon it. The rest of the book then spans the development of statutory school provision from its mid-nineteenth-century beginnings to present-day practice and policies. Elementary and primary, secondary and special education, associated welfare services, schools' curricula and examinations, teacher training and the administrative structure all receive appropriate attention. Additionally, there is a final postscript on the current scene and some future prospects, a useful appendix giving a list of Education Ministers and their governments since 1856 and a select bibliography to provide further reading.

Whilst the book lays no claim to quality of literary style or original scholarship, it does presume to provide students with a more summary and systematic presentation of the relevant material than is commonly found available in other texts. The substance of each chapter is clearly divided into a number of major parts, with each part designated by a main heading. A quick look at these main headings affords a ready appreciation of the basic aspects which compose the whole of the topic concerned. In like fashion each major part is sub-divided into subsidiary sections and other constituent elements; this allows the chronological sequence of events and developments, the legislative provisions of various Acts, the recommendations and results of official reports, the analyses of underlying influences and determinant factors, the structural or institutional components of a given framework and other such matters to be presented in a summary and systematic manner which can be easily understood. Yet considerable trouble has been taken to ensure that this form of presentation (with its peculiar advantages) does not exact too high a price in terms of sheer readability. I hope I have succeeded in this respect.

Finally, may I express my gratitude to those who have helped me to produce this work. Professor Lawton contributed to its conception and welcomed it to his series. Mr G.F. Crump, the Director of Education for the County of Avon, kindly gave me the benefit of his expert comments on the first draft of Chapter 11 on 'The Present Structure of the English Educational System'. My thanks are also due to my wife for help with the typing and other clerical chores. And throughout the long haul leading to final publication Mrs Diana Simons of Hodder and Stoughton has been a continuing source of efficient editorial support. Whilst acknowledging the generous help obtained from these various quarters, I must, however, emphasise that any shortcomings the book may have are my sole responsibility.

Bolton, Lancashire   KEITH EVANS
1984

Note on Acronyms

To save space a number of acronyms have been used on a routine basis. Some are instantly recognisable and all are well-established in current educational usage. The complete list is as follows:

ATO	Area Training Organisation
APU	Assessment of Performance Unit
AMMA	Assistant Masters and Mistresses Association
AEC	Association of Education Committees
CEE	Certificate of Extended Education
CPVE	Certificate of Pre-Vocational Education
CSE	Certificate of Secondary Education
CNAA	Council for National Academic Awards
CLEA	Council of Local Education Authorities
DES	Department of Education and Science
GCE	General Certificate of Education
GCSE	General Certificate of Secondary Education
LEA	Local Education Authority
MSC	Manpower Services Commission
NAS/UWT	National Association of Schoolmasters/Union of Women Teachers
NUT	National Union of Teachers
TVEI	Technical and Vocational Education Initiative
UDE	University Department of Education
YTS	Youth Training Scheme

1 The Context of English Educational Development

The foundations for and the core of any modern educational system consist in the provision of formal schooling for the child and adolescent. The growth of such provision and educational development in the widest sense do not take place in a vacuum; they occur within, and are part of, the whole context of the parent society. Thus the nature of an educational system varies according to time and place. The aims, the extent, the organisation, the curricula and the methodology of education will reflect the existing institutions and the dominant attitudes, values and forces which characterise a particular society. In this sense the history of English education since 1800 is not simply the superficial story of expanding and changing provision in various fields and at different levels; it also involves an understanding of nineteenth- and twentieth-century English society, especially in terms of the forces working within it that help to explain the developments and problems which emerged in the field of education. In other words, the development of the English educational system and its schools cannot properly be understood unless it is seen in societal perspective and related to the overall context of the time. To facilitate clearer examination, this complex context may be somewhat arbitrarily divided into various dimensions.

1 Demographic

Variations in the growth and distribution of population have exerted a considerable influence upon the educational scene since the late eighteenth century.

(a) Nineteenth Century

This was a period of unprecedented growth during which the population of England and Wales rose from nine to thirty-three millions. The associated process of urbanisation ensured that this growth was concentrated in the towns; for example, the combined populations of Birmingham, Liverpool, Manchester, Leeds and Sheffield expanded nine-fold during the nineteenth century. At times, especially the 1840s, substantial Irish immigration increased the pressures. The sheer size of the younger generation ultimately broke the monopoly of voluntary provision in elementary schooling and necessitated the direct intervention of the State. Once the Factory Acts began to take real effect, the growing number of children on the streets produced an urban social problem which helps to explain the 1870 Elementary Education Act and the subsequent drive for compulsory attendance.

(b) Inter-War Years

This was a period during which the birth-rate fell to its lowest level in British history, with the possibility of a stagnant or declining population emerging. This was associated with a critical sex imbalance amongst those of marriageable age, resultant of the heavy loss of male lives on the Western front during the First World War. The new demographic context relieved the previous pressure on school places and made available the life-long services of a very large group of dedicated spinster teachers. Although the educational system encountered other serious difficulties during the inter-war period, it was never faced with a shortage of teachers. Indeed, in these years, for a female teacher to announce her forthcoming marriage was tantamount to handing in her resignation; at a time when there was often the threat of unemployment within the profession, this was a policy which it was felt could be afforded and justified.

(c) Post-War Period 1945–70

This period provided a difficult demographic context for educational advance. Already required to raise the school leaving age (to fifteen years) and to provide secondary education for all, the authorities were suddenly faced with a significantly higher birth-rate, featured by an immediate post-war 'bulge' and a sustained rise 1955–64. This situation was exacerbated by the growing influx of Commonwealth immigrants and by an acceleration in the geographical redistribution of population. Meanwhile the correction of the former sex imbalance, the move towards earlier marriage and the consequent high wastage rate among young female teachers, produced an acute shortage of teachers which was only slowly overcome. The 1944 Education Act's provision for the further raising of the school leaving age to sixteen years was progressively put off, and its county college scheme to establish compulsory part-time continuative education for the 15–18 age group was shelved indefinitely.

(d) Recent Years

The mid-1960s heralded a radical change in the demographic context. During the period 1964–77 there was a continuous and cumulative fall of 35 per cent in annual live births in England and Wales. After 1977 the total school population became subject to serious contraction and by the 1980s the problem of falling rolls was resulting in the closure and reorganisation of schools, staff redeployment, the limitation of teacher employment and promotion opportunities, early retirement and redundancy. Inevitably, it was the system of teacher training which suffered most; from 1975 savage cutbacks were combined with major reorganisation to meet the new situation. Although the birth-rate took an upward turn 1977–80, this has not been sustained and underlines the difficulties involved in predicting future educational needs.

2 Economic

Educational development and economic matters have come to have an increasingly close relationship because any modern system of education both provides for the needs of the economy and inflicts a heavy charge upon it.

(a) Needs of the Economy

One of the major functions of the educational system is to subserve the basic manpower needs of society. This function emerged with the Industrial Revolution and became increasingly important as the economy became more advanced and sophisticated. The present need is for a highly skilled and differentiated labour force, able to promote and capitalise upon scientific and technological advance for the economic benefit of the nation. Thus the demands made by the economy and its developing occupational structure upon the educational system have changed with time.

(i) Mid-Nineteenth Century

The need for a disciplined labour force for the factory system and a growing pool of skilled artisans and clerks partly explains the developing interest of employers in elementary education as a means of instilling obedience and minimal learning into the younger generation of the working class.

(ii) *1880–1939*

The increasing concern over the provision of technical and secondary education was partly attributable to economic influences. The challenge to Britain's industrial supremacy and the beginnings of her comparative decline in the last quarter of the nineteenth century provoked a new sense of urgency in the field of technical education. The rise of new scientifically-based industries, the growth of the welfare state and its attendant bureaucracy, and the increasing importance of tertiary (especially professional) occupations in the early twentieth century combined to encourage the expansion of secondary grammar and higher education.

(iii) *Post-War Era*

The need for a much more highly skilled and finely differentiated labour force (rather than an 'elite' plus the 'mass') has supported the drive for comprehensive secondary education and the remarkable expansion of further and higher education since 1945. In the 1960s it became widely accepted that economic strength depended upon avoiding the previous wastage of talent associated with the inadequacy and inequality of educational opportunity. The vastly increased post-war expenditure on education was justified by its being a long-term investment in human resources which the country could not afford to neglect. But from the early 1970s this simple confidence evaporated as the educational system's accountability and supposed contribution to the country's economic well-being was seriously questioned. Against the background of a depressed economy and a growing pool of unemployed school-leavers, it is significant that, since 1977, the role of providing ordinary teenagers with the experience and training relevant to economic needs has been increasingly assumed by the Manpower Services Commission (MSC), a non-educational agency operating under the Department of Employment.

(b) Cost to the Economy

For educational development the price of growing dependence upon public funds has been increased vulnerability to economic vicissitudes and to the constraint of what the nation is able and prepared to afford. Thus the state of the economy and the priority enjoyed by education at any particular time have had a direct bearing on the nature and extent of educational development.

(i) Late-Nineteenth Century

The official commitment to economic retrenchment following the Crimean War helps to explain the introduction of the stringent 'payment by results' for grant-aided elementary schools, whilst the dual system of voluntary and State provision introduced by the 1870 Elementary Education Act was partially justified by W.E. Forster in terms of 'sparing public money'. Not until 1891 was the principle of free elementary schooling finally accepted. Meanwhile the reluctance and failure to embark upon the development of a national system of secondary education is also partly explained by the widespread opposition to the cost of doing so; indeed, when the venture was at last undertaken after the turn of the century a substantial part of the cost was to be defrayed by parental fees, an arrangement which continued to operate until 1944.

(ii) Inter-War Years

This period provides a classic instance of educational development being at the mercy of changes in national economic fortunes. The unprecedented enthusiasm and high hopes for education which found expression in Fisher's 1918 Education Act foundered on the rocks of Britain's serious economic difficulties. The post-war slump and later the world economic depression constrained successive governments to curtail national expenditure, and educational development was singled out on two occasions for particularly rough treatment. The Geddes Committee (1922) recommended that educational spending be cut by one-third and the May Committee (1931) was no less severe. The projected day-continuation schools, the free-place system for secondary grammar education, the new percentage grant arrangements devised by Fisher to encourage more generous provision, and teachers' salaries and superannuation were all, in one way or another, victims of the economic backlash. The Hadow reorganisation process, which pointed forward to secondary education for all and was launched upon in 1928, inevitably made very slow headway in the face of a serious lack of funds.

(iii) Post-War Era

The remarkable rise in public expenditure on education after the Second World War was a reflection of the much higher priority accorded to it by governments and the community at large. For the first time educational development became a major burden on the economy. At the end of the 1960s education surpassed defence as the largest single item of public expenditure. The point had been reached where further significant educational advance, if not based on an improved economic growth rate, could only be made at the expense of other social services or the already overburdened tax-payer. By this time the various sectors of education were in sharp competition for funds (e.g. 'priority for primaries' policy) and there was the danger of administrative cost-effectiveness rather than educational considerations determining development (e.g. in respect of decisions for or against open-plan schools and between various patterns of comprehensive reorganisation).

But it was not until after 1975 that education really began to suffer, largely as a consequence of its loss of political priority and the onset of economic depression. From that date educational expenditure began to fall in real terms and as a proportion of total public spending. Although falling rolls have helped to offset such spending cuts, the educational system has not faced comparable financial stringencies since the 1930s. A sign of the times is the interest of educational publishers in the sale of school books direct to parents and their acute concern over the illicit duplication of copyright material for teaching purposes.

3 Scientific and Technological

The industrialisation and urbanisation of Britain involved an ever-increasing dependence upon scientific and technological developments, to the extent that they came to underpin and impinge upon our very way of life. Yet traditionally English education had neglected these fields of study and consequently pressures were brought to bear upon it.

(a) Late-Nineteenth Century

The 'scientific movement', pioneered and led by Prince Albert, Lyon Play-fair, Bernard Samuelson, Herbert Spencer and Thomas Huxley, challenged the prevailing neglect of scientific and technical studies and helped to produce the higher-grade elementary schools, the organised science schools, the early technical colleges and the new civic universities. The foundation and development of the Department of Science and Art for the official encouragement of scientific and technical instruction of utility to industry and commerce was a foremost expression of the movement's influence. The gradual widening of the elementary curriculum and the limited concessions made to the study of the natural sciences in the grammar schools and the ancient universities may also be ascribed to its existence.

(b) Post-War Era

Following the Second World War the 'technological movement', punctuated by the Percy (1945) and Robbins (1963) Reports, emphasised the need for the educational system to produce more scientists, technologists and technicians if the country's industrial future was to be safeguarded. Whilst giving some encouragement to the development of secondary technical schools, the main result was that technical and technological education at the further and higher levels became the most impressive single growth area in English education during the period 1955–72. Additionally the Industrial Training Act (1964) provided a framework within which individual industries, in co-operation with local education authorities (LEAs), developed schemes for the training of apprentices and other young people.

But the momentum was not sustained. The secondary technical schools, never large in number, began to disappear in the 1960s. Spending cuts ultimately hit technical education and even the technological universities. In 1982 most of the Industrial Training Boards (accused of waste and ineffectiveness) were wound up.

Certain new initiatives have been forthcoming from the MSC. The Youth Training Scheme (1983) is to provide a year's work experience, training and related education for a large proportion of sixteen to seventeen-year-old school leavers; it is part of a long-term plan to modernise the training system as well as a means of responding to youth unemployment. And, impressed by Continental example, the government has directed the MSC to mastermind a pilot (potentially national) scheme to develop technical and vocational courses for students aged fourteen to eighteen in full-time education.

Although the needs of science, technology and industry have been pressed upon the English educational system from various quarters for well over a century, the unfortunate fact is that such pressure has generally met with a reluctant and tardy response. The root cause has been, and still is, the entrenched position of the 'liberal' (previously 'classical') tradition in English education. This tradition elevates academic learning and devalues technical, vocational and practical studies. At the senior elementary level it helped to postpone the introduction of practical subjects until the 1890s and subsequently to stifle the growth of vocational courses. At the secondary level it dominated the independent schools and did much to shape the curriculum of the State grammar schools after 1902. It placed the stamp of inferiority on the junior technical schools of the inter-war period and upon the secondary technical schools of the post-war era. Its commitment to the prior claims of a 'general' education condemned the secondary modern schools to a diluted version of the grammar curriculum and to an unsuccessful quest for a distinctive role. Even in the comprehensive secondary schools technical and vocational studies enjoy only limited scope and low prestige. At university level the 'liberal' tradition has always favoured scholarship rather than functional learning, pure science rather than applied, humanistic studies rather than technology and engineering. Even the polytechnics, dating from 1966, have been partly seduced by its influence. Finally, most of the teachers and senior staff working in our schools and other educational institutions are themselves the products of this long-istablished tradition. It is hard to break the vicious circoe and so the educationsl system's capacity to subserve the needs of the economy rimains rather weak.

4   Social

The technological and economic transformation of the country during this period had important social connotations which bore upon educational development.

(a)   Class Stratification

The triumph of industrial capitalism resulted in the crystallisation of deep-rooted class divisions and the pyramid-like stratification of Victorian society:

   (i)   the working class or proletariat (with its own 'elite' of skilled artisans);
  (ii) the middle class or bourgeoisie (with its various sub-divisions);
 (iii) the upper class of landowners and gentry (a declining minority slowly fusing with the wealthier middle class).

The development of education in nineteenth-century England was very closely tied to this class structure. Elementary schooling, narrowly conceived and self-contained, was all that working class children could hope to receive. Secondary and higher education were the preserve of the well-to-do, with the very wealthy looking to the public schools and the universities and the comfortably off to the endowed grammar schools and private secondary institutions. Thus there developed two parallel and mutually exclusive systems of education to mirror the class-conscious nature of Victorian society. Within this rigid framework even the benefits of an elementary education were seriously curbed by the social factor. After 1870, when universal elementary provision finally became a reality, School Boards operating in poor working class areas (e.g. London's East End) found that the need to socialise and succour their deprived charges supervened upon their responsibility to educate them. The result was a long, determined effort to secure regular attendance and the pioneering of embryonic welfare services for such pupils towards the close of the century.

It was the need to open 'other than elementary' education to outstanding talent irrespective of social class background which gradually changed the situation. During the twentieth century the basis of social class stratification has become less plutocratic and more meritocratic, with the educational system becoming a major vehicle for upward social mobility. This process has its meagre beginnings in the 1880s and 1890s with the short-lived appearance of the higher-grade elementary schools which provided improved opportunities for a small number of working class pupils. In the period 1902–44 the process was mainly associated with the development of the educational ladder linking the elementary schools to the growing system of State grammar schools. But the benefits which accrued to able working class children were strictly limited. Even by the late 1930s only half of the State grammar school places were available to scholarship winners – with the rest still dependent upon fee-paying. Material poverty in the Edwardian and inter-war periods ensured that the parents of many able working class pupils refused a scholarship place when it was offered. And increasing lower-middle class competition for such places made matters worse.

After 1944 the process gathered momentum and was closely associated with the provision of secondary education for all, the abolition of the State grammar fee-paying places and the widening of opportunities to enter further and higher education. For more than twenty years, however, the selective system operated as a serious barrier to educational opportunity; there was a high correlation between eleven-plus examination success and children's social class. The continued dominance of the State grammar entry by middle class pupils did much to set the stage for the comprehensive reorganisation of secondary education from the mid-1960s. The raising of the school-leaving age to sixteen in 1972 was also justified in terms of improving the educational prospects of the working class child. But, over a decade later, the social factor remains the most important differentiating influence upon the student's capacity to stay in and benefit from the educational system. In terms of GCE 'O' level entry and performance, sixteen-plus participation, 'A' level entry and performance and, finally, entry into higher education, the lower the student's socio-economic grouping the less likely he is to 'succeed'. At one end of the scale (socio-economic Group 1) the child is likely to receive a private schooling and a university education; at the other end (socio-economic Group 5) the child from a deprived working class background is likely to leave school at sixteen without any educational qualifications and become one of the young unemployed. The social factor also finds expression in regional terms. Whilst the South East and the Home Counties, with their relatively higher proportion of managerial and professional parents, score best on all the aforementioned counts, the North East and the West Midlands, with their more marked industrial and working class character, do significantly less well.

Although the advance of the welfare state, especially since 1945, has done much to overcome the sort of material deprivation once suffered by many working class children, there is still a residual problem of serious social and educational disadvantage occurring on a significant scale. The Child Poverty Action Group, established in 1965, has shown that within our welfare state well over a million children live in poverty or close to it. The Plowden Report (1967) highlighted the situation in many inner city areas where increasingly adverse social and environmental factors gave rise to crippling educational disadvantage – and recommended a policy of 'positive discrimination', starting with pre-school provision, to meet the problem. The worst affected, and hence those in most need of such compensatory education, have been children of single, coloured and unemployed parents. By the 1970s, with the marked rise in the post-war divorce rate, one-parent families accounted for one-tenth of those with children. Ever since 1945 the children of coloured parents have constituted a growing minority of the school population, especially in certain towns and cities. And latterly the proportion of pupils with unemployed parents has grown substantially. Whilst their predicament has aroused much sympathy and fulsome enquiry, there has been a marked reluctance to provide the resources to make the post-Plowden 'educational priority area' policy (even in the crucial field of pre-school provision) an effective instrument for the diminution of disadvantage. The initially hopeful response from central and local government gave way during the 1970s to a sustained decline of real concern. Recent symbols of this retreat are the 1980 Education Act's affirmation that the provision of nursery education is not a statutory requirement and, in the same year, the closure of the short-lived Centre for Information and Advice on Educational Disadvantage. Meanwhile, as cuts in educational spending bite deeper and the tendency to accept parental financial help grows, it is the schools in which disadvantaged children are concentrated which inevitably suffer most. And in the longer term, given the conviction in certain quarters that compensatory educational policies will produce only limited effect at great expense, it seems that there will be little real progress along this particular road in the forseeable future.

(b)   Working Class Movements

The unenviable plight of the proletariat within Victorian society naturally gave rise to such developments as the co-operative movement, the trade union movement and the Labour movement, all dedicated to improving the lot of the workers. These movements took a growing interest in education as one of the essential means of securing a better deal for the working class, pressing for State intervention and provision on a broadening and increasingly generous front. At the close of the nineteenth century the influence of the Trades Union Congress was exemplified in the introduction of free elementary education and the first demands for secondary education for all. Thereafter, and especially following the Second World War, the organised working class movement exercised a steadily growing influence upon educational policy and development at both and central and local levels. This whole process was facilitated by political and religious changes and by a transformation of public attitudes which combined to produce a context increasingly favourable – until very recently – to collectivist designs and the advance of the welfare state.

(c) Emancipation of Women

This important social process was both a cause and an effect of educational change. In the nineteenth century girls and boys from working class homes were equally restricted to a limited elementary schooling, although the growth of the elementary schoolteaching occupation afforded an outstanding means of advancement for a minority of able working class females. Meanwhile girls from more well-to-do families were denied the educational opportunities available to their male counterparts until the advent of proper girls' secondary schools and the beginnings of university access later in the century. In the first half of the twentieth century the improving position of women in society was reflected in girls' equal opportunity of access to the State grammar schools and some improvement in the proportion of university places taken by female undergraduates. But able girls issuing from the grammar Sixth Forms tended to move on to teacher training college rather than university. With schoolteaching still the main avenue to professional status for females the National Union of Women Teachers 1909–60 fought a long and finally successful campaign for equal pay. Except in the field of further education and training, the post-war era has seen a further marked improvement in educational provision and opportunity for females. By 1980 girls accounted for just over 50 per cent of 'O' level and about 43 per cent of 'A' level passes; and some 40 per cent of university undergraduates were female. Throughout the last century the gradual strengthening of the female position in the qualification stakes has done much to assist the general progress of women's emancipation.

5 Political

The field of education was markedly affected by the radical changes taking place in this critical context during the period concerned.

(a) Rise of Democracy

Within a century the parliamentary system was gradually transformed so that by 1930 true political democracy had been achieved in terms of 'one adult, one vote' and the supremacy of the elected House of Commons. Before the first Reform Act (1832) the landed oligarchy monopolised political power, whilst in the mid-nineteenth century they shared it with the rising manufacturing and commercial middle class. Not until after the second Reform Act (1867) did the working class begin to receive the vote and a share of political power, although it was to take many years before this class could properly organise and capitalise upon its superiority of numbers. But the gradual change, completed after the First World War by the enfranchisement of women, was in the long-term full of consequences for education, especially as it provided the seed-bed for the emergence of the modern Labour party.

This period also witnessed the advent of an effective local democracy. Although the Municipal Corporations Act (1835) produced some measure of improvement in the towns, it was not until later in the century that major advances were made in this field. From 1870 the elected School Boards provided an important vehicle for the extension of local democracy, but they added to the growing confusion of *ad hoc* bodies operating at that level. In fact it was the local government enactments of 1888–94, introducing the new county, county borough, municipal borough and urban district councils, that provided the great step forward. Elected by the ratepayers, these multi-purpose bodies attracted a wide range of responsibilities and soon became involved with education at the local level. In the twentieth century this modern framework (which lasted until 1974) provided the means by which party political influence and the expertise of appointed officers were brought to bear upon local educational concerns.

(b) Influence of Political Parties

Here one must distinguish between the three major political parties and their attitudes towards and influence upon educational development.

(i) *Tory or Conservative Party*

In the nineteenth century this party tended to display less interest in education and more opposition to State intervention than its Liberal counterpart. It supported voluntary provision and denominational schools, being tied to the Anglican cause in elementary education and to the independence of the public and endowed grammar schools in secondary education. Nevertheless, the Conservatives were responsible for the epoch-making Balfour Act (1902), which laid the foundations of a national system of State education. During the twentieth century the party has tended to maintain a fairly 'conservative' position in relation to changes in secondary schooling and the widening of higher educational opportunity. In the inter-war period the party's dominance was effectively used to limit the expansive intent of the 1918 Education Act and to stifle and distort the movement towards secondary education for all. In the post-war era its support of the selective against the comprehensive approach to secondary education, of the maintenance of the private sector and of the university as the 'model' higher educational institution all symbolised an elitist outlook on education. Conservative policy since 1979 – including unprecedented cut-backs in post-war educational spending, the abolition of the Schools Council and the 'assisted places scheme' for helping independent schools – has led some commentators to question the party's commitment to the State system of education. Yet the far-reaching 1944 Education Act, which established secondary education for all and abolished fee-paying places in the State grammar schools, was the work of a war-time coalition government led and dominated by the Conservative party. And the greatest concern over the erosion of traditional objectives and standards in education has usually emanated from this political quarter. In recent years this sort of Conservative interest has been stretched to bear more directly upon such matters as the school curriculum, public examinations, teacher competence and the quality of teacher training.

(ii) *Whig or Liberal Party*

In the nineteenth century it was this party which showed most interest in education (e.g. 1833 parliamentary grant, 1870 Elementary Education Act), with its Radical left leading the way in terms of pressing for State intervention and provision. In the actual field the party tended to be tied to the Nonconformist and secularist causes in elementary education, being the main support for the School Boards and undenominational religious instruction. Conversely the Liberal party was unsympathetically disposed towards the Anglican and Roman Catholic denominational schools, especially in respect of giving them increased financial support from public funds. This party was the major progressive influence in the Edwardian era, laying the foundations of the welfare state (e.g. 1908 Old Age Pensions Act, 1911 National Insurance Act) and broadening the approach to education (e.g. school meals, school medical service, free-place system) in the years before the First World War. The Liberals were also mainly responsible for the 1918 Fisher Act, which, although ill-fated, was not without significance in the process of educational advance. Rather unhappily, the party's rapid decline in the inter-war period (to only seventeen seats in the Commons by 1935!) then robbed it of further major influence on educational develop-ment. However, Liberal support for comprehensive secondary organisation and the widening of higher educational opportunities has aided the Labour party since the 1960s. Conversely, the Liberal party's traditional concern for personal liberty and consequent refusal to support any serious action against the post-war independent schools has been welcomed by the Conser-vatives. Whether the current Alliance partnership with the new Social Democratic Party will provide an effective vehicle for the resurgence of Liberal political and educational influence remains to be seen.

(iii) *Labour Party*

Arising out of the trade union movement and various socialist intellectual groups (e.g. the Fabians), this party was not established until 1900. In its early days the growing Labour party was content to wield influence through Liberal governments, but after 1918 it emerged as an independent force in British politics. Disillusioned by the Fisher Education Act, it officially embraced secondary education for all as part of its political programme (1922), briefed the Hadow Committee to investigate provision for senior ele-mentary pupils, attempted to raise the school-leaving age (1930), supported multilateral schools as an alternative to tripartite secondary organisation and campaigned for the abolition of the private sector. After 1944 the Labour party clearly emerged as the main source of support for the populist concep-tion of education, condemning the eleven-plus examination and the asso-ciated selective pattern of secondary schooling and promoting the rapid expansion of further and higher education in the public sector. Thus, from the mid-1960s, the advance of comprehensive reorganisation and the rise of the new polytechnics owed much to its influence. Typically, the Open Uni-versity (1969) was very much a Labour party initiative. And, for much of the post-war period the Labour party gave its uncritical support to the profes-sional autonomy of teachers in respect of the school curriculum and teaching methods, even where progressive change gave rise to the suspicion of a lowering of standards. However, since 1976 the party has pressed the case for teachers' accountability, arguing that such important matters should be subject to public consensus and some sort of a nationally agreed framework.

Meanwhile its interest in secondary examination reform (especially the idea of a common sixteen-plus arrangement), dating from the late 1960s, and in the provision of a new 'tertiary' deal for the education and training of the 16–19 age group continues. Finally, having got rid of most of the State grammar schools and all the direct-grant grammar schools, the Labour party is now fully committed to abolishing the private sector.

6 Religious

The nature and strength of this influence on English education changed greatly during this period. In the nineteenth century elementary education was dominated by church interests which did so much to provide, maintain and control the schools involved. And, until the 1890s, they monopolised the provision of teacher training through their denominational colleges. Many of the nineteenth-century secondary schools, especially those that were endowed, also had continuing or historic connections with the churches. It was only slowly and reluctantly that they accepted the developing role of the State in the elementary field. Yet it is clear that nineteenth-century religion in England was a middle and upper class concern; the 1851 census reveals a very low church attendance on the part of the urban proletariat which was already religiously apathetic. Thus the religious struggle in English elementary education was fought over the heads of working class parents, though it was a struggle to determine the atmosphere of the schools which their children might attend. The nineteenth-century 'religious difficulty' was an obstacle to educational advance and inevitably produced a secular reaction demanding a State take-over in the elementary sector, but this was never strong enough to defeat religious influence as it did in France. Instead, the difficulty was met (from 1870) by the resort to a 'dual system' of elementary education within which schools provided by both State and Church were to co-exist. Later extended to the provision of teacher training as well, the dual system is still operative today.

During the twentieth century religious apathy spread far beyond the urban working class and the organised churches have had increasing difficulty in maintaining their position and power in the educational field. The proportion of voluntary (i.e. church) school places in the dual system declined sharply from 53 per cent in 1900 to 30 per cent in 1938. Since the Second World War the proportion has fallen still further to the present 22 per cent – with the further weakness that one-third of this provision is in the post-1944 category of voluntary controlled schools which lack any denominational atmosphere. The grave weakening in the churches' position in the total framework has been particularly associated with the dismantling of the old elementary school system and the development of secondary education for all. A parallel and similar loss of ground has faced the churches in the important field of teacher training which has long afforded them their only significant stake in post-school education.

Yet paradoxically, to maintain the dual system in being, this comparative decline in importance was accompanied by a major improvement in the financial arrangements for voluntary schools and denominational training colleges. During the period 1902–44 all voluntary schools had to meet their own capital costs in full; today the voluntary controlled schools are completely State-financed whilst the voluntary aided schools are committed to only 15 per cent of their capital costs. And the clauses of the 1944 Act which still require all maintained schools to provide a daily act of corporate worship and regular religious instruction are (despite numerous evasions) a reminder of the influence which the churches can still command. The compulsion involved has attracted severe criticism from various quarters since 1944, but the legal position has not been changed.

Finally, in recent years there has been a developing attempt to add a new dimension to denominational school provision. The growing Muslim community has sought the right to establish its own voluntary aided schools on the terms long available to the Anglicans and Roman Catholics. Groups of Hindu and Sikh parents have made similar representations. So far, in the interests of racial integration, the LEAs have resisted such a potentially divisive departure and it has been confined to small-scale experiment in the private sector. But such non-Christian religious pressure has affected, and will continue to affect, the maintained schools, especially those in areas where the child population is markedly multi-cultural (e.g. Manchester, Bolton, Bradford, Birmingham and Leicester). The daily act of worship, the nature of religious education, school meals, uniform and clothing requirements for pupils and the question of single-sex versus co-educational secondary schools are all important issues to the ethnic minorities concerned.

However, in considering the religious context one must always distinguish between the attitudes and influence of the various groups within it.

(a) Church of England

Claiming prior rights in education inherited from the mediaeval church, the Anglican community was the most important single religious pressure group in English education. The neglect of its educational responsibilities by the established Church in the eighteenth century was followed by a sudden rejuvenation of interest thereafter. During the nineteenth century the Church's influence exemplified itself in the National Society's work in the growing provision of Anglican elementary schools and training colleges.

By 1870 over three-quarters of the grant-aided, inspected elementary schools were Anglican and a similar dominance had been established in teacher training. After 1870 the Church of England led the opposition to the School Boards and the longer-term demand for increased financial aid for voluntary schools at both the elementary and secondary levels which found a major response in the 1902 and 1944 Education Acts. Despite its weakening position in the twentieth century, it was largely Anglican influence which ensured the continuance of the dual system at the time of Hadow reorganisation and the acceptance in 1944 of compulsory religious worship and instruction in all the State maintained schools. The Church has also been closely involved in the post-war development of Agreed Syllabuses for the teaching of religious education in the County and voluntary controlled schools. To many aspiring parents, irrespective of religious dispositions, the Anglican voluntary aided schools have recommended themselves in terms of traditional standards of discipline and work, ensuring that their entries are often over-subscribed. In very recent years, against the backcloth of falling rolls and greater concern for parental choice, these schools have been accused of manipulating the situation to avoid their full share of contraction and to obtain an improved share of able pupils. This poses the Church a difficult dilemma – the choice between a strictly denominational admissions policy to offset such accusations and the continuance of rather loose procedures which allow its schools to form an integral part of the whole local community but with the danger of parental manipulation and 'creaming' over entry.

(b) Roman Catholic

Following the Catholic Emancipation Act (1829) and the large Irish influx of the 1840s the Roman Catholic community grew in strength and was accepted back into the main stream of English life. In 1847 the Catholic Poor School Committee received its first instalment of State financial aid for elementary education purposes. Thereafter, the Roman Catholic interest continually strove to increase the number of its own denominational schools and to obtain the maximum possible public financial aid for their support. In this respect the Roman Catholics were the allies of the Anglicans and supported the latter in their hostility to the School Boards and the rate-aided public elementary schools. During the twentieth century, whilst accepting the integration of its schools into the State system (1902 Act), the Roman Catholic Church has successfully defended the maintenance of the dual system and the denominational atmosphere of its schools, without having to pay a high price for this.

Indeed, with its flock less affected by the growth of irreligion and the fall in average family size, only the Roman Catholic Church has progressively raised its number of voluntary school places. Consequently its share of total church school provision 1903–79 increased from 12 to 41 per cent. Always vitally concerned about the distinctive denominational character of its schools, this Church rejected the financially tempting voluntary controlled option of the 1944 Act and reluctantly accepted the 50 per cent capital cost obligations associated with the voluntary aided and special agreement categories (for details see pages 103–5). Since then, however, ecclesiastical pressure has reduced such capital obligations to a mere 15 per cent (from 1975) and the 'promised land' may now be in sight – a denominational system of Catholic schools completely financed from public funds and providing a place for each and every Catholic child.

(c)   Nonconformist

The considerable influence of the Free Churches upon education in the eighteenth century crystallised itself at the elementary level in the establishment of the British and Foreign School Society in 1814. Supported by the various Nonconformist sects, this body strove to expand elementary educational provision for the children of Dissenters. Though it received State assistance from the central government after 1833 on the same terms as the Anglican National Society, it was outstripped by the latter in the actual provision of places. Worried by the dominant position of the established Church in elementary education, the Nonconformists switched from the ideal of providing their own schools to the support of the case for undenominational public elementary schools provided and controlled by the State. Between 1870 and 1914 the Nonconformists (linked politically with the Liberal party) were a major pressure group in the field of English elementary education; they welcomed the 1870 Act, they supported the School Boards and they opposed rate-aid or increased central grants to help the denominational schools. By the inter-war years, however, the Nonconformists had ceased to be of major importance in English politics and no longer enjoyed their former influence on the educational scene. Since 1870 the great majority of their schools had been handed over to the State. However, they were consulted over those provisions of the 1944 Act which related to the future of the dual system and were also involved in the construction of Agreed Syllabuses for compulsory religious instruction.

(d)   Secularist

This group emerged in the nineteenth century as a result of the growth of irreligion and of irritation with religious obstructionism in the field of education. The secularist ideal was the establishment of a State system of secular elementary schools devoid of all religious influences and connections. The Birmingham Education League, formed in 1869 to press for universal, compulsory, free and unsectarian elementary education, drew upon much secularist support; although unsuccessful the pressure at least resulted in the 1870 Act's allowing the School Boards to opt for the abandonment of religious worship and instruction in their schools, even if only very few did so in practice. The secularist cause was later taken up by the trade union movement and the Labour party (1895–1911), but was quietly dropped by them because of the opposition of their own Roman Catholic members. Thereafter, the secularist cause made little or no headway, with both politicians and the public content to contain the old 'religious difficulty' in education by timely adjustments to the working of the dual system. Although post-war secularist criticism of the 1944 Act's requirement for compulsory religious worship and instruction in all maintained schools has attracted some support, there is now the hope of a resurgent influence based upon more recent developments. In the last few years the ability of voluntary-aided church schools to avoid the full impact of falling rolls and to improve the quality of their intake has excited opposition. And, given the growing multi-ethnic nature of society, the Anglican and Catholic schools attract more hostility and envy than they have for a long time. But it is unlikely that the secularist camp and associated elements can win enough influential support to threaten seriously the deep-rooted place of the church schools within the educational system.

7 Philosophic

There has been a significant change in the basic philosophy underpinning social attitudes and practices. In particular there was the move from the 'individualism' of the nineteenth century to the 'collectivism' of the twentieth century.

(a) *Laissez faire* Philosophy

With its emphasis on individual freedom and the strict limitation of State activity to the defence of the realm, the maintenance of law and order and the saving of public money, the influence of this philosophy proved double-edged. Whilst it challenged the continuance of antiquated and unreasonable laws and worked in favour of legal, religious and political reform, it produced a backlash effect in the socio-economic field, setting the stage for the 'jungle' capitalism of the early and mid-nineteenth century in which the stronger could tread upon the weaker on a class basis. The *laissez faire* philosophy was conveniently embraced by the upper and middle class ruling oligarchy; it justified governmental indifference to the condition of the proletariat at the close of the Industrial Revolution on both economic (Adam Smith's ideas) and demographic (theories of Thomas Malthus) grounds. According to this philosophy the improvement of social conditions was to be left to humanitarian and philanthropic activity and to individual exertion and 'self-help'. In relation to education the *laissez faire* philosophy favoured little being done rather than very much, blessed voluntary efforts whilst condemning State provision, and supported the independence of the public and endowed grammar schools from State interference. Yet simply to brand the nineteenth century as an 'age of *laissez faire*' is to distort the facts, not least in relation to education. Whilst *laissez faire* influence remained entrenched in the economic field to the end of the century, in areas of social concern (e.g. factory conditions, poor relief, public health and education) inroads upon it date from the 1830s, and fifty years later it was in full retreat. In the middle years of the century elementary schooling was increasingly recognised as an expedient means through which social control could be exerted, economic strength could be bolstered and political democracy safely introduced. Thus, whilst *laissez faire* ensured the failure of Roebuck's ambitious Education Bill in 1833, paradoxically its rejection was the prelude to the first phase of State involvement in elementary education. And during this phase, 1833–69, the work of Kay-Shuttleworth and Lowe made that involvement increasingly marked and influential; yet the continuing influence of *laissez faire* helped to circumscribe the State's role which was developed within the existing denominational framework and fell short of actually providing either elementary schools or training colleges. But during the second phase, 1870–1902, elementary education was subject to direct State provision and growing intervention, progressively giving rise to the School Boards, compulsory attendance, free tuition and, finally, the first non-denominational teacher training institutions. By the 1880s the State was also assuming a substantial role in the field of technical instruction. However, the compromise of the dual system (1870 +) and the State's predisposition to further its interest in elementary and technical education via local agencies (i.e. the School Boards and Technical Instruction Committee) owed something to *laissez faire* influences. And even in the late nineteenth century *laissez faire* was still strong enough to secure both secondary and university education in England from any significant State incursion.

(b) 'Collectivist' Philosophy

With its emphasis on the needs of society and the rights (socio-economic as well as political and religious) of the majority of its members, and especially of the younger generation, the influence of this philosophy was broadly socialist. Given the initial artificial inequalities of Victorian society, individual freedom was rejected as a solution; the emphasis shifted to the equalisation of advantages through collective action, justifying State intervention and the curtailment of individual rights in the interests of the welfare of the mass of the community. Locked in a dire struggle with *laissez faire* throughout the later nineteenth century, this philosophy won its first clear victory in the field of factory and mines reform and went on finally to win the day. It became the very basis of the Labour party's political programme, and greatly influenced the changing attitudes of the other two major parties (the Liberals more so, the Conservatives less so). The turning point was the Edwardian era, when inspired by this philosophy the Liberals laid the foundations of the welfare state. But the Liberal party commitment to 'collectivist' attitudes and policies was inevitably more confined than that of Labour and after the First World War the latter was able to outbid the former for working class votes to become the main opposition to the Conservatives. The philosophy gained added strength from the egalitarian impact of the Second World War during which both the Conservatives and Labour subscribed to the Beveridge Plan (1942) for the extension of the welfare state. Since then the philosophy has found its most forthright expression in the work of the post-war Labour governments, although their Conservative counterparts – until very recently – found it necessary to embrace its spirit to a large extent. Obviously the rise of the 'collectivist' philosophy and associated policies has proved extremely favourable to the development of education in terms of both objectives and actual provision. Collectivist influence in the late nineteenth century was already strong enough to bring about direct State intervention, compulsory attendance and free provision in elementary education. During the present century it has served to sanctify the developing State system of education as such, to secure the development of educational welfare services, to broaden the conception of the educational process, to bring about secondary education for all and to expand opportunities in further and higher education. Its progressive influence was at its most intense during the quarter century which followed the 1944 Act – the wartime measure which was itself a clear expression of this philosophy.

However, the foregoing analysis now calls for an important postscript. In more recent years the 'collectivist' philosophy and approach has lost some of its former strength. Initially, in respect of education, this was a function of the greatly expanded post-war educational system's relative failure to deliver the social and economic benefits expected of it. Since the early 1970s none of the political parties have accorded to education the high priority it enjoyed in the 1950s and 1960s. And now the welfare state itself is facing the critical scrutiny of the political right, with an increasing emphasis upon the need to cut its enormous cost and to check its erosion of individual self-reliance. The last decade has not been an auspicious one for educational development and the current ideological signs are that the statutory system could face an even rougher passage in the years ahead.

In the nineteenth and early twentieth centuries the role of education was basically conservative and passive: the system of education grew out of the contemporary society, either mirroring the established social and culture pattern or slowly and painfully responding to any shifts in that pattern. The mechanics of change were as follows:

> Various forces (demographic, economic, scientific, technological, political, religious and philosophic) → changes in the nature of society → delayed effects on the system of education.

In more recent times education emerged as a progenitor as well as a derivative, as a progressive influence as well as a conservative force. The educational system was no longer simply shaped by society, but helped to shape that society by exercising a growing influence upon it. The extent to which the educational system can and should be used as a means of social engineering and change is a controversial issue, but clearly the relationship between society and education became increasingly two-way. The rise of meritocracy over the last half century was largely facilitated by the widening of secondary and higher educational opportunities. For many the quest for an egalitarian society begins with the educational system, hence the post-war interest in secondary education for all, comprehensive schooling, compensatory education and nursery provision. That a 'brave new world' could be built on educational foundations was a widespread conviction after the Second World War. But the extent to which educational developments, even if generously funded and effectively undertaken, can secure social justice and economic well-being is limited. By the 1970s public disillusionment began to have an adverse effect on the priority given to education and its capacity to influence wider concerns. In this regard the schools' seeming failure to provide a really satisfactory curriculum to meet contemporary social and economic needs, especially in respect of less able pupils, has been and remains a serious handicap. If the teaching profession and the statutory system can respond to the current demand for greater accountability and for a more functional and effective school curriculum, the lost ground may be ultimately regained. Failing this, there is the danger of certain future initiatives being left to outside agencies – such as the MSC – and, under favourable political conditions, of a significant extension of private education and training.

2 Developments in Elementary Education 1800–70

The development of elementary education in England and Wales during the period 1800–70 may be considered in three major parts.

1 The Situation at the Turn of the Century

The evidence of an official investigation (the report of the parliamentary Select Committee on the Education of the Lower Orders of Society, 1818) led Lord Brougham to describe England at this time as the worst educated country in Europe. It showed that only one quarter of the child population was receiving any education at all, and for the great majority of these its duration was very short. Moreover, many of those privileged to receive some elementary education were attending the ineffectual dame and common day schools or merely going to Sunday school one day per week. A very large number of poor children, estimated at over one and half million, were wholly without any means of elementary instruction, with the rapid growth of population and demand for child labour both calculated to make the situation worse. The traditional means available for bringing about an expansion of provision were extremely meagre; private individuals and voluntary bodies working in the field were dependent on the limited and unreliable funds obtained from endowments, donations and parents' pence. Nor was such expansion generally agreed to be necessary or desirable. Against the backcloth of the French Revolution most of the propertied governing class feared the possible consequences of educating the poor more than the possible dangers and disadvantages of not doing so. In particular they were concerned lest the provision of elementary education for the poor should produce a growing dissatisfaction with their lot in life at the close of the Industrial Revolution. Better to let sleeping dogs lie.

But within early nineteenth-century English society various influences

and considerations were combining to help the cause of elementary education for the lower classes.

(a) Humanitarian

As the Industrial Revolution concentrated and sharpened the misery of the
poor there was a remarkable development of private benevolence throughout the country in the early decades of the new century. This growth of
philanthropy found a focus in the Society for the Bettering of the Condition
of the Poor which gave a place to elementary education in its overall design.
Humanitarian opposition to the employment of child labour and support for
factory reform legislation was also of long-term significance for the development of elementary education.

(b) Religious

Stimulated by the Methodist example, the Church of England underwent a
marked revival in the early nineteenth century and through the Evangelical
movement found a new Christian purpose which had important educational
results. The establishment of the National Society in 1811 heralded the start
of a new Anglican drive in the field of elementary education, which drew its
inevitable response from the Nonconformists who founded the British and
Foreign School Society in 1814 for the same purpose. In this way the
religious revival and the denominational rivalry of the early nineteenth
century pumped additional interest and resources into the provision of
elementary education.

(c) Social

The brutish ignorance and behaviour which characterised the backstreets of
the growing industrial towns and the riots and disorders which sprang out
of contemporary social conditions could not be ignored or repressed
indefinitely. Gradually an increasing number of the governing class became
apprehensive and turned to elementary education as a possible civilising and
steadying influence on the turbulent mass of the urban proletariat. Their
interest was in an elementary schooling deliberately aimed at the religious
and social conditioning of lower class children.

Thus the cause of expanding elementary education obtained increasing
support: the great problem was how to bring this expansion about.

2 Efforts to Expand Elementary Education 1800–33

Although the practical results were limited, these years saw considerable efforts being made to increase the provision of elementary educational facilities. Such efforts took three main forms.

(a) Projection of the Sunday School Movement

The pioneer work of Robert Raikes to meet the needs of pin-factory children in the town of Gloucester was quickly followed by the founding of the Society for the Establishment and Support of Sunday Schools in 1785. As a result of support received from most denominations and from factory-owners interested in insuring themselves against any loss of child labour during the working week, the Society achieved a national impact. By the turn of the century there were over three-quarters of a million children attending Sunday schools up and down the country; thirty years later the figure had reached about one and half million. Although in terms of numbers the achievement of the Sunday school movement was impressive, its practical effects were much more limited. Many of the volunteer teachers were inexperienced and poorly educated and secular education (in the three Rs) was gradually drowned by sectarian religious instruction. The real significance of the Sunday school movement was threefold:

(i)   it raised the ideal of universal elementary education and pointed the way towards it;

(ii) it kindled the denominational rivalry between Anglicans and Nonconformists which was to provide in double-edged fashion so much of the drive and difficulty in the field of nineteenth-century English elementary education;

(iii) it pioneered the monitorial system; Raikes met Joseph Lancaster and some believe that the latter developed his system from the beginnings made by the Sunday schools.

(b) Development of the Monitorial System

Shortage of money and shortage of teachers were the two fundamental problems facing any attempt to expand elementary education in the early nineteenth century. The solution provided was the monitorial system, elaborated and popularised by Andrew Bell, an Anglican clergyman, and Joseph Lancaster, a Quaker schoolmaster. Although their respective systems differed in detail they rested on the same basic principles, the foremost of which was that of mass-production in elementary education by applying the division of labour to the process of simple instruction. The central idea was to enable a single schoolmaster to cope with a very large number of children by the employment of monitors, i.e. making use of the older and abler pupils to teach the others. The monitorial system depended on the schoolmaster taking responsibility for the organisation and discipline of the school and for the clear instruction of the monitors in particular elements of the three Rs, so that they could duplicate the exercise with their different monitorial groups. Membership of such groups was determined by attainment rather than age and promotion from one group to another took place as proficiency increased. Lancaster boasted that the system made it possible for one master to teach a thousand pupils. The major attraction was its cheapness; the annual cost of instructing a child in a typical Lancasterian school was 7s 6d, whilst the more austere arrangements of Bell's system reduced the sum even further.

The churches were quick to take advantage of the opportunity offered by the monitorial system, the charity schools of the eighteenth century being adapted to its use as well as new schools established for its introduction. The National Society for Promoting the Education of the Poor in the Principles of the Established Church (1811) adopted Bell's system to extend rapidly the provision made for elementary education by the Anglicans; simultaneously the British and Foreign School Society (1814) adopted Lancaster's system to expand the opportunities available for Nonconformist children and others. The resultant denominational rivalry drove both sides to strenuous efforts and helped to attract considerable funds to the task. Both societies set up 'normal' schools for the swift training of schoolteachers who would operate the monitorial system. By 1830 the system was enabling the National Society to provide elementary education for about one-third of a million children.

In spite of its shortcomings the monitorial school was a considerable improvement on the dame, the common day and charity schools inherited from the eighteenth century; the children did obtain a superficial smattering of the three Rs and were conditioned to a sense of good order and discipline. The subject of much contemporary interest and enthusiasm, the monitorial schools did much to popularise elementary education and encouraged those who thought in terms of making such provision universal. But in certain respects the influence of the monitorial system was far from beneficial:

   (i) little worthwhile education resulted from the mechanical instruction of younger by older pupils;
  (ii) denominational rivalry became very bitter, thus crystallising the 'religious difficulty' in elementary education which was to prove such an obstacle to future progress;

(iii) the mould was set for the elementary school of the later nineteenth century with its mechanical methods, low standards, large classes, cheapness and narrow educational ideals.

(c) Demands for State Involvement

The spread of the Sunday schools and the monitorial system was accomplished by the efforts of voluntary bodies without a single penny of public money being subscribed thereto by the State. But a minority of progressives, unkindly described as the 'education mad' party, recognised that voluntary resources were too limited and pressed for State involvement in one form or another. Gradually the government policy of non-intervention in relation to child labour and elementary education was undermined by the work of various pioneers both inside and outside Parliament. There were a number of signal events in this developing process:

(i) 1807 Whitbread's Parochial Schools Bill: this suggested the establishment of a national system of rate-aided parish schools to be run by elected local committees and providing two years' free elementary schooling for poor children. Emasculated in the Commons, it was thrown out of the Lords.

(ii) 1818 Parliamentary Select Committee Report on *The Education of the Lower Orders of Society*: inspired by Lord Brougham and the outcome of a two-year inquiry, this premier official report on elementary education provided much ammunition for those favouring State involvement.

(iii) 1820 Brougham's Parish Schools Bill: this envisaged a national system of elementary education based on the provision of buildings by the manufacturers, with running costs being met by local rate-aid, redistributed endowments and small fees. An ill-designed religious compromise was attempted by placing the control of staffing and curricula under the established Church, whilst suggesting that religious teaching should be undenominational. The Bill inevitably foundered on the combined opposition of the employers and the churches.

(iv) 1833 Roebuck's Education Bill: in the more favourable setting resultant of the first Reform Act (1832), John Roebuck, a Radical member of Parliament, submitted a plan for 'the universal and national education of the whole people'. The Bill provided for a Minister of Public Instruction, elected School District Committees, central and local financial aid to supplement parents' pence, compulsory attendance from six to twelve years of age and normal schools for teacher training. But, even for a reformed Parliament, Roebuck's Bill was too ambitious and expensive; the Commons decided not to proceed with it.

(v) 1833 First Parliamentary Grant: whilst rejecting Roebuck's measure, the House of Commons showed it was not completely indifferent when (a few days later) it provided a grant of £20,000 for 'the erection of elementary schools'. In the event, as this offer was not an isolated but a continuing one with no fixed ceiling, it was of the utmost significance. Indeed, although the 'religious difficulty' would long continue its obstructive influence, the 1833 parliamentary grant was the beginning of State assistance for and involvement in the provision of elementary schooling. Moreover, the failure of Roebuck's Bill had also been balanced by the passage of the 1833 Factory Act which resulted in the first effective regulation and limitation of child labour, a development of acute importance for the future of elementary education. The very first inroads upon the established philosophy and policy of *laissez faire* had now been made.

3   The Era of Voluntary Initiative and State Assistance 1833–70

The annual parliamentary grant for elementary education rose from £20,000 in 1833 to £30,000 in 1839. The exact nature of and means of dispensing the grant at this time is noteworthy. It was essentially in 'aid of private subscriptions', thus being available only to those voluntary bodies which could first raise 50 per cent of the total cost of the projected school building and guarantee to meet the running costs thereafter. Thus in practice State assistance was limited to those localities possessing the requisite interest and resources to muster half the cost, which discriminated against the poorest urban areas where the need was greatest. Initially all the public funds made available were channelled through the National Society (about 80 per cent) and the British and Foreign School Society (about 20 per cent) which vetted applications for assistance on behalf of the Treasury. There was no attempt to inspect the schools receiving grant money or to control the appointment of staff or the curriculum. Because the Treasury wielded so little real control over the sums expended, the central government determined in 1839 to set up a special body to exercise its responsibilities in the field of elementary education: the establishment of the Committee of the Privy Council for Education set the stage for the work of Dr Kay, later Sir James Kay-Shuttleworth, who did so much to improve the situation in the middle years of the century before the report of the Newcastle Commission (1861) and the introduction of the Revised Code (1862).

(a)   Sir James Kay-Shuttleworth

Doctor, poor law commissioner, social reformer and educationist, he was appointed first Secretary of the new Committee and for ten years he worked twelve hours a day to improve the state of elementary education, thus impairing the state of his own health. During the 1840s and 1850s his energy and influence brought about a major advance, though he was always acutely aware of how much more needed to be done.

His *achievements* were varied and considerable:

(i) the initial development of a central administrative agency for dispensing State financial assistance to elementary education, through the religious organisations, and for maintaining contact with the growing number of grant-aided schools. This agency, located at Whitehall and responsible to the Committee of the Council, grew into the Education Department of the later nineteenth century and was the original forefather of the present Department of Education and Science (DES).

(ii) the establishment of Her Majesty's Inspectorate (1839), which, with the agreement of the religious organisations, was to serve as the link between Kay-Shuttleworth's central agency and the grant-aided schools. Kay-Shuttleworth's influence, as expressed in the first instructions to HM Inspectors, worked in favour of a wide-ranging and diplomatic role, rather than a narrow, inquisitorial one, for this new body. Whilst ensuring that grants were put to proper use, the inspectors were to be more concerned with affording 'assistance' and 'encouragement' than with 'exercising control': they were, on request, to offer advice to the promoters of elementary schools not aided by public grants and were to collect any information calculated to shed light on the general state of elementary education in England and Wales.

(iii) the impressive increase in the annual parliamentary grant to elementary education, which rose from £30,000 to over £800,000 during the period 1839–61, and the development of a system of specific grants for a widening range of items and purposes. Following the Committee's Minutes of 1846 State assistance was extended well beyond the original 50 per cent building grant; public moneys became available to help defray current costs, especially after the introduction of capitation grants (tied to minimal attendance requirements) in the mid-1850s.

(iv) the dilution of the key problem of teacher training and supply, which was at the root of limited provision and poor standards in elementary education. Through the 1846 Minutes Kay-Shuttleworth launched the pupil-teacher system which was to serve English elementary education down to the end of the century. The new arrangements were based on a five years' apprenticeship for interested and able thirteen-year-old pupils who engaged in 'on the job' training in approved grant-aided schools; the best pupil-teachers were then offered Queen's Scholarships to undertake a further two-year course at a denominational training college. With the State providing financial assistance for the support of training colleges, the religious organisations responded well and by 1859 there were some thirty-odd such institutions offering places. By this time the new system had produced more than 7,000 trained certificated teachers, whilst twice as many pupil-teachers were in the schools. Significant inroads were made into the shortage of teachers and monitorial methods began to retreat before the advance of class teaching.

His *disappointments*, resulting from the contemporary 'religious difficulty', are also noteworthy in certain respects:

(i) the failure to bring about the establishment of a State Training College, as a forerunner of others, free of denominational influence and control. This idea had been canvassed in the late 1830s, Parliament had voted the sum of £10,000 for the project and the new Committee was commissioned to make it a reality. But when Kay-Shuttleworth drafted a detailed scheme for a 'purely civil' Training College it quickly foundered on the religious issue. He then turned to the establishment of Battersea Training College as a private venture in 1840, to show the possibility of developing teacher training in a broad Anglican setting which would not offend tender consciences. However, personal and financial difficulties, combined with the narrow sectarian influence of the Oxford Movement within the established Church, led him to surrender the college to the National Society in 1843. Until very late in the century the field of teacher training was monopolised by the denominational colleges which, especially after the 1870 Act, were unable to provide enough places to meet the growing needs of the elementary schools.

(ii) the failure to provide special help for those poor urban areas unable to muster 50 per cent of the cost of a new school building. In 1843 Kay-Shuttleworth helped to devise a Factory Bill which not only extended the regulation of child employment but provided for a developing system of elementary schools in factory areas. Government loans were to be made available for the establishment of such schools, but the real cost was to be largely defrayed by the employers through the parish rates. Control of the schools was vested in the Church of England, and Anglican religious worship and instruction were provided for, albeit with a 'conscience clause' to make the arrangements more generally acceptable. However, such was the violent outcry from the Nonconformist ranks that a political crisis arose and the government withdrew the Bill. The Nonconformist reaction was so strong that it resulted in the 'Voluntaryist' movement: intensely suspicious of government intentions in elementary education, the Congregationalists and others refused State grants and campaigned for a reversion to the purely voluntary principle. Had this ploy succeeded the Anglican schools would also have lost their State financial assistance, but in practice the result of this masochistic exercise was to put the Nonconformists at a serious disadvantage in the denominational school race and later to incline them to the support of direct State provision. Meanwhile the failure of the 1843 Factory Bill postponed a further major government initiative in the field of elementary education for over a quarter of a century.

Obviously these were difficult times for developing the State's role. The strength of the established Church and, to a lesser degree, the Nonconformists in these years ensured that any attempt at direct State provision or control was defeated; by 1846 it was recognised that the only way forward was for the State to work strictly within the existing denominational framework. But, in this frustrating context, the faith and fortitude of Kay-Shuttleworth was nothing less than heroic; in spite of the disappointments his contribution was absolutely critical to the progress of elementary education in the nineteenth century. When nervous strain forced his resignation in 1849, he was succeeded by R.R.W. Lingen who went on to become Permanent Secretary (1856–70) to the new Education Department. Although the expansive momentum of Kay-Shuttleworth's work continued into the 1850s the original dynamic was not maintained. Lingen, albeit an able man, lacked his predecessor's crusading spirit and became increasingly preoccupied with containing the rising level of his Department's spending.

(b) Newcastle Commission 1858–61

The Report and significance of this body may be considered in the following terms:

(i) *Context*

The need for financial stringency after the expense of the Crimean War and the serious shortcomings of elementary education in State-assisted schools as revealed in inspectors' reports, combined to bring the parliamentary grant under close scrutiny in the late 1850s. As the new Education Department created in 1856 was directly responsible to Parliament it was now essential to justify the moneys annually expended on elementary education and to ensure their proper and effective use.

(ii)   *Terms of Reference*

'To inquire into the present state of popular education in England, and to consider and report what measures, if any, are required for the extension of sound and cheap elementary instruction to all classes of the people.' In spite of the unfavourable context the commissioners adopted a more liberal approach than is generally appreciated or acknowledged; in their work they showed much more interest in the extension and improvement of the existing provision than in cheapening its cost.

(iii)   *Findings*

These gave qualified approval to the existing situation. On the credit side the report pointed to the considerable improvement which had taken place since 1818 as a result of voluntary efforts and State assistance. The significant rise in the proportion of children receiving some sort of elementary education and the beneficial influence of the pupil-teacher system were particularly noted. But on the debit side the report spotlighted the sheer inadequacy of provision in the poorer areas, the unsatisfactory nature of the unassisted schools, the short duration and irregularity of attendance and the early leaving age of the great majority of pupils. The report further emphasised the widespread incidence, even in grant-aided schools, of inefficient teaching simply for the want of sufficient concentration on the task of giving the children a thorough grounding in the three Rs; too much attention was being focused on the older children and on non-essential subject matter.

(iv)   *Recommendations*

That the commissioners were the prisoners of their age found expression in their conservative response to a number of critical issues. They rejected the idea of State provision and control in favour of the continuance of voluntary initiative and self-help; whilst State assistance was acceptable, any attempt to introduce compulsory attendance or free elementary schooling was condemned. Beyond this the Commission based its positive recommendations on two essential requirements. Firstly, it underlined the need for more financial assistance for the voluntary bodies, and even for the extension of such aid to previously unassisted schools, especially in the poorer areas. To this end State aid in the simple form of block capitation grants was to be supplemented by local rate-aid channelled through a new framework of County and Municipal Education Boards. Secondly, it insisted on the need to ensure that the public funds so provided were put to proper use and accordingly suggested that grant assistance should be tied to minimal attendance requirements for the capitation allowance and to annual examination requirements for the receipt of rate-aid. The total result of adopting the recommendations would be to increase the resources available to the elementary schools, to raise their standards of attainment and to simplify and partly decentralise the administration of grant-aid.

(c)   Robert Lowe and the Revised Code (1862)

The report of the Newcastle Commission was duly considered by Robert Lowe, Vice-President of the Council and head of the Education Department 1859–64, who was an efficient administrator with an aristocratic outlook rather than a visionary educationist with a real sympathy for popular education. Both he and Lingen were impressed by the report's emphasis on the need to ensure value for money rather than by its insistence on the need for more to be made available. The result was the Revised Code of 1862, which stressed the former and ignored the latter. In any case the introduction of rate-aid for the support of elementary education was a religiously explosive issue which neither Lowe nor his Whig masters were prepared to face. The Revised Code, which was to survive in a progressively modified form for some thirty years, introduced a new set of regulations which subjected the grant-aided elementary schools and training colleges to a strict 'payment by results' system.

Its *features*: the detailed regulations of Lowe's Code ensured that the new system had a number of distinctive features:

(i)   the abolition of the specific grants for furniture, books and apparatus, of pupil-teacher stipends and of teachers' merit grants and pension rights introduced by Kay-Shuttleworth;

(ii)   the sharp reduction of State grants to the training colleges partly through the curtailment of the number of Queen's Scholarships;

(iii) the strict relation of State grants for elementary education to attendance and attainment. HM Inspectorate was henceforth committed to the task of annually examining the registers and the proficiency in the three Rs of all children of six years and over in State-assisted elementary schools which now had to earn their grant. Each child could earn the school the sum of twelve shillings; according to the average number in attendance throughout the year four shillings per pupil was paid, whilst successful examination performance earned a further eight shillings (i.e. 2s 8d per child for each of the three Rs). The

good quote

examinations were conducted at six graded levels (Standards I-VI) and no pupil could be entered at more than one level or repeat a grade already successfully undertaken.

Lowe boasted of the new system: 'If is not cheap, it shall be efficient; if it is not efficient, it shall be cheap.' In fact the annual parliamentary grant for elementary education fell by 23 per cent during the first five years of the Code's operation, but recovered thereafter as the grant-aided schools adjusted to the demands of the new system.

Its *advantages*: these were substantial and included:

(i) a considerable rise in the school population and greater regularity of attendance;

(ii) an improvement in school organisation and in competence in the three Rs, especially amongst those grant-aided schools which had been the weakest;

(iii) a dilution of the previous stress on religious teaching in favour of secular instruction as the former was not eligible for grant;

(iv) a much-needed reduction in the administrative burden of the Education Department now that it ceased to deal directly with teachers, pupil-teachers and the earlier wide range of specific grants;

(v) a crucial shift in the balance of power between State and Church in the elementary arena which was unfavourable to the religious interests. HM Inspectorate became more closely bound to the Education Department and the way was prepared for even more positive State action via the 1870 Act.

Its *disadvantages*: the system came under increasing criticism and challenge because of the retrogressive influence it wielded in various directions:

(i) the over-pressurisation of the children and the comparative neglect of the fast and slow learners in favour of the 'bread and butter' middle section;

(ii) the narrowing of the elementary curriculum as a result of the inevitable concentration on the three Rs, with its corresponding and derivative effect upon the character of training college courses;

(iii) the demoralisation of teachers who lost their semi-Civil Service status and were reduced to the role of hired drill instructors, attendance officers and register falsifiers whose income came to depend on the results they achieved in circumstances often beyond their control;

(iv) the rapid growth of distrust and hatred for HM Inspectorate by the majority of elementary teachers as the latter were subjected to the former's new inquisitorial role;

(v) the fall in the recruitment of pupil-teachers and the output of trained certificated teachers, associated with a rise in average class size and a decline in the standards of entry into elementary teaching.

In the final analysis both the Newcastle Commission and Robert Lowe were content to rely on the voluntary bodies to bear the main burden of providing for the expansion of elementary education. The Revised Code was not calculated to increase the number of elementary schools or to improve their geographical distribution; it merely tended to make the existing grant-aided schools more efficient. But by the late 1860s the changing context was making it increasingly clear that the voluntary organisations could not manage and that there was a need for much more direct involvement by the State. The stage was being set for the 1870 Elementary Education Act, by which at long last the poorer districts would receive the attention hitherto denied them.

3 Elementary Education in the School Board Era 1870–1902

The study of the very considerable subject matter involved in this topic may well be divided into two major parts.

1 1870 Elementary Education Act

This critical landmark in our educational history formed the watershed between mere State assistance for, and direct State provision of, elementary education. It represented the first bold and effective legislative initiative undertaken by government in English education, involving the creation of the earliest local authorities for education and opening the way to the development of a more positive and widening role for the State in this field.

(a) Underlying Causes

By the late 1860s various influences had combined to make elementary education a national issue and to convince many important people that a radical extension of State involvement was now vitally necessary. It was the work of such influences which prepared the way for the introduction and acceptance of the 1870 Act.

(i) *Demographic*

The continued population explosion, especially in the major towns and cities was swamping the efforts of the voluntary organisations to provide adequate elementary educational facilities under existing arrangements. Even Edward Baines, the Congregational protagonist of pure 'Voluntaryism', was forced to admit defeat and accept the idea of State provision.

(ii)   *Social*

As the Factory Acts progressively raised the minimum age of child employment in a growing range of occupations, centres of dense population were
faced with the problem of thousands of children on the streets, with nothing
better to do than turn to petty crime or otherwise misapply their energies. It
has been estimated that the 1867 Factory Act alone debarred an additional
one-fifth of a million children from paid employment. Having demonstrated
the connection between idleness and ignorance on the one hand and vice and
crime on the other, W.E. Forster asked Parliament. 'Dare we then take the
responsibility of allowing this to continue one year longer than we can help?'
(*Hansard*, cxcix, 17 February 1870). The answer was to get the urchins into
school.

(iii)   *Political*

The 1867 Reform Act extended the franchise to the industrial working class
and convinced even the aristocratic Robert Lowe that it would now 'be
absolutely necessary (to) prevail on our future masters to learn their letters'
(*Hansard*, clxxxviii, 15 July 1867). Thus the dangers of an illiterate electorate helped to marshal opinion favourable to the cause of universal elementary education.

(iv)   *Economic*

The Paris Exhibition of 1867 gave grounds for foreboding in relation to
Britain's long-established industrial lead and commercial supremacy. The
rapid advance of some of Britain's continental competitors was explained by
the greater priority they gave to educational development. Introducing his
Bill to the Commons, W.E. Forster insisted, 'We must not delay. Upon the
speedy provision of elementary education depends our industrial prosperity'
(*Hansard*, cxcix, 17 February 1870). Industrialisation had reached a more
complex stage and the need for literate and skilled workers was growing both
absolutely and comparatively.

(v)   *Military*

During the 1860s contemporary observers were much impressed by the
results of the American Civil and Austro-Prussian Wars and by the
emergence of modern Germany. Military strength and national power
clearly seemed to benefit from the provision of universal elementary education; it was even declared that the dramatic victory in the Seven Weeks' War
was forged in the elementary schools of Prussia. Given Britain's recent
mediocre performance in the Crimean War, these were considerations
which could not be lightly ignored.

(b) Contemporary Ferment

Whilst the Manchester Education Aid Society (established 1864) and similar urban organisations elsewhere campaigned nationally for more public funds and more vigorous State action, and supported the ill-fated attempts of certain private members (e.g. H.A. Bruce) to institute new legislation, W.E. Forster, the new Vice-President of the Council and head of the Education Department in Gladstone's first Liberal ministry 1868–74, mounted a parliamentary investigation into the state of elementary education in four large cities. The report submitted on the situation in Liverpool, Manchester, Leeds and Birmingham confirmed the government's worst fears: the total extent of provision was quite inadequate, the available schools were unevenly distributed, the unaided schools virtually worthless and the benefits of instruction seriously undermined by irregular attendance and very early leaving. The inquiry's statistical returns showed that of the six to twelve years age-group in the cities concerned, nearly one-half received no elementary schooling at all whilst a mere one-third attended inspected schools. It was assumed that this depressing sample picture was typical of the condition of elementary education in the growing urban industrial areas.

The Gladstone government determined to 'grasp the nettle' and Forster was elevated to Cabinet position to prepare and present the necessary legislation. Meanwhile the different interests organised themselves to bring pressure to bear on the government in the hope of securing a legislative solution in accordance with their particular viewpoint.

(i) *Birmingham Education League (1869)*

Representing the Nonconformist, secularist and radical cause, the League campaigned energetically for 'universal, compulsory, free and unsectarian' elementary education in the months before and during the passage of the Act. The success of this nationally-organised body would have meant the displacement of the existing denominational schools, the great majority of which were Anglican, by direct State provision throughout the country; thus the tradition of religious initiative and control in English elementary education would have been overthrown. However, the League was weakened somewhat by its own internal divisions; whilst the secularist minority pressed for the complete abandonment of religious worship and instruction in the State elementary schools, the majority of supporters favoured its retention in unsectarian form. Moreover, the public at large were unlikely to accept the sheer expense of the Birmingham programme or its extremely rough treatment of the established Church.

(ii) *National Education Union (1870)*

Representing the Anglican interest mainly, but supported by the Roman
Catholics and the Methodists, this body campaigned for the continuance of
the denominational monopoly in elementary education, with the churches
simply receiving more generous financial help to do the job. The Union
pressed for the introduction of local rate-aid for the denominational schools
to supplement the central grants already available. The majority of elementary teachers lent their support to the Union against the League at this time.
But the Union also suffered from internal dissension especially in relation to
the conscience clause issue; the moderates felt that the acceptance of a conscience clause, giving parents the right to withdraw their children from
sectarian religious worship and instruction, was a reasonable price to pay for
the public financing of denominational schools, but the more extreme
elements denounced such a course of action as inimical to the denominational identity and atmosphere of the Anglican and Roman Catholic
schools.

Gladstone and Forster were unprepared to give way to either pressure
group. Instead they embraced a compromise solution suggested by Robert
Lowe which would allow the churches a 'period of grace' to meet the country's elementary educational deficiencies and would provide for direct State
provision where such deficiencies were not completely eliminated. Thus the
government opted for a dual system inevitably calculated to draw an
unfavourable reaction from both the League and the Union; nevertheless it
proved to be a way forward basically acceptable to most moderate opinion
both inside and outside Parliament.

(c) Main Aims and Provisions

The declared purpose of the 1870 Act was to 'cover the country with good
schools' and so enable all parents to secure elementary education for their
children. This was to be done, not by dismantling the existing system, but
by the State simply 'filling the gaps' left by voluntary effort, thus 'sparing
the public money where it can be done without' and retaining the 'co-operation and aid of those benevolent men who desire to assist their neighbours'
(*Hansard*, cxcix, 17 February 1870). The main provisions of the Act followed naturally from this basic strategy.

(i)   The country was divided into several thousand school districts, pend-
      ing an investigation into existing facilities in each one and a possible
      declaration of deficiency by the Education Department.
(ii) Where the existing facilities were not 'sufficient, efficient and suitable'
      the churches were given a six months' 'period of grace' to rectify the

situation, with 50 per cent State building grants made available during this time but not beyond.

(iii) School Boards, elected by local ratepayers, were to be established in all districts where a deficiency remained once the six months' period had elapsed. These Boards were given the responsibility of covering the residual deficiencies and were presented with a wide range of associated permissive powers. They could accept the transfer of voluntary schools into their hands, establish their own new elementary schools, levy local rate-aid for their work, compulsorily acquire land, decide for or against religious instruction in their schools, remit the fees of poor children, enforce compulsory attendance through the by-laws and appoint their own permanent officials.

(iv) The Board schools were to be financially supported by central grants, parental fees (maximum 9d per week) and rate-aid, whilst the voluntary schools were expected to defray their costs from central grants, parental fees (no maximum prescribed) and church subscriptions, with rate-aid being deliberately denied them. For both types of school the amount which could be earned in central grants under the 'payment by results' system was increased.

(v) The 'religious difficulty' was met by two important and distinct clauses of the Act. The Cowper-Temple clause related to the School Boards only, giving them the choice between undenominational religious instruction and none at all; the former option was defined as worship and instruction devoid of any 'catechisms or religious formularies distinctive of any particular denomination'. The main intention was to secure the rate-aided Board schools from the threat of sectarian religious teaching, although in practice the clause was more susceptible to manipulation by denominationally controlled School Boards than is generally appreciated. The right of each School Board to abandon religious worship and instruction was of much less practical importance; predictably, in the climate of late Victorian times, it was rarely acted upon and, apart from the short-lived Birmingham experiment (1873–9), no major School Board took up the secular alternative. The timetable conscience clause affected both the Board and the voluntary schools; it laid down the parents' right to withdraw their child from religious worship or instruction, and to facilitate this the schools were required to timetable religious teaching at the beginning or end of the day. This was designed primarily to meet the difficulty of single-school areas where the only elementary school available was a denominational (usually Anglican) one, but it also met the needs of atheist and agnostic parents sending their children to Board schools giving undenominational religious instruction.

(d)   Reaction to the Act

The original Bill as first presented to Parliament included the provision of rate-aid for denominational schools and gave the churches a period of twelve months to cover deficiencies. Accused of a sell-out to the Anglican interest by its own Nonconformist and Radical supporters, Gladstone's government was forced to make amendments unfavourable to the churches. Nevertheless, some Liberal members felt unable to support the Bill in its amended form and the Act, which received the royal assent in August 1870, was viewed with dissatisfaction from both ends of the politico-educational spectrum.

(i) *The National Education League* saw the Act as nothing more than a short step in the right direction, with free, compulsory and unsectarian elementary education in a purely State system of schools having eluded its grasp. In spite of the amendments which its influence had helped successfully to press upon the government, the league still considered the measure was far too soft on the denominational interests and had lumbered the country with a dual system which would be hard to get rid of. For the next quarter-century the Nonconformist, secularist and radical supporters of the National Education League agitated for the acceptance of the original Birmingham programme.

(ii) *The National Education Union* could only find consolation in the fact that the Liberal government had dealt less severely with the church interests than many of its supporters had demanded. At least they had obtained a six months' 'period of grace' during which, with the aid of State building grants, they would be given the first opportunity to make up the deficiencies. Thereafter a significant increase in the central grants which the denominational schools could earn would become available. The denominational atmosphere of the Anglican and Roman Catholic schools would remain unimpaired; it was recognised that the practical significance of the right of withdrawal would prove minimal anyway. In a word, Gladstone's solution was a dual system which retained a very important place for the denominational schools, not a purely statutory system which absorbed or ostracised them. But the churches also had strong grounds for dissatisfaction with the new settlement. The cessation of building grants after the 'period of grace', the prospective competition of the rate-aided and potentially 'godless' Board schools and the prior right of established School Boards to meet ensuing deficiencies were all very ominous. They seemed to portend a gradual erosion of the churches' influence in the field of elementary education. Naturally the Anglicans and Roman Catholics were anxious to stimulate more generous subscriptions from church members for the support of their own schools, to capture control of School Boards established in deficiency areas and to persuade some future Conservative government to change the arrangements in a way much more favourable to them.

But to the nation at large the objections from these sources were of secondary importance: the 1870 Act was to make available to all parents an elementary education for their children and that was what really mattered.

(e) Significance and Limitations of the Act

Forster's measure established a new framework for the provision of elementary education which ensured that deficiencies were gradually overcome and a school place made available to all children in the country. In the context of that time it was a major triumph to devise and implement legislation which established the first local authorities and infringed the former monopoly of provision held by the churches; to overcome the hostility of the established Church and the employers of child labour, and to persuade a traditionally reluctant Parliament to accept the introduction of rate-aid for elementary education, was no mean feat. The 1870 Act put new life into the efforts of the voluntary organisations and produced educational pace-setters at the local level in the shape of the larger, progressive School Boards.

But the 1870 Act did not provide for compulsory or free elementary education. Nor did it make any fundamental difference to the 'payment by results' system which was accepted in principle and thus perpetuated in practice for a further quarter-century. From the outset the denominational schools were at a disadvantage because of their lack of rate-aid. Worst of all, whilst setting the stage for the provision of many more elementary places, the Act did nothing to ensure a parallel expansion in the supply of suitably-trained elementary teachers. Thus, although Forster's measure amounted to a critical breakthrough, there were many loose ends to be tied up in the years that followed its passage through Parliament.

2   Subsequent Developments in Elementary Education

The passage of Forster's Act gave rise to the School Board era 1870–1902, a period during which the elementary educational scene was characterised by much change and many problems.

(a) Expansion of Provision

The inevitable competition between the School Boards and the church interests within the new framework ensured a rapid increase in available elementary school places. In 1870 the voluntary system had afforded less than one and three-quarter million places; by 1900 the dual system was providing five and three-quarter million and the ideal of universal elementary education had been realised. The Anglicans and Roman Catholics made a supreme effort during the 'period of grace' and tenaciously clung to their schools in succeeding years. As a result of almost doubling their provision the churches were still providing (without rate-aid) 53 per cent of the total elementary places available in 1900. Meanwhile, by filling the gaps not covered by the increased effort of the churches the School Boards had gradually come to provide well over two and a half million places. Some of these places arose from the British and Foreign Schools Society happily transferring many of its Nonconformist elementary schools to the local School Board, but the bulk of them were the outcome of new and direct provision by the Boards themselves. Starting as they did from nothing it was an impressive achievement by these new local authorities and one not really envisaged by the denominational interests in the early 1870s.

(b) Compulsory Attendance

The 1870 Act simply authorised, but did not require, the School Boards to frame local by-laws for the enforcement of attendance between five and thirteen years. The London School Board took full and immediate advantage of this power and its example encouraged other Boards to follow suit; but the majority proved extremely laggard and as more places became available the government took further action.

1876 *Sandon's Act*: this provided for the establishment of School Attendance Committees, with power to frame and enforce by-laws for compulsory attendance, in those districts still without a School Board and made it the parents' legal obligation to ensure that their children received 'efficient elementary instruction'. Employers were forbidden to employ children under ten years and were only to hire those over ten years on the production of a labour certificate issued by one of HM Inspectors authorising release from school. But even this measure proved unsatisfactory in practice because the passage and enforcement of suitable by-laws was not made a statutory requirement; the rural areas in particular did not respond adequately to Sandon's measure.

1880 *Mundella's Act*: this measure adopted a more direct approach by requiring all School Boards and School Attendance Committees to pass by-laws for compulsory attendance and to enforce them. They were to require unconditional attendance from five to ten years, whilst providing exemption arrangements for the ten to thirteen year olds on grounds of proficiency (i.e. reaching a given Standard under the 'payment by results' system) or satisfactory attendance during each of five consecutive years (the so-called 'Dunce's

Certificate'). No child could be held at school beyond his thirteenth birthday.

Thus from 1880 compulsory elementary education was a legal reality throughout the country, though it was only gradually that the magistracy and parents were conditioned to accept the new situation. Attendance officers continued to fight an uphill struggle in many areas until the turn of the century and the 'half-time' system (under which the older pupils were allowed special exemption to divide each day between work and school) lingered on in the textile areas until 1918. Meanwhile, the context was thought sufficiently improved to raise the minimum school-leaving age permitted under the by-laws to eleven years (1893) and then to twelve years (1899). And in 1900 it became permissible for pupils to be kept at school until their fourteenth birthday. Beyond the minimum, the age of actually leaving school varied considerably according to the exemption conditions laid down for the district concerned. This unsatisfactory situation continued until the 1918 Education Act ended the exemption arrangements and simply provided for a national minimum school-leaving age of fourteen years.

(c) Free Tuition

The 1870 Act expected parents to contribute towards the cost of providing their children with elementary education, although an the case of the Board schools an inflated upper limit of 9d per week per child was imposed. However, Section 25 did provide for the remission of fees for necessitous children in both Board and denominational schools, but this became a source of controversy when certain School Boards refused to remit such fees for children in church schools, whilst those Boards dominated by the Anglican interest remitted to these same children on a generous scale. In 1876 the anomalous situation and the bitter controversy surrounding it was resolved by transferring the responsibility for remitting the fees of necessitous children in church schools from the School Boards to the Poor Law Guardians; the price of this move was to attach a social stigma to those parents unable to pay for their children's elementary education at a church school. Meanwhile the payment of school fees bore hard upon many working class parents, especially those with large families suffering from the economic vicissitudes of the Great Depression. By the mid-1880s, with compulsory attendance now taking effect, elementary school fees had become a burning issue and the Trades Union Congress demanded their abolition. The London School Board, faced with much truancy and absenteeism, identified the continuance of fees as an obstacle to educational progress. In 1891 the government responded to the growing pressure with an Act which required all school districts to provide within twelve months free places for the children of all parents requiring these. The loss of income sustained by the schools was compensated from central sources by an extra capitation grant of 10s per child per annum; on balance this proved of most advantage to the Board schools where the fees had tended to be lower. Not all working class parents took advantage of the new situation, some preferring to pay fees for the privilege of sending their children to the more respectable or exclusive (e.g. Methodist) elementary schools. By the end of the century one-sixth of the elementary school places were still fee-paying, but no parent was paying such fees without desiring to do so. This residue of elementary school fees was not finally abolished until 1918.

(d) 'Payment by Results'

The 1870 Act accepted the basic principles underlying the Revised Code and even sanctified the sytem by giving it statutory authority. At the same time, however, Forster's measure made the actual grants payable more generous and thus began the slow and irregular process of liberalising Lowe's creation. The trend was for the Education Department to dilute the former stress on the three Rs and to widen the elementary school curriculum by offering grants for the teaching of other examinable subjects. The 'New Code' of 1871 offered a range of 'specific' subjects to be undertaken by individual children who had reached at least Standard IV in the three Rs; in 1875 various 'class' subjects were made available for the examination of all pupils in Standards II-VI. Thus elementary school children came to be taught English grammar, history, geography, simple science and practical subjects as successive codes widened the range of grant-earning possibilities. Gradually there was a significant shift in the curricula pattern and in the philosophy underlying elementary education which pointed forward to the enlightened Code of 1904. During the 1880s the annual examinations in the three Rs were placed on a sample (one-third minimum) basis, whilst the schools were given the opportunity to earn an additional 'merit' grant for organisation, discipline and general quality. In the mid-1890s Sir George Kekewich, appointed Permanent Secretary to the Education Department in 1889, finally abandoned the 'payment by results' system in favour of a single grant based on attendance and a satisfactory 'general inspection' report. At last the teachers had room for some manoeuvre in terms of curricula and method, whilst the children were delivered from the worst aspects of the mental drudgery promoted by the Revised Code. Meanwhile, the process of liberalisation had been accompanied by a remarkable rise in the Education Department's annual expenditure on elementary education, from less than £1 million in 1870 to over £5 million by the end of the century.

(e) Pioneering Influence of the School Boards

Some of the larger School Boards emerged as pace-setters in the develop-ment of elementary education, their claim upon the rates in highly developed urban areas facilitating such a role. In the last quarter of the nine-teenth century this progressive minority of public authorities was responsi-ble for various forms of educational advance:

(i) the introduction and expansion of higher-grade elementary education which afforded a secondary-type schooling (with a scientific, technical or commercial bias) for abler working class children who were pre-pared to stay on beyond the age of twelve. The Sheffield School Board pioneered this development in 1880 and the example was followed by Bradford, Nottingham, Halifax, Manchester, Leeds, Birmingham and London; by the late 1890s there were some seventy higher-grade schools with over 25,000 pupils and many more 'higher tops' in ordinary elementary schools, a development encouraged by the intro-duction of a new Standard VII in 1882. A trickle of students was even able to reach university by this new avenue of advance.

(ii) the establishment of pupil-teacher centres for the more effective pre-paration of pupil-teachers for the Queen's Scholarship examinations and training college entry. These centres, the first of which was established by the Liverpool School Board in 1874, began to afford something approaching a secondary education for teacher trainees undergoing apprenticeship between thirteen and eighteen years of age. This approach for raising the level of the trainee's personal education was adopted by other large School Boards in densely populated urban centres.

(iii) the improvement of teachers' salaries and conditions of service. The larger, progressive School Boards paid certificated teachers more generously, did not tie their salaries to annual examination results and laid down conditions of employment safeguarding them against capricious dismissal or unauthorised extraneous duties (cf. denomina-tional school managers and small rural School Boards).

(iv) the recognition of health, nourishment and disability as matters directly related to the success or failure of elementary schooling. It was the larger, progressive School Boards which pioneered the provision of schools meals, school baths and school medical inspection and the development of rate-aided special education for the handicapped, initially for the benefit of blind, deaf and mentally defective children. This pointed the way towards the legislation of the Edwardian era and the general acceptance of a concern for physical welfare as part of the State's responsibility to the younger generation.

(v) the raising of standards in respect of school buildings, the supply of
     books and equipment and the teacher-pupil ratio, resulting in a much
     higher *per capita* expenditure than was acceptable to the denomina-
     tional managers or the small School Boards. Over the years the latter
     bodies came under increasing pressure from the Education Depart-
     ment to match their standards of provision more closely to those of the
     pace-setters.

(f) Difficulties of the Church Schools

Throughout the School Board era the denominational schools laboured
under the disadvantage of having no rate-aid available to them. Once the
challenge of the 'period of grace' was passed the Anglican and Roman
Catholic communities did not take too kindly to the long-term need for
generous subscriptions as the only alternative to rate support. For many
denominational schools a vicious circle developed; being short of money,
they could not afford to employ the best teachers or provide satisfactory
facilities, and this resulted in second rate examination results and reduced
central grants, which in turn came full circle to affect adversely the schools'
ability to escape this situation. As already shown, the displacement of fees by
an extra capitation grant in 1891 was a mixed blessing to the Anglican
schools; too many of them lost more in fees than they gained from the new
'fee grant'. Meanwhile, the pace-setting School Boards and the rising
demands of the Education Department combined to increase progressively
the annual *per capita* cost of elementary education. In the face of this growing financial pressure a considerable number of Anglican schools gave up
the struggle and transferred their buildings to the local School Board.
Thoroughly alarmed, the churches turned to the Conservative government
of Lord Salisbury (elected to office in 1895) and pressed for the extension of
rate-aid to their schools. In fact, this long cherished hope was not met until
1902 and the denominational schools had to face another seven years of
financial difficulty and deteriorating provision. At the close of the century
the Board schools were spending 25 per cent more than their denominational counterparts on the elementary education of each child.

(g) Report of the Cross Commission 1888

Sixteen years after the passage of the 1870 Act and amidst the subsequent
developments just considered, a Conservative government appointed a
Royal Commission under the chairmanship of Lord Cross to investigate the
operation of the elementary education acts and to make recommendations
for any improvements. Most of the commissioners were past supporters of

the voluntary system, with Cardinal Manning, Roman Catholic Archbishop of Westminster, and Dr Temple, Anglican Bishop of London, predictably determined to push the ecclesiastical viewpoint very hard. But some of the commissioners were equally strongly committed to the further development of the School Boards' role and to the limitation of church influence and control in elementary education. Thus the division of opinion in Parliament and the country was sharply reflected in the composition of the Commission; unable to agree upon certain vital matters the commissioners were forced to draw up separate Majority and Minority reports duly signed by two-thirds and one-third of the members respectively. There were three areas of serious disagreement.

(i) *The Religious Issue*

The Majority report stressed the importance of positive religious and moral training for all children and the conviction that parents desired this. Whilst conceding the conscience clause, it recommended the repeal of the Cowper-Temple clause to enable denominational religious teaching to be introduced into the Board schools. The church interest was to be further secured by extending rate-aid to the denominational schools, freeing them from the payment of rates on their premises and giving them an equal right with the School Boards to fill any emergent gaps in provision in their school districts. But these demands were rejected by the Minority report which defended the Cowper-Temple clause and suggested that church schools in financial difficulty should simply surrender themselves to the local School Board. Moreover it also recommended that undenominational schools under public control should be available for every child whose parents desired them; this demand resulted from anti-denominational dissatisfaction with the continuance of many single-school areas in which parents were obliged to send their children to an Anglican school.

(ii) *The Higher-Grade Elementary Schools*

Sympathetic to the complaints of the endowed grammar schools and not well disposed towards the Schools Boards, the Majority report questioned the legality of the development of rate-supported secondary-type schooling in higher-grade elementary schools. It recommended that the term 'elementary education' as used in recent legislation should be more stringently defined so as to protect the grammar schools and other *bona fide* secondary institutions from unfair competition. But the Minority report championed the cause of higher-grade elementary education and encouraged the School Boards to expand such provision; it admitted the need to clarify the meaning of elementary education, but only in a way which would recognise and regularise this progressive and worthwhile development.

(iii) *The Pupil-Teacher System*

The Majority report backed its maintenance as the only 'available (and) trustworthy' source of teacher supply, although insisting that pupil-teacher centres and half-time attendance at them should become a standard part of it. The Minority report condemned outright the continuance of 'on the job' training and advised the complete abandonment of the system in favour of extended full-time education for would-be teachers. But such a radical suggestion could only be considered as part of the much larger question of the future of secondary education in England and Wales.

Because of the highly controversial nature of these issues it is not surprising that, apart from the development of more pupil-teacher centres, no immediate action was taken in relation to them. The line of least political resistance was to leave things as they were. But the longer-term significance of the Cross Commission can be discerned from the ultimate solutions once these particular nettles were really grasped after the turn of the century. In 1902 the Majority report's recommendations materialised in respect of rate-aid for the church schools and the abolition of the higher-grade elementary schools, whereas in the case of the pupil-teacher system the Board of Education finally applied the solution recommended by the Minority report.

However, the Cross Commissioners did share some common ground as well and *recommendations* were made which had a greater and more immediate effect than is usually appreciated:

  (i) the 'payment by results' system was sharply criticised and its further relaxation called for in order, amongst other things, to give room for greater curricula attention to science, technical and manual instruction of an elementary sort and for an improvement in the relationship between teachers and HM Inspectorate. The Education Department quickly responded with the liberal Code of 1890 and within a decade had gone on to abandon the whole system.

 (ii) the duration of compulsory schooling caused dissatisfaction and the Commission recommended that it should be extended by raising the minimum age at which exemption arrangements could apply. The Acts of 1893 and 1899, already mentioned earlier in this chapter (page 45), were in line with the Commission's desire.

(iii) the Commission underlined the need for more generous elementary provision in terms of accommodation, playgrounds, books and equipment; this demand was written into the annual Codes of the 1890s although often to the discomfiture of the denominational schools.

(iv) the need to increase the supply of trained certificated elementary teachers and to raise the standard of training college courses was recognised by the Commission and various means of achieving this were suggested. To supplement the efforts of the forty-odd rather small voluntary colleges already in existence, the Commission recommended the establishment of undenominational day training colleges in association with the universities and university colleges. The latter institutions would provide the academic training whilst special lecturers would be responsible for the principles and practice of education; this would enable prospective elementary teachers to study for a degree whilst undergoing their professional training. In accordance with the latter possibility it was further suggested that some student teachers would benefit from a three-year course of training. By the end of the century there were some sixteen such institutions which pointed the way to the University Education Departments of the future. Indeed, the new day training colleges quickly came to supply a quarter of the trained certificated entrants to elementary teaching (1900). If the Minority commissioners had had their way, day training colleges would have been established under the auspices of the larger School Boards as well as the universities. This was not to be, but the idea later found expression in the municipal training colleges established by the new LEAs under the 1902 Act.

Thus the report of the Cross Commission, as well as throwing much light on the divisive issues of the School Board era, wielded a quite significant influence upon later developments in elementary education.

4 Developments in Secondary Education during the Nineteenth Century

Any attempt at a clinical treatment of the present topic is beset by certain difficulties which should be recognised at the outset. Firstly, the term secondary education did not come into general and official use in England and Wales until the close of the century; and secondly, throughout the period concerned there was no clear dividing line, especially in respect of non-classical instruction, between secondary education on the one hand and elementary and technical education on the other. Nevertheless it is convenient and helpful for the historian of nineteenth-century English education to use the term secondary, looking upon such education as that traditionally associated with classical studies and possible entrance to university and increasingly provided on a fee-paying basis for the almost exclusive benefit of the upper and middle classes. This said, the study of the development of secondary education in nineteenth-century England may be divided into two major aspects.

1 The Condition of Secondary Education in the Early Nineteenth Century

Contemporary sources of evidence show that secondary-type educational provision at this time was both inadequate in its extent and generally most unsatisfactory in its substance. However, any further analysis must distinguish between the various and distinct sources of secondary education then available.

(a) Endowed Grammar Schools

There were some seven hundred or more of these schools, originally endowed by pious founders for the free education of local inhabitants in the learned languages and still maintaining their traditional connection with the established Church. Whilst the great majority were still only small local grammar schools, a tiny minority of them, led by the mediaeval foundations of Winchester and Eton, had emerged as national institutions depending largely on fee-paying boarders drawn from the ranks of the aristocracy and gentry; by the beginning of the nineteenth century the latter were already being referred to as the 'great public schools'. Authoritative contemporary sources of evidence, both official and otherwise, are most severe in their strictures on the endowed grammar schools at this time. The personal investigations of Nicholas Carlisle, covering almost five hundred of these institutions and leading to the publication of his *A Concise Description of the Endowed Grammar Schools in England and Wales* (1818), proved highly unfavourable and his impression was later confirmed by the official inquiries of the Charity Commission 1818–37. As late as the 1860s the Clarendon and Taunton Commissions found much ground for serious criticism when they were called to report upon the schools concerned. Such evidence has been the basis of the orthodox historical viewpoint that by the early nineteenth century a hundred years or more of growing neglect and malpractice had reduced these schools to their lowest ebb in terms of educational efficiency and public esteem. Only recently has further research provided reason to question whether the picture was quite as bad as it has been painted and particularly whether the condition of the schools was the result of the negligence and cupidity of those entrusted with their functioning rather than the result of overwhelming educational, social and economic pressures. Whilst space will not permit an elaboration of the intricacies of this argument, it is possible to affirm the fact that the endowed grammar schools had suffered a decline during the eighteenth century and to attempt a balanced analysis of the main symptoms and causes of this decline.

(i) *Inadequate Provision*

Even if the condition of the endowed grammar schools had been sound, the extent and distribution of provision would have been a weakness. The rapid growth and shift of population in the age of the Industrial Revolution aggravated the shortage of such schools and crystallised their maldistribution. In Tudor times there had been one endowed grammar school for every six thousand inhabitants; by the early nineteenth century the ratio had deteriorated to one school to every twenty-four thousand people. Not only had the country's population risen greatly but the rate at which new endowed grammar schools were founded had fallen very markedly. The charity school movement which attracted philanthropic support towards purely elementary education and the rising demand for non-classical instruction combined to make the eighteenth century an inauspicious period in the growth of the endowed grammar school system. Meanwhile, most of these schools, founded usually in Tudor or Stuart times, were located in southern market towns, but the growing need for secondary education was in the developing industrial and commercial centres of the north.

(ii) *Unsatisfactory Government*

Falling standards in the social and official life of Hanoverian England, finding particular expression in political corruption and ecclesiastical indifference, reached their height in the later eighteenth century. Since the Restoration the endowed grammar schools had become subject to narrow Anglican control and increasingly reflected the laxity and abuses of the Church. Many trustees, drawn largely from the landed gentry, the established Church and the unreformed municipal corporations, became negligent and irresponsible in the performance of their duties. Some of the schoolmasters, most of whom were Anglican clergymen, were similarly affected. Official investigations into the administration of all charitable endowments as a prelude to Gilbert's Poor Law Act (1786) pointed to considerable irregularity in the management of trust property. The inquiries of Brougham's parliamentary Select Committee (1816–18), following the widening of its terms of reference to include endowed grammar schools, and subsequently of the Charity Commission (1818–37), revealed many flagrant abuses, including the misappropriation of endowment income and the existence of numerous sinecures and pluralist arrangements whereby schoolmasters drew salaries without performing any teaching duties. At the close of the eighteenth century Lord Chief Justice Kenyon, pronouncing upon a legal case concerning one of the endowed grammar schools, thought fit to comment upon their 'lamentable condition' and to deplore the neglect of everything except the receipt of incomes. In 1812 Parliament finally registered its concern by accepting in principle the need for the inspection and stricter control of charitable endowments.

(iii) *Financial Difficulties*

Inflationary conditions in the later eighteenth century and during the period of the French wars subjected the endowed schools to pressure in two ways. Firstly, many schools on small fixed endowments faced a heavy and continuing fall in the real value of their annual income. At the turn of the century only a dozen schools enjoyed an endowment income of over £1,000; some 60 per cent of them were endowed to the extent of only £100 or less which was hardly sufficient to pay a satisfactory stipend to the master. Secondly, given the rise in the age of university entry since Tudor times (i.e. from fifteen to sixteen years to eighteen to nineteen years), inflation gnawed at the ability and willingness of the parents of potential foundationers (i.e. those receiving free education) to afford their sons a full grammar education. Thus many schools were faced with a choice between the continuance of their classical tradition and the maintenance of their charitable function. Various results flowed from this unhappy conflict. To continue as a classical school usually involved the introduction of entry fees and extra charges for 'free' foundationers and increasing resort to the attraction of fee-payers (often boarders from further afield) to the neglect of free scholars. To maintain the charitable function often meant the acceptance of dilapidated buildings, inadequate books and equipment and serious understaffing. Sometimes for the sheer lack of local classical scholars a free grammar school would be degraded to the position of an endowed elementary school in which new capacity it would carry on its charitable role.

(iv) *Outdated Curricula*

As late as the early nineteenth century the bulk of the endowed grammar schools had failed to widen and modernise their curriculum which had originated in the Renaissance and which was based on the teaching of Latin and Greek supported by religious worship and instruction acceptable to the Anglican Church. Even the study of the learned languages had been reduced to an arid exercise in grammar and syntax, with far too little concern for the much greater educational benefits to be derived from an exploration and understanding of the life, thought and times of ancient Greece and Rome. Although many of the small number of new eighteenth-century foundations provided for English as well as classical studies and a minority of the older schools did introduce such subjects as mathematics, French, history and geography, well over two-thirds of the existing endowed grammar schools had undergone no curricula change. And at the beginning of the nineteenth century, in spite of the growing demand for a more modern and useful curriculum, any attempts to alter the situation still faced serious obstacles. Few of the schoolmasters serving the endowed grammar schools were either qualified or prepared to make the necessary adjustments. Secured in many cases by a freehold tenure of office which protected them from dismissal, and able to make a satisfactory living from the endowment salary and receipts from fee-payers, they had no interest in pioneering or accepting change. The majority were content to ignore the demands of both trustees and local parents in the knowledge that the foundation deeds usually justified such a stand and that they would be upheld in the Court of Chancery. Indeed the progressive trustees of Leeds Grammar School, who were interested in pushing curricula reform against the opposition of the schoolmaster, had their efforts stymied by the Eldon judgement of 1805 which pronounced it illegal to switch an endowment to the support of purposes other than those laid down in the founder's trust deeds. As the grammar school was defined as an institution 'for teaching grammatically the learned languages', this decision did much to bolster the position of the classics and their defenders. Even the Grammar School Act (1840), ostensibly designed to encourage and facilitate curricula change by the trustees, was so riddled with provisos that its impact was very limited. Thus the law served to support the conservative stand adopted by the schoolmasters. What curricula reform was achieved in the endowed grammar schools at this time took place on a very narrow front as a result of introducing other subjects as extras requiring additional fees, which usually denied them to the free scholars. Where such change occurred the additions were more likely to be elementary than modern subjects. The main business of the endowed grammar schools remained the teaching of the classics.

(v) *Low Moral Tone*

The ethos of many of these institutions was very unsatisfactory, being at its worst in the public schools and those few local grammar schools with a significant number of boarders. The boarding arrangements were characterised by scanty food and rough living. The system of fagging and the universal bullying ensured that all pupils in the public schools began as slaves and ended up as tyrants. A contemporary critic described these schools as a 'system of premature debauchery' which provided an early initiation into aristocratic insensitivity and vice. Shortage of staff left dormitory life virtually unsupervised and senior pupils took to drinking, gambling, cruel amusements, homosexuality and even association with prostitutes. There was little or no provision made for the boys' free time, organised games still being a thing of the future; outside classroom and dormitory, fighting and blood sports were the main physical outlets. The headmaster's authority was maintained by means of terror and certain heads became renowned floggers. Most memorable was Dr Keate, headmaster of Eton 1809–34, around whom many legends grew. It was said that on one occasion he flogged a batch of Confirmation candidates because the list of names was submitted on a sheet of paper very similar to the usual punishment slips! In his sixtieth year Keate still found the energy to flog eighty boys in one day. The serious understaffing is the main explanation of this resort to such punitive discipline; at Eton there were only nine masters to almost six hundred pupils and sometimes Keate himself took control of one-third of these in the upper schoolroom. Of course the boys did not take kindly to such régimes and mounted several serious rebellions against authority in the late eighteenth and early nineteenth centuries. In 1797 Dr Inglis, then headmaster of Rugby and endearingly called the 'Black Tiger' by his pupils, had his study door blown off with gunpowder and only the reading of the Riot Act and the appearance of the military cowed the young insurgents. An outburst at Eton in 1818 persuaded even Keate to vacate the premises whilst his charges took a sledgehammer to his fine oaken desk! Winchester was recurrently affected by serious disturbances, a rising there in the same year requiring the intervention of soldiers armed with fixed bayonets before order was restored. Both pupils and masters regarded each other as natural enemies and acted accordingly; Keate expected all his pupils to lie to him and they rarely disappointed him in this respect. Clearly these institutions had their own corporate character and were described by Gladstone, one of their contemporary products, as 'the greatest pagan schools in Christendom'. Yet ironically many of the great statesmen of the age passed through these public schools and survived all their educational deficiencies; surely they emerged as national figures in spite of their schooling rather than because of it. Happily the majority of the endowed grammar schools, not being boarding institutions, did not have this problem to exacerbate their other shortcomings.

(b)   Private Institutions and Means

The characteristic features of the endowed grammar and public schools were hardly calculated to recommend them to the rising middle class with its strong Nonconformist element or to the more discriminating families of the upper class. The result was an increasing resort to other means of obtaining a satisfactory secondary education.

(i)   *Private Tutors*

A growing number of the aristocracy and wealthier gentry hired private residential tutors to teach their sons, whose education was sometimes rounded off by a grand tour of Europe. Middle class parents took to sharing the services of a private visiting tutor. In both cases these private tutors tended to give their charges a more modern and broader education than was available in the old grammar schools and the ancient universities.

(ii)   *Private Classical Schools*

Usually run by Anglican clergymen for fee-paying pupils and sometimes including boarders, these small schools still placed the classical languages at the centre of the curriculum, but attracted the support of the gentry and professional people because of their respectable atmosphere, satisfactory boarding arrangements, somewhat wider curricula and greater teaching efficiency. Some two hundred such schools were in existence as the turn of the century.

(iii) *Private Academies and Schools*

By the early nineteenth century there were thousands of non-classical institutions of every size, kind and quality aspiring to provide secondary-type education for the emerging middle classes. Anglican domination of the endowed grammar and private classical schools as well as the ancient universities had produced the Dissenting academies of the eighteenth century; pioneering the widening and modernising of the traditional curricula, they provided the best secondary and higher education then available, but were in sharp decline by the early nineteenth century. Their progressive spirit had been passed on to the private academies offering an encyclopaedic range of subjects to the older student and the ubiquitous private schools providing a more practical education for the sons of merchants, manufacturers and superior tradesmen. Both types of institution were run by private individuals for profit although some of the private schools were founded and supported by particular religious sects. The Quakers, Methodists and Presbyterians, particularly active and prosperous in the field of business and industry, developed a small number of exclusive private schools, sometimes with boarding arrangements, which educated men like John Bright and others destined to play a significant role in the future public and economic life of the country. It was the private schools which supported the few educational experiments of the time: particularly noteworthy in this respect was the Hazelwood School in Birmingham run by the Hill family, with its wide curricula, main and optional subjects, progressive teaching methods based on the spirit of emulation and pupil self-government in matters of discipline and control. The common elements which distinguished the majority of private schools from their endowed grammar counterparts were the close supervision of pupils and the teaching of non-classical subjects. These were the features which attracted the middle classes to the financial support of such schools. But the private schools of the early nineteenth century had serious shortcomings. Depending on individual enterprise they were ephemeral in nature and strongly subject to profit motives rather than educational considerations in their development. Too many were conducted on a small scale in poor accommodation and with inadequate equipment. Those trying to attract the support of the lower ranks of the middle class gave a very limited education which was hardly
rior to an elementary schooling. Even in the better schools there was no
nception of how to develop non-classical secondary education. It was
ell to condemn classical studies and exalt useful and practical
it was a much more difficult matter to develop the teaching of
way that was educationally beneficial. At this time the
lly a barren catechetical one based on rote-learning and

teacher questioning. In defending their own position the supporters of classical studies made the most of this palpable weakness.

(c) Secondary Education for Girls

This was provided on a limited but expanding scale for the daughters of upper and middle class parents by means of private governesses or private academies and schools of variable exclusiveness. Girls were debarred from the endowed grammar and public schools and there was no attempt to develop their intellect through the classics for their intelligence was considered inferior anyway. For the more socially distinguished there were very expensive boarding establishments in such places as Brighton; here young ladies would remain until about the age of eighteen preparing themselves for entry into Regency society. The main concern was for those feminine accomplishments considered important for the marriage market – dancing, singing, instrumental music, deportment, embroidery, painting, French, Italian and German. This was combined with a smattering of general knowledge obtained from catechisms of historical and geographical facts and some English and arithmetic. Time was allocated in inverse proportion to the educational importance of the subject and everything was pursued at a shallow level. In the towns there were cheaper day schools to serve the needs of the lower middle class whose daughters would leave at fourteen or thereabouts. Here the emphasis was on teaching the girls reading and writing, plain needlework and some arithmetic; beyond this they might use various catechisms to acquire a superficial knowledge of English grammar, history, geography and even science. Many such establishments were inferior to the better elementary schools. Of course, no real improvement was likely until the restrictive attitude towards female education was changed. But early feminists like the author Mary Wollstonecraft, who demanded a new approach to female education, were simply dismissed as eccentrics.

2 Reform, Reorganisation and Expansion

During the middle years of the nineteenth century the endowed grammar and public schools faced growing criticism from various quarters. The utilitarians, hostile to the maintenance of outmoded practices and traditional institutions which no longer served the needs of contemporary society, condemned their useless curriculum. Supporters of the 'scientific movement' were particularly disgruntled at their almost total neglect of the natural sciences. The Evangelicals deplored the low moral tone and lack of

Christian ethos displayed by some of them. The rising middle classes with their business interests and background demanded value for money in terms of educational relevance and efficiency. As the wealthy manufacturers sank their differences with the landed interest to form a composite upper-middle class, the rehabilitation of the public schools as a bulwark to their social supremacy became a matter of urgency. Meanwhile, the less wealthy elements of the middle class looked to the rejuvenation and transformation of the endowed grammar schools as a means of securing their social position in relation to that of the lower orders of society. The resultant developments were inevitably calculated to remove free scholars from the schools concerned and to make secondary education the almost exclusive preserve of the well-to-do, leaving the working classes with only elementary education available to them.

(a)   Reform of the Public Schools

By the close of the century the upper-middle class had a considerable number of reputable and expensive public boarding schools available to them. Brought into close association by the Headmasters' Conference (established in 1869), these independent schools enjoyed a strong connection with Oxford and Cambridge with which they combined to educate and character-train the social elite of late Victorian times. The rehabilitation and expansion of the public school system hinged upon several developments.

(i)   *Reforming Headmasters*

Internal changes in the public schools were largely the result of the efforts and example of a growing number of reforming headmasters. The beginnings of such influence can be seen in the work of Samuel Butler at Shrewsbury (1793–1836) and Charles Butler at Harrow (1805–29). It was critically advanced by the headmastership of Thomas Arnold at Rugby (1828–42) who made his school the generally accepted model for reform. In the middle years of the century it blossomed in the work of Hawtrey at Eton (1834–52), Kennedy at Shrewsbury (1836–66), Vaughan at Harrow (1845–59) and Cotton at Marlborough (1851–8). Later on, the cause of internal reform centred upon the outstanding contribution and influence of Edward Thring of Uppingham (1853–87). Gradually the material standards of provision were raised to afford a more favourable physical environment for the life of the schools. Helped by the reform of the old universities during the 1850s it was possible to improve staffing quality and ratios so as to secure more efficient teaching and supervision. A less arid approach to the teaching of the classics and some widening of the curriculum developed, although advance in these respects was rather limited before the report of the Clarendon Commission (1864). Most important, however, was the marked improvement in the moral tone of the public schools; the reforming head-masters effectively used the school chapel and the prefect system as a means of diffusing Christian values and responsible attitudes amongst the pupils.

Although the Arnold 'myth' (the idea that the reform of the public schools in the nineteenth century was the work of one outstanding man) is no longer tenable, his personal influence was very great and in some respects even critical to the future of the public schools. It is true that one of his pre-decessors at Rugby had done much to improve the buildings and accommodation of the school, but its atmosphere remained tyrannical and amoral and it was left to Arnold to transform Rugby into the ideal to be followed by countless numbers of future public school headmasters and teachers. His process of reformation, conducted in a highly impressionist fashion, was characterised by several noteworthy features. Firstly, he placed his trust in the Christian faith and a liberal culture as the foundation stones of a satisfactory education: the school chapel services and his own sermons, the study of the classics and the humanities were all central to life and work at Rugby where the aim was to produce Christian gentlemen. Secondly, he brought about a radical improvement of the school's internal organisation with particular emphasis upon ensuring more effective supervision of pupils; to this end he raised the staffing ratio on the basis of full-time residential appointments, arranged for smaller dormitories and a more civilised fagging system and developed a strong sense of mutual trust and respect between himself and the senior pupils to support the operation of a proselytising prefect system. Finally, he developed a wider curriculum with history, choir singing and organised games achieving a prominent place; the study of classics was revitalised by using them as a vehicle for the teaching of ancient history, literature, philosophy, politics and geography as well as the Latin and Greek languages. The impact of the Arnold tradition was initially strongest in the new public schools and only later began seriously to affect the older ones. From the public schools his reforming influence finally spread to the endowed grammar schools once they received a new lease of life from the work of the Taunton Commission (1864–8). His influence did much to restore public confidence in the traditional secondary institutions and his broad Christianity encouraged a growing number of wealthy Non-conformists to support them.

(ii) *Clarendon Commission 1861–4*

The rehabilitation of the public schools was also helped by the work and influence of the Clarendon Commission 1861–4, appointed to investigate the condition of the nine 'great' public schools. In spite of the positive lead given by Arnold, the situation was recognised as still unsatisfactory with Westminster and Charterhouse suffering continued decline. Although the criticisms and recommendations made by Lord Clarendon and his colleagues were rather muted, the Commission's report did result in certain limited improvements. Firstly, it led to the reform of the governing bodies to ensure a broader membership and more professional responsibility; hitherto their pursuance of pecuniary and clerical interests had been a serious source of weakness in the running of these schools. The need for such reform received the statutory backing of the Public Schools Act (1868) which established a small commission to undertake the task. But once reformed the governing bodies were to be trusted to proceed with other reforms without any further State interference. Secondly, the report led to a gradual broadening, though not a transformation, of the traditional curriculum. The classics remained the core, consuming over half of the teaching time, but their treatment was revitalised in 'Arnold fashion'. Beyond this, increasing importance was attached to the study of subsidiary subjects such as English, modern languages, mathematics and science. This was in line with the Prussian gymnasium programme recommended by the report and did something to dilute the traditional dominance of Latin and Greek in these schools. Thirdly, the report resulted in the reform of the foundation statutes so as to remove anachronistic restrictions upon the use of endowment funds; but the most important single result of this was to abolish the right of children of local inhabitants to enjoy a free education at these institutions in favour of open competition for fee-paying places. As very few scholarships were offered in lieu of the foundation places lost, this development was in line with the Clarendon Commission's expressed desire to rehabilitate these schools for the exclusive benefit of the upper-middle class.

(iii) Rise of New Public Schools

These schools, based on the reformed model, made a major contribution to the process of rehabilitating and expanding the system. These new public schools emerged during the middle and later years of the nineteenth century in one of two ways. In the 1830s the wealthier and more discriminating elements of the middle class had supported the development of proprietary day schools characterised by an absence of religious teaching, a wide and modern curricula, optional subjects and a respectable ethos. The prototypes, such as Liverpool Institute (1825) and University College School, London (1828), were very successful and the movement spread. With the coming of the railways the next stage was to use joint-stock enterprise to develop proprietary boarding schools to meet the growing demands of the same clientele. The result was the establishment of Cheltenham (1841), Marlborough (1843), Rossall (1844), Wellington (1853), Epsom (1855),

Clifton (1860), Malvern (1862), Haileybury (1864) and Bath (1867). Contemporaneously the Woodard Foundation, associated with the Anglican church, set up middle class boarding schools at Lancing, Hurstpierpoint and Ardingly. Whilst modelling themselves in many respects upon Arnold's Rugby, these new schools were more progressive in their approach to the curriculum. They aimed at providing an efficient education for professional and business careers at a time when more exacting entry requirements were being demanded for careers in the civil service, the army, medicine and the law. At Rossall non-classical courses were organised from an early date with particular professional destinations in mind. In most of these schools, whilst Latin was retained, Greek was usually omitted from the curriculum. Such was the movement which by the end of the century had added considerably, both quantitatively and qualitatively, to the public school system. The other source of expansion was the aspiring endowed grammar schools some of which, assisted by the aftermath of the Taunton Commission report (1868), gradually broke their links with their own locality and emerged as boarding schools enjoying a national reputation. Once they obtained membership of the Headmasters' Conference these endowed grammar schools became part of the public school system. Edward Thring transformed Uppingham in this way and Repton, Sherborne and Tonbridge are other good examples of such translation.

The continued growth of the upper-middle class with its social sensitivity, the coming of the railways giving easy access to the countryside and the growth of the Empire resulting in many well-to-do parents living abroad combined to ensure that the reform and expansion of the public school system could and would be taken full advantage of. A concomitant Victorian development was the rise of satellite preparatory schools. These spread across the country and increasingly specialised in preparing their eight to thirteen-year-old fee-paying pupils for entry into the public school system. In 1892 the headmasters involved formed the Incorporated Association of Preparatory Schools and eleven years later the 'Common Entrance Examination' was established.

(b)   Reform of the Endowed Grammar Schools

It was not until the last quarter of the century that the provision of secondary education for the lesser-middle class and more prosperous skilled artisans took a distinct turn for the better. Aware of continuing failure to meet the needs of this important section of the population, the government appointed the Taunton Commission 1864–8 to investigate the position fully. As well as the procuring of written evidence and the oral examination of witnesses, the inquiry involved the dispatch of assistant commissioners to selected districts (e.g. James Bryce to Lancashire). Nearly eight hundred endowed schools and over one hundred proprietary and private schools were visited. As expected the findings revealed a most depressing situation. Whilst the proprietary schools earned a fair report, the unsatisfactory state of the endowed schools purporting to provide a secondary education was relieved only by the even worse shortcomings of the typical private school – of which, it was estimated, there were some ten thousand now spread across the country! Accordingly this extremely thorough report made a number of positive and far-reaching *recommendations*:

  (i) the establishment of a national system of secondary education based on a proper administrative framework which would include a central agency and a number of provincial authorities. Within this co-ordinative framework individual schools would retain their own governors with responsibility for appointing the headmaster, managing the finances and determining the curricula.

 (ii) the differentiation of the schools into three categories (first, second and third grades) according to the existing socio-economic divisions within the middle class. The school fees, the school leaving age (eighteen, sixteen and fourteen respectively) and the curricula would vary according to category. It was emphasised that the greatest need was for third grade secondary schools to serve the lower-middle class and skilled artisans.

(iii) the need to rationalise the use of educational endowments to improve provision, to change trust deeds where they inhibited reform and to reform governing bodies as a means of infusing new life into the schools. Within this context the report recognised the particular need to extend and transform the provision of secondary education for girls.

(iv) the introduction of a 'scholastic register' for competent secondary teachers and of a national system of examinations for secondary pupils. Both these recommendations were designed to improve the efficiency of teaching and to check the dilution of the profession and the proliferation of local examinations.

If the Taunton recommendations had been implemented in their entirety, England would have obtained a national system of secondary education some thirty odd years before it was actually launched. Perhaps unhappily the stiff opposition of the headmasters (led by Thring) to any form of State interference in the secondary field received political support from the ranks of the Tory party. Given the Gladstone government's preoccupation with elementary education, this ensured that the immediate results of the Taunton Report were meagre and disappointing. But, in an unspectacular way, it wielded a slow reformative influence right down to the end of the century and thus in the longer term produced a number of significant *results*.

(i) The Endowed Schools Act (1869) authorised the long and painful process by which the Endowed Schools Commission (1869–74) and later the Charity Commission (1874–99) reformed and redistributed the educational endowments and reconstituted the governing bodies of the endowed grammar schools. The result was to strengthen the financial base of the schools and to exert some indirect influence in favour of a wider curricula and more efficient teaching.

(ii) The redrafting of trust deeds facilitated the alienation of the grammar schools from their original purpose (i.e. the free education of children of local inhabitants). Whilst the Commissioners' schemes made provision for a small number of scholarships, the existing foundation places were scrapped and even endowments for elementary education were transferred to the local grammar school. This whole process was extremely unfavourable to the working class but was slowly driven to its conclusion in spite of protests. It secured the endowed grammar schools as a source of subsidised secondary education for the middle class and enabled a minority of them to pass into the public school system.

(iii) The Taunton emphasis on the need for third grade secondary schools and the possibility of granting some form of public financial aid to them helps to explain two important developments in the later nineteenth century. Firstly, the rise of higher-grade elementary education by which the larger, more progressive School Boards provided a secondary-type schooling at low cost was in tune with the Taunton idea. Secondly, an increasing amount of financial help from public sources was made available to the endowed grammar schools. At the price of widening their curriculum they were able to earn grants from the Department of Science and Art for the teaching of science, technical and modern subjects and to obtain funds from the new Technical Instruction Committees empowered after 1889 to dispense rate-aid for the support of local technical and secondary education.

(iv) The influence of the Taunton Commission made a major contribution to the improvement and extension of secondary provision for girls. Miss Frances Mary Buss at North London Collegiate School (1850) and Miss Dorothea Beale at Cheltenham Ladies' College (1853) had already emerged as pioneers in the field and both were able to impress the Commission with their evidence. Thus the needs of middle class female secondary education received considerable attention in the Report and in the years that followed real advance took place. In redistributing endowments the Endowed Schools Commissioners and the Charity Commissioners were authorised and encouraged to use any surplus funds for the establishment of new endowed grammar schools for girls. Bradford Girls' Grammar School and Leeds Girls' High School were two of the earliest such foundations and by the close of the century over eighty were in existence. But this process was a slow one, leaving much room for supplementation by private enterprise. In 1872 another pioneer, Mrs Maria Grey, encouraged by the concern shown by the Taunton Commission, founded the Girls' Public Day School Trust on a joint-stock basis. Over the succeeding quarter-century this body was responsible for the establishment of nearly forty reputable girls' secondary schools in London and the main provincial towns. After 1883 similar efforts to promote secondary education for girls were made by the Church Schools Company, although the number of new schools resulting was much smaller. In all these new foundations the old emphasis on female accomplishments gave way to the more 'solid instruction' recommended by the Taunton Commission; although the curriculum was modelled on that of the boy's grammar schools, the tendency was for the new girls' schools to adopt a more markedly modern approach. Indeed by the close of the century the girls' schools were setting the example in the development of new teaching methods and the recognition of the importance of professional training as a complement to academic knowledge.

By 1900 the condition of the public and endowed grammar schools had certainly improved, even though the lower classes (the sons of skilled artisans excepted perhaps) were now virtually denied entry to them. Girls' secondary education had benefited from a remarkable improvement during the last quarter of the century. But, failing the full implementation of the Taunton Commission recommendations, Britain still did not have a national system of secondary education resting on a proper administrative framework, nor, in an increasingly competitive world, was the extent of the provision adequate to meet the socio-economic needs of the time. Any decisive intervention by the State had been successfully resisted by those interested in protecting the public and endowed grammar schools from any real measure of public control. Matthew Arnold's repeated exhortation, 'Organise your secondary education', had not been met and this contributed very greatly to the administrative muddle in English education as a whole which had become intolerable by the 1890s. Meanwhile the Welsh Intermediate Act (1889), which did so much to organise and support a State system of secondary education in the principality, served to underline the need for further radical measures in England. All this led to the report of the Bryce Commission on *Secondary Education* (1895) which set the stage for the 1902 Education Act and the subsequent development of State secondary schools in England.

5 The Forging of a National System: the 1902 Act

Any attempt at a thorough understanding of why and how a national system of education was at last forged for England and Wales must rest on a satisfactory knowledge of the quarter-century which preceded the outbreak of the First World War (1914–18). Within this context the origins, the provisions and the results of the 1902 Education Act must be subjected to particular examination. The relevant subject matter may be considered in four main parts.

1 The Need for a National System

The need for a national system and hence for decisive legislative action had become very pressing by the close of the nineteenth century. That this need was increasingly recognised and supported by a growing consensus of influential opinion has various explanations.

(a) Administrative Muddle

The piecemeal development of State interest and involvement in education had produced a multiplicity of largely separate and unco-ordinated agencies working in the field. Central administrative responsibilities were wielded by the Education Department, the Department of Science and Art and the Charity Commission. Local administrative responsibilities were in the hands of the School Boards, the School Attendance Committees, the Technical Instruction Committees of the new County and County Borough Councils, the governors of the public and endowed grammar schools, and the managers of the voluntary elementary schools. As their respective spheres of responsibility had not been clearly defined the result was overlap, confusion and conflict. The need was for rationalisation aimed at the establishment of a single central department and a single type of local authority which could ensure co-ordination and efficient provision throughout the whole educational field and provide a satisfactory administrative foundation for the development of a national system of education.

(b) Position of the Voluntary Schools

This gave rise to increasing concern as the financial and administrative implications of the 1870 Act for these schools became clear. Denied the advantage of rate-aid the voluntary schools were hard-pressed to maintain the minimal rising standards of elementary provision: by the mid-1890s the Anglican Church claimed that for want of money the very survival of its schools was at stake. As the denominational schools were right outside the jurisdiction of the School Boards, the central government had continued to maintain direct administrative contact with their voluntary managers; by the end of the century there were over fourteen thousand such managing bodies for the over-worked Education Department to deal with and it had become an intolerable burden only marginally eased by the end of the 'payment by results' system. The need was to end or mend the dual system, the choice depending on one's attitude to the denominational schools as such. Whilst the Tory party and the Anglican and Roman Catholic Churches pressed for a new deal for the voluntary schools, the Liberals, supported by the working class movement and the Nonconformists, were unsympathetic and disposed to resist any attempt by the State to rescue them from their financial difficulties.

(c) Inadequacy of Secondary and Technical Educational Provision

The first sure signs of a threat to Britain's industrial supremacy had appeared at the Paris Industrial Exhibition of 1867, since when the growth of foreign competition and the comparative decline of British economic strength had given cause for growing alarm. Slowly but surely it was recognised that Britain's main commercial rivals, such as modern Germany, were equipped with superior systems of secondary and technical education. Various official investigating bodies and widely travelled individuals like Matthew Arnold insisted that our industrial and commercial future would remain increasingly vulnerable until such time as higher education was organised and expanded. Meanwhile the pupil-teacher system was being subjected to growing criticism because of its failure to provide prospective elementary teachers with a satisfactory level of personal education; Robert Morant and many others were convinced that the only proper solution was for the State to abandon the old system and provide a secondary education for those concerned. Another recognised weakness was the insufficiency of training college places resulting from the long-established reliance upon voluntary initiative in this field; the argument in favour of developing a system of State training colleges had become too strong to be denied any longer. Thus for one reason or another there was a need for much more vigorous and systematic State involvement in the 'other than elementary' field of education.

(d)   Mounting Opposition to the School Boards

Whilst many of the small rural School Boards had proved inefficient and a source of embarrassment to the Education Department, the larger, progressive School Boards had aroused the growing hostility of the denominational interests, the endowed grammar schools and the new Technical Instruction Committees. To the sharp mind of Robert Morant, a rising professional administrator at Whitehall, the *ad hoc* School Boards were a serious obstacle to administrative efficiency and the creation of a national system of education. They did not cover the whole country and were not designed to undertake responsibility for the whole field of education. Worse still perhaps, they had become the objects of bitter political and religious conflict and as such were no longer calculated to serve the best interests of education. The new County and County Borough Councils seemed to offer a much sounder basis for the development of effective educational administration and provision on a broadening front at the local level.

2   Towards the 1902 Education Act

At the close of the nineteenth century a number of significant and successive developments combined to set the stage for the Balfour Act of 1902.

(a)   1888 Local Government Act

This established the multi-purpose County and County Borough Councils which were destined to become the vital base of a national system of education in England and Wales. In the following year the Technical Instruction Act took advantage of the new local government framework to project local rate-aid into the provision and support of technical education. By the late 1890s many of the resultant Technical Instruction Committees were widening their role to develop a growing interest in secondary education as well.

(b) 1889 Welsh Intermediate Act

This was the delayed result of the Aberdare report on *Intermediate and Higher Education in Wales* (1881) which had revealed the lamentable state of Welsh secondary education. Much worse off than England for endowed grammar schools, the strong Nonconformist community in Wales was disinclined to use them anyway because of their established Church connection; nor were there many reputable proprietary secondary schools available to fill the gap. The Act created joint education committees in each county and county borough of the Principality for the development of secondary and technical education. Rate-aid support was to be matched by treasury grants (subject to inspection) and supplemented by existing endowments. Within six months the Act was being effectively applied and at a later stage the Central Welsh Board (1896) emerged to co-ordinate the work and to undertake responsibility for inspection. By the end of the century almost one hundred new Welsh secondary schools had resulted from this State initiative. The success of these measures pointed the way towards a similar rationalisation of English secondary education.

(c) 1893 Annual Code

This new code radically altered the existing regulations for evening class work undertaken by the School Boards. By removing the previous limitations on age and subject content, A.H. Acland, then Vice-President at the Education Department, allowed the School Boards to provide post-elementary evening instruction. This development was not welcomed by the endowed grammar schools or the new Technical Instruction Committees as it was seen as a threat to their preserve. Thus another source of administrative conflict and of hostility to the School Boards emerged.

(d) 1895 Report of the Bryce Commission

Although its terms of reference were limited to the field of secondary education, this Report inevitably concerned itself with the total administrative context and its recommendations and results accordingly assumed a wider significance. Whilst acknowledging the improvements which had taken place since 1868, the Report regretted the failure to implement fully the suggestions of the Taunton Commission. In order to establish 'a well-organised system of secondary education in England' the Bryce Commission made a number of far-reaching *recommendations:*

  (i) the merging of the three separate central agencies into a single Ministry of Education to overlook the whole field of State education. To cushion national educational development from the vicissitudes and effects of party politics, it was further suggested that the Minister should be advised and assisted by a strong Educational Council of professional and independent members. The Minister himself would be responsible to Parliament for general policy and administrative control.

(ii) the establishment of new Local Authorities for Secondary Education in all County and County Borough areas to take responsibility for all types of secondary schooling. The members of these *ad hoc* bodies were to be nominated rather than elected. In County Borough areas the local Council and the local School Board were each to nominate one-third of the membership. But in County areas the Councils were to nominate over half the members and there was to be no place for School Board nominees. In both cases there would be provision for a minority of co-optees. Whilst the higher-grade schools were to be transferred to the jurisdiction of the new authorities, the School Boards would continue to operate within the confines of proper elementary education. Significantly, a minority of commissioners favoured the outright abolition of the School Boards to enable one single type of body to assume overall responsibility for education at the local level.

(iii) the expansion of secondary education by granting wide powers to the new local authorities to 'supply, maintain and aid' appropriate schools. Backed by rate-aid (2d in the £) and treasury grants, they were to develop and supervise an adequate system of secondary education for the needs of their respective areas. Although fees were certainly to be retained to help defray the considerable cost, it was recommended that there should be an 'adequate supply of scholarships' to provide an educational ladder for exceptionally able elementary schoolchildren.

(iv) the improvement of secondary education through the extension and rationalisation of external examinations for secondary pupils, the encouragement of professional training for secondary teachers and the introduction of a register of teachers to control the quality of staffing. It was further suggested that all secondary schools, including those remaining independent of public financial aid, should be subject to local recognition and central inspection.

Although its immediate implementation did not occur and its *ad hoc* recipe for local educational administration was set aside, the Bryce Commission Report was generally well-received and its recommendations proved a major influence upon the legislative action taken at the turn of the century and upon other subsequent developments.

(e) 1895 Return of the Tories to Power

With the Liberal party seriously weakened by Gladstone's retirement and its internal dissensions over Irish Home Rule and imperialism, Lord Salisbury's decisive electoral victory in 1895 was the prelude to a decade of uninterrupted Conservative rule at Westminster, a context which proved favourable for the Church interests and threatening for the School Boards. The Tories were committed to saving the denominational schools but were highly conscious of the explosive situation which would result from any attempt to rescue them from their difficulties or to cut the School Boards down to size. Thus there was much to be said for trying to cloud the critical issues by combining changes in the operation of the dual system with wider administrative reforms and provision for the expansion of secondary education. If the latter two issues could be used to engineer the abolition of the School Boards and the extension of rate-aid to the voluntary schools so much the better. But the tactical execution of this strategy was to prove a complex and difficult matter.

(f) 1896 Gorst's Education Bill

Sir John Gorst, the new Vice-President of the Council and head of the Education Department, introduced a measure calculated to truncate and erode the influence of the School Boards in favour of the multi-purpose County and County Borough authorities and to strengthen the financial and denominational position of the Anglican interest in elementary education. Although he did not dare to provide for the outright abolition of the School Boards or for the extension of rate-aid to the voluntary schools, the Bill nevertheless foundered on the opposition of Tory members from municipal boroughs which did not welcome any increase in the power of the county authorities and on the horrified reaction of the Nonconformists to the repeal of the Cowper-Temple clause to facilitate denominational teaching in the Board schools. The controversial Bill was finally withdrawn and the Salisbury government forced to think again: in the following year it was content to increase central grants to the voluntary schools and to any 'necessitous' Board schools. But this was recognised as a temporary expedient and the future of the church schools remained uncertain.

(g) 1899 Board of Education Act

As educational reform at the local level and the modification of the dual system posed so many thorny problems, the line of least resistance was to deal with the administrative muddle at the central level. Based on the Bryce recommendations, the Board of Education Act (1899) provided for two significant developments:

(i) the displacement of the Education Department, the Department of Science and Art and the Charity Commission by a single Board of Education commissioned with 'the superintendence of educational development in England and Wales';

(ii) the establishment of an associated Consultative Committee to advise the new Board upon any educational matter referred to it.

Although the Act was criticised for not giving exact expression to the Bryce recommendations for an orthodox Ministry and a strong Educational Council, the measure did rationalise the situation at the central level and resulted in the pressures for reform at the local level becoming even more insistent.

(h)   1900 The Cockerton Judgement

Having identified the continued existence of the School Boards as the most serious obstacle to thorough-going administrative reform, Robert Morant shrewdly judged that these bodies were more vulnerable to legal attack than to direct political assault. Established under the 1870 Act the School Boards had been empowered to use rate-aid for elementary education purposes; it followed that their support of secondary-type instruction in the higher-grade schools and more advanced evening classes was questionable in law. The Cross Commission (1888) had already alluded to his possibility and Morant determined to capitalise upon it. Assured of Gorst's unofficial support, he surreptitiously encouraged the London Technical Education Board to challenge the legal rights of the London School Board in respect of its rate-aided post-elementary provision. The result was the Cockerton judgement, in which the local government auditor so-named surcharged the London School Board with the amount spent from the rates on higher-grade schooling. Two subsequent appeals against this decision were turned down in the courts; worse still, the court decisions declared against the use of rate-aid for evening continuation classes as well as higher-grade schools. Although the presiding judges recognised the blurred limits of elementary education, their final pronouncements were tantamount to a legal condemnation of the position taken up by the larger, progressive School Boards. Given the illegality of the existing situation an emergency Act was quickly passed in 1901, authorising such Boards to continue their work under the auspices of the County and County Borough Councils until such time as the anomalous position had been thoroughly reviewed and dealt with. Whilst Gorst further reduced his declining political stature by hastily drafting an inadequate Bill, his private secretary, Morant, cultivated the friendship of the future prime minister Arthur Balfour and prepared the ground in detail. With the close of the Boer War in March 1902 the time was finally opportune for major legislative action by the Conservative government. For the church interest it had been a long, hard wait.

3   The 1902 Education Act

Although the new prime minister Balfour took responsibility for the drafting and the passage of this highly controversial measure, its real architect was Robert Morant who later served as Permanent Secretary to the Board of Education 1903–11. Thus the form and implementation of this critical enactment owed much to the vision and influence of one ambitious and clear-sighted professional. The provisions of the Balfour Act were designed to generate the necessary Conservative support through the religious issue whilst attracting more general support through their reform of local administration and secondary education. Thus the Act may be divided into three major aspects.

(a)   Local Administrative Reorganisation

The existing School Boards, School Attendance Committees and Technical Instruction Committees were swept away and replaced by some three hundred LEAs which covered the whole country. Each such authority was instructed to appoint a local education committee through which to exercise its responsibilities under the Act.

These new authorities were of two types.

(i)   *Part II Local Education Authorities*

The second part of the Act designated the County and County Borough Councils as LEAs to assume overall responsibility for elementary and 'other than elementary' education (i.e. secondary, teacher training, technical and adult education) in their respective areas.

(ii)   *Part III Local Education Authorities*

The third part of the Act authorised any municipal borough with over ten thousand people or any urban district with more than twice that number to undertake responsibility for elementary education *only* in their own areas. About one hundred and eighty such authorities emerged from the Act as a result of this provision.

The resultant division of administrative responsibility in county areas where Part III enclaves arose was not to Morant's liking and he would have much preferred the County and County Borough authorities to have enjoyed a monopoly of control; but this was the political price which had to be paid by Balfour to obtain the support of Conservative members from many municipal boroughs and urban districts about to lose their School Boards.

(b) The Modification of the Dual System

The 1870 settlement was revised, ostensibly in the interests of educational efficiency, along certain lines:

(i) rate-aid was extended to the voluntary schools so as to cover their running costs completely; henceforth the churches were simply faced with the capital expenditure involved in the establishment of new schools and the extension or repair of old buildings. Costs arising from 'fair wear and tear' were to be charged to the LEA. Thus the financial difficulties of the denominational schools were greatly eased and their survival ensured; it was anticipated that the new arrangements would enable them rapidly and significantly to raise their standards of elementary provision.

(ii) the voluntary schools were now to be administered as well as financed by the new LEAs. Renamed 'non-provided schools' they were placed under the jurisdiction of the LEA in relation to the secular aspects of the elementary education they provided. Their trust deeds were to be altered to allow for one-third of their managers to be nominated by the parent authority and the latter was given the power of veto upon the appointment of unsuitable teachers. Thus the denominational schools were to be much more closely incorporated within the State system. But they maintained a foundation majority on their managing bodies with the right to appoint the head and assistant teachers and continued to enjoy their denominational atmosphere and identity. The appointment and dismissal of staff for religious teaching purposes was placed outside the jurisdiction of the authority.

A significant omission from this aspect of the Act was any provision designed to override the Cowper-Temple clause. The High Church party had pressed very hard for access facilities to allow denominational teaching to be given to Anglican children attending the schools provided by the LEAs. But Balfour and Morant rightly judged this to be an extreme demand and the 'provided schools' (as the old Board schools were now renamed) were left to continue with the Cowper-Temple tradition of undenominational religious worship and instruction.

(c) Expansion of Secondary and Further Education

The Part II LEAs were required to investigate existing facilities in the field of 'other than elementary' education and were empowered as far as 'seemed desirable' to use rate-aid for its support and development. In particular, the County and County Borough authorities were allowed to take action in a number of important directions:

   (i) to support existing endowed grammar schools in return for representation on their governing bodies, to buy out private and proprietary secondary schools, to convert higher-grade schools and pupil-teacher centres and to establish their own County grammar schools. All these were means by which the Part II authorities could contribute to the launching and development of a State system of secondary education.

  (ii) to provide scholarships for able elementary schoolchildren to transfer to secondary grammar schools where the majority of places would still be fee-paying. This would develop an educational ladder between the elementary system and the new State secondary schools which would be especially helpful to working class pupils intent upon a career in teaching.

 (iii) to establish and maintain municipal training colleges for elementary teachers. The denominational monopoly in this field had already been broken into by the establishment of day training colleges under university auspices during the 1890s; the Part II authorities could now make their contribution to the further expansion of this non-denominational sector.

 (iv) to expand technical education provision and support the efforts of recognised organisations (e.g. the Workers' Educational Association) active in the field of adult education. In this way the Part II authorities not only inherited the responsibilities of the previous Technical Instruction Committees but were commissioned to develop a wider field later categorised as 'further' education.

Thus the Part II local education authorities were to cover the whole field of State educational provision and were expected, in particular, to expand and improve that provision in the 'other than elementary' sector. Nevertheless the latter responsibility was permissive rather than mandatory, the means and extent of expansion and improvement being left to the discretion of individual Part II authorities.

The passage and implementation of the 1902 Act inevitably proved stormy and difficult. It took fifty-nine days of bitter debates to force the measure through Parliament, the great bulk of this time being consumed by argument over those sections of the Act concerned with the religious issue.

The clear design to rehabilitate the denominational schools by placing them on the rates excited the combined wrath of the Nonconformists and secularists who had been relying on their slow financial strangulation to destroy the dual system. In the House of Commons Lloyd George led the Liberal opposition to the measure almost clause by clause, whilst in the country at large the Baptist preacher Dr Clifford marshalled huge Nonconformist demonstrations and warned the Balfour government of the dire consequences of 'putting Rome on the rates'. Once the Act became law its opponents refused to pay the education rate and a number of Welsh LEAs simply refused to advance public monies to Anglican and Roman Catholic elementary schools in their areas. Some seventy thousand individual passive resisters were met by prosecution and even the distraint of their belongings, whilst the recalcitrant authorities were outflanked by the special Education (Local Authorities Default) Act of 1904. The latter measure allowed the Board of Education to finance any denominational school directly at the expense of central grants due to the offending authority in respect of all its schools. Gradually the opposition began to subside and the position was regularised. But the Liberal landslide electoral victory early in 1906 suddenly threatened to undo Balfour's work before it had had a chance to prove itself. During the period 1906–8 no fewer than three major Education Bills were introduced to withdraw rate-aid for church schools or simply to abolish the dual system. The day was saved for the denominational interests by the Tory majority in the House of Lords. Because of the resistance of the Upper House the church schools continued to enjoy the favourable terms extended to them by the Balfour Act, in spite of the new Liberal government's hostility to such arrangements. By the time the power of the House of Lords had been curbed by the Parliament Act of 1911, the context had changed again in a way favourable to the maintenance of the 1902 settlement. The Balfour-Morant system was working well and the more moderate elements on both sides increasingly recognised this fact. The secularist stance of the working class movement, which had lent more strength to the Liberal and Nonconformist position in the early years of the century, had now weakened and was on the threshold of official abandonment. The earlier religious bitterness had died down somewhat and, pressed by the emergence of a number of other serious problems, the pre-war Liberal government was much less inclined to risk another political storm by meddling yet again with the Balfour arrangements. When Morant left the Board of Education in 1911 he must have had the satisfaction of feeling that the Balfour Act and the framework it had set up and which he had done so much to develop was now reasonably safe from successful attack.

4   Retrospective Assessment

Whatever the contemporary opposition to and the possible criticisms of the 1902 Act, it must be regarded as one of the really major landmarks in the history of English education. Any balanced assessment of its significance must take into account a number of considerations.

(a)   New Administrative Framework

In conjunction with the Board of Education Act (1899), it established a new administrative framework incomparably more cohesive and effective than its predecessor. At a stroke the long-standing weakness of the small rural School Boards was eliminated. The *ad hoc* approach to local educational administration was finally abandoned and local responsibility for education was henceforth devolved upon the maturing multi-purpose Councils. And the particular interests of education within the multi-purpose framework was secured by the requirement that the parent Councils set up local education committees to discharge their new functions. On this sound basis Morant forged the crucial partnership between central and local government which has since remained fundamental to the English educational system. Through the new framework the State projected itself much more decisively into the field of 'other than elementary' education.

(b)   State System of Secondary Education

It launched a State system of secondary education (albeit on traditional grammar lines) which enjoyed considerable expansion in the Edwardian era and during the First World War. Although the system was developed on a fee-paying basis, the Act's provision for scholarship awards to enable elementary schoolchildren to transfer to secondary grammar schools pointed the way towards the 'free-place' system (1907) and the ultimate rejection of the nineteeth-century concept of secondary education as the prerogative of the middle and upper classes. In its concern for the establishment of an educational ladder, however narrow initially, the Balfour Act reflected the beginnings of a contemporary shift from the plutocratic to the meritocratic rationale of secondary education.

(c)   Elementary Education

It benefited elementary education by strengthening the financial resources of the voluntary or non-provided schools and subjecting them to a greater degree of public control, thereby setting the stage for an overdue

improvement in their standards of provision. Further benefit accrued from
the opportunity provided by the Act for the Part II authorities to develop
teacher training facilities through the establishment of municipal colleges,
twenty-two of which were founded in the years before the outbreak of the
First World War.

(d)   Administrative Dichotomy

It gave rise to the administrative dichotomy between Part II and Part III
LEAs which was to prove such a weakness in many County areas. Once the
1902 Act met the demands of the municipal boroughs and larger urban
districts for a major say in local educational development, it was difficult
thereafter to deprive them of the privilege even in the interests of educational efficiency. Thus the disappearance of the Part III authorities under
the 1944 Education Act was accompanied by the emergence of divisional
executives and excepted districts which continued to confuse and dilute the
power of the County LEAs for a further thirty years. Morant favoured functional efficiency to local democratic influence; political considerations
resulted in his being overruled and some would say that the educational
price was considerable.

(e)   Progressive School Boards

It abolished the larger, more progressive School Boards which had championed the cause of educational advance in the closing decades of the nineteenth century. With these Boards went the higher-grade schools and the
widening opportunity for secondary-type education on the cheap provided
by them. As a result of the 1902 Act these schools were absorbed into the fee-
paying system of State grammar schools or reverted to the strictly elementary role. The impetus given to technical and scientific education by the
higher-grade and evening continuation schools of the progressive Boards
was largely lost in the subsequent preoccupation with the development of
State secondary education along traditional grammar lines. Finally, the local
education committees, through which the new LEAs were to exercise their
responsibilities, were not directly elected like the School Boards and were
seen by the Labour movement as less democratic institutions. Brian Simon,
in his fine book *Education and the Labour Movement 1870–1902*, has
condemned the 1902 Act as a reactionary measure because of the fate of the
progressive School Boards and their higher-grade schools. This is an
interesting viewpoint that deserves consideration; it deplores the way in
which Morant's administrative measures capitalised upon the Act to define
rigidly the distinctions between elementary and secondary education which

the higher-grade schools had done so much to blur, and it implies that the 1902 Act was a development calculated to injure the immediate educational interests of the working class. Such an interpretation explains the fact that of the many elements composing the contemporary Labour movement only the Fabian Society gave its support to the Balfour Act.

(f) Dual System

It entrenched the dual system and so perpetuated the problem of balancing the claims of the State and the interests of the churches in a changing social and educational context: the survival of the voluntary schools with their 'special position' caused serious difficulties for the Hadow reorganisation process after 1928, for the drafting of the 1944 Education Act, for the process of comprehensive reorganisation and for post-war educational finance. By the close of the inter-war period the problems associated with the dual system were present in secondary education as well as in the elementary and teacher training fields. In 1944 the church interests were still strong enough to negotiate the introduction of compulsory religious worship and instruction into all State maintained schools. The secularist would argue that the 1902 Act would have served posterity better if the denominational schools and colleges had been forced to contract into or out of a purely State system. But such a radical solution was impracticable at the turn of the century. The voluntary schools accounted for over half the available places in the public elementary system. To dispense with their services would have left a huge and quite unacceptable gap in provision. To let them simply wither away from financial attrition would have been grossly injurious to the educational interests of the many children attending such schools.

If the 1902 Education Act did not immediately create a national system of education in England and Wales, it certainly laid the foundations of one, especially in the administrative sense and in relation to secondary provision. Although it may be argued that the Balfour Act had some short-term reactionary effects, in the long run it provided a sound and elastic framework within which progressive educational development could and did take place.

6 The Broadening Conception of State Schooling 1902–44

During the period 1902–44 the overall context in which educational development takes place was now changing more rapidly and markedly than ever before. By the turn of the century the age of *laissez faire* and individualism was crumbling before the inexorable advance of the collectivist approach to human affairs; in the years that followed the State assumed an increasingly wide and decisive role in the development and ordering of various aspects of national life, the hope and belief being that such intervention would serve the best interests of the majority of the population. The Liberal party was able to lay the foundations of the welfare state in the years before the First World War and the new Labour party, committed to a socialist programme designed to raise the quality of life of the working class, was able to grasp political power at Westminster on two separate occasions during the inter-war period. Once the Liberals went into headlong decline and the Labour party emerged as the new source of alternative government, electoral considerations persuaded the Conservatives to adjust their stance somewhat to accommodate the collectivist view. The traumatic experience of two World Wars, in which all classes had to pull together as never before in order to survive, produced a strong egalitarian tide to challenge traditional assumptions and practices; the final extension of the franchise to all adults, the increasing emancipation of women, the growing pressure for real equality of opportunity regardless of sex or social class and the quest for a 'brave new world' were all symptomatic of the changing outlook which emerged. The rise of educational psychology to maturity and respectability in the early decades of the new century provided an increasingly firm basis for the child-centred approach to education, with its emphasis on pupil needs and interests, individual capacities and differences, and the nature of child development and learning processes.

Meanwhile, the philosophy of education, subjected to the influence of Deweyan ideas from across the Atlantic, became much more interested in and concerned about the social aims of education; the gradual transition was exemplified in the move from Sir Percy Nunn's education for individuality thesis in the 1920s to Sir Fred Clarke's education for society argument during and after the Second World War. The rise of new industries and the continued growth of tertiary occupations 1902-44 also provided a stimulus for educational change and advance; the main effect was upon the growth and improvement of post-primary education and to a lesser extent upon technical college/school provision.

But not all the influences bearing upon the State educational system and its schools during this period were favourable. Progressive advance on a broadening front was subject to serious challenge from restrictive economic and unsympathetic political forces which frequently checked or diluted it. After 1918 stiffening foreign competition and the decline of Britain's old staple industries produced serious economic difficulties which ensured that the resources available for educational development were often limited or prone to sudden cuts. The post-war slump following the First World War savaged many of the hopes which had found legislative expression in the Fisher Act (1918), whilst the world economic depression gave rise to a period of acute financial stringency in the early 1930s. As the inter-relationship between the industrial and educational systems continued to be a very loose one, with industry tending to prefer early leaving and on-the-job training whilst the schools neglected technical and vocational subjects, the economy found it that much more difficult to adjust to changing needs and market conditions. The inter-war period was also one of Conservative political dominance, at a time when this party was increasingly ruled by business interests intent upon resisting radical change and the generous development of social services. During the period 1918-45 the only years in which the Conservatives were not in a majority in the Commons were 1924 and 1929-31 when short-lived Labour governments held office. Moreover, the political opposition was generally weak. After 1918 the Liberals rapidly lost their former strength and the new Labour party, still feeling its way, suffered a serious setback when the MacDonald government (1929-31) was broken by the world economic depression. Meanwhile, the failure of the General Strike (1926) proved a serious blow to the trade union movement and further weakened the Labour cause. Although certain industrial areas sustained Labour strength in the field of local government, the 1930s saw the Labour movement in considerable disarray. Thus the political context was one in which the Conservative party and elitist Board of Education officials could combine to restrict the extent and control the shape of educational change. Until the egalitarian impact of the Second World War changed the situation, those who championed educational reform were faced with an uphill struggle.

Given the overall context just described, the broadening conception of

State schooling during the period 1902–44 may be considered in terms of three broad avenues along which it developed.

1   The Emancipation of the Elementary School

The nineteenth-century conception of elementary education, crystallised in the Revised Code of 1862, was a narrow utilitarian one and rigidly class-based. But the abandonment of the 'payment by results' system near the century's end opened the way for a more liberal approach to elementary schooling. The next fifty years witnessed considerable change for the better and by the 1930s the transition from the old elementary system to modern primary education had begun in earnest. This process of evolution was consequent upon and punctuated by a variety of influences and developments.

(a)   Educational Psychology

The broad progressive influence of educational psychology came to enjoy a place of increasing importance in the teacher training colleges. The result was the gradual rise of the child-centred approach to education which had its initial and greatest impact upon the teaching of younger children. Educational psychologists stressed the importance of individual differences and pupil motivation in relation to learning at school. They felt that what was taught, and how, should be reconsidered in the light of pupil needs and interests and the nature of child development. Their influence certainly undermined the largely repressive and rote-learning tradition inherited from the nineteenth century. Thus the inter-war period was characterized by a fair amount of experimentation and re-examination of curricula and teaching methods, although the widespread practical fruits were postponed until after the Second World War. The greater attention given to the physical and socio-emotional development of younger children and certain organisational changes which affected their education may also be attributed in part to the influence of educational psychology.

(b)   Progressive Practitioners

The particular contributions of certain progressive practitioners who were themselves well versed in educational psychology and even helped to develop it, began to be felt. Margaret McMillan, who had served the Bradford School Board in the 1890s and later ran an open-air nursery school in Deptford, underlined the importance of physical well-being and creative activity

to the satisfactory development of young children and even won Robert
Morant and H.A.L. Fisher to her viewpoint. In her book *Education through
the Imagination* (1905) the need to sustain the child's emotional development is stressed and expressive work in art, music, movement, handicrafts,
poetry and imaginative story-telling are suggested as the best means to this
end. Underlying her whole outlook was the conviction that the child's intellectual development depended on a sound emotional base.

Maria Montessori, an Italian doctor who became interested and involved
in the infant schooling of deprived children in Rome, emphasised practical
and individual activity as the vital basis for learning. Her approach was more
clinical and scientific than Margaret McMillan's but lacked its aesthetic
dimensions. The teacher's function according to the 'Montessori method'
was to organise the classroom environment by providing all sorts of purposeful materials to attract the young child's interest and to facilitate its mastery
of basic concepts. She favoured the vertical grouping of infants and juniors
as a socially beneficial arrangement and was opposed to the use of rewards
and punishments. By 1914 she already had numerous disciples in Britain
and her influence spread further afield after the First World War.

The ideas of Margaret McMillan and Maria Montessori in many ways
looked back to those of Froebel, the nineteenth-century pioneer of the kin-
dergarten; their work helped to revitalise the efforts of the Froebel Society
(established 1874) in Britain in the early decades of the new century. The
main impact of all this was upon nursery and infant education, but in the
long run the effects were destined to assume wider significance. In this latter
regard a third and later practitioner, Susan Isaacs, was influential. Infant-
trained and a qualified psychologist, she painstakingly evaluated her own
attempts (1924–7) to teach children of 'junior' age on an informal and individualised basis. Although this work was conducted within the untypical
context of a private school, it helped to provide the basis for persuasive writ-
ings. Two of her books, concerned with the intellectual growth and social
development of young children, were important expressions of the child-
centred rationale. More specifically, in *The Children We Teach* (1932), she
argued that throughout the years of primary schooling children's self-acti-
vity is the key to their full development and the teacher's role must be
shaped accordingly. Thus the challenge to formal class teaching along traditional lines passed from the infant to the junior stage of schooling.

(c) Official Change of Attitude Towards the Elementary Schools

An official change of attitude towards the elementary schools was
announced by the Board of Education and inspired by Robert Morant
shortly after the 1902 Act. The publication of the 1904 Elementary Code

and the 1905 *Handbook of Suggestions for the Consideration of Teachers engaged in the Work of Public Elementary Schools* heralded the dawn of a new era for the elementary schools and their teachers. The new Code was responsible for a complete and wholesome restatement of the purpose of the elementary school which was certainly calculated to improve its public image. The *Handbook*, by its very title (suggestions *not* instructions, consideration *not* direction), symbolised the burial of the traditions and official attitudes associated with elementary education in the late nineteenth century. Taken together they introduced a new spirit and in various ways pointed towards a new ideal:

 (i) by projecting elementary education as a vital public service to the nation and abandoning the old concept of its being a charity service for working class children;
 (ii) by stressing the importance of developing individual abilities and interests and the building of character and moral training, thereby identifying a much broader purpose for elementary education;
 (iii) by exalting the freedom and responsibility of the individual elementary teacher in the field of curricula and method and by revising the role of HM Inspectorate accordingly.

Of course it was easier to state new policy than to change the old ways of teachers who had been otherwise conditioned over many years. Thus in 1911, Edmond Holmes, recently retired from the office of HM Chief Inspector no less, rebuked the majority of elementary teachers and local inspectors in his publication *What Is and What Might Be*. The prevailing teacher-centred approach with its emphasis on class teaching (equated to 'the path of obedience') was roundly condemned in favour of a more child-centred approach involving individual activity and expression (equated to 'the path of self-realisation'). During the inter-war years the reports of the Consultative Committee were significantly influenced by the evidence invited from or the ideas developed by educational psychologists (e.g. Burt and Piaget) and progressive practitioners (e.g. Montessori and Isaacs); and meanwhile the revised versions of the original *Handbook of Suggestions* which were issued from time to time (e.g. 1927) also reflected the advance of child-centred ideas. Thus the Board of Education gave an encouraging lead and slowly but surely it met with a growing response.

(d)   Education Act 1918

The 1918 Education Act accepted the extension of State responsibility into the field of nursery education, although the post-war financial climate ensured that the response of the LEAs to this new opportunity was disappointingly limited. Fisher's measure (1918), which raised the minimum school leaving age to fourteen, also required the LEAs to provide special arrangements for the education of senior elementary pupils. Accordingly, by 1925 the Board of Education (via Circular 1350) was positively recommending a break at eleven years in the provision of elementary schooling and – where possible – the formation of separate 'junior' and 'senior' schools. Both developments pointed the way forward to a separate primary stage for the younger children.

(e)   Hadow Report on *The Education of the Adolescent* (1926)

The Hadow Report on *The Education of the Adolescent* (1926) recommended the abandonment of the elementary/secondary dichotomy in English education, in favour of a continuous educative process divided into primary and secondary stages. This gave rise to the modern concept of primary education as a self-contained stage for children aged five to eleven years. The Hadow reorganisation, begun in 1928, presaged the death-knell of the term 'elementary' and its unhappy connotations in English education.

(f)   Hadow Report on *The Primary School* (1931)

The Hadow Report on *The Primary School* (1931) gave official expression and encouragement to many of the new ideas being put forward for the education of young children. It suggested that primary education should be seen, not in terms of subjects to be taught and facts to be learned, but in terms of experiences to be undergone and activities to be engaged in. Learning by listening and mechanical exercises was condemned in favour of learning by doing through the medium of purposeful practical and expressive activity. But the report did not go overboard in favour of the progressive approach; it also asserted there was an 'indispensable place' for 'well tried methods of corporate teaching' and a continuing need for 'an adequate amount of drill in reading, writing and arithmetic'. Furthermore, the report supported the streaming of older junior children in order to cope with widening ability differences, although it recommended that the demands of the eleven-plus examination should be resisted in the interests of a pupil-centred approach. Of course, this was easier said than done. Any overt tendency to give progressive methods precedence over the quest for eleven-plus scholarships made the primary school concerned liable to intense pressure from anxious middle class parents. But, helped by falling rolls and somewhat reduced class sizes in the 1930s, many teachers did make some response to the new official outlook. The report also had significance for the future organisation of primary education in that it recommended the separation of infant and junior children. Indeed, in one way or another, the ripples of this important Consultative Committee report have continued to influence development right down to the present day.

(g)   Hadow Report on *Infant and Nursery Schools* (1933)

The Hadow Report on *Infant and Nursery Schools* (1933) reiterated the need for separate infant schools and backed the progressive influences already at work in infant education. Whilst not ignoring the need of the six- and seven-year-olds for formal instruction in the three Rs, the report condemned rigid timetables for infants and underlined the importance of natural activities and expression training. The Froebelian and Montessorian approaches were woven into an official rationale for the infant school. The report also pressed the desirability of a State system of nursery education and emphasised the particular need for such provision in deprived areas; in this respect it anticipated the recommendations of the Plowden Report (1967) by over thirty years, but unhappily it failed to make any real impact upon the existing situation.

By 1939 about half the pupils aged five to eleven were in separate primary schools which afforded a more favourable organisational basis for developing the child-centred approach. And, by this time, such an approach to the schooling of younger children had the strong support of HM Inspectorate, training college lecturers and many LEA chiefs and inspectors. Predictably the 1944 Education Act then gave statutory recognition to the new primary stage and its associated schools and reflected the widening conception of primary education in particular by declaring the object of the educational process to be the development of the spiritual, moral, mental and physical capacities of each and every child. This was indicative of a broad and enlightened approach to education, which contrasted starkly with the much narrower conception holding sway at the beginning of the century.

2   Secondary Education for All

As long as the nineteenth-century conception of elementary education survived, secondary schooling would remain the preserve of upper and middle class children. Significantly, and perhaps inevitably, the first State secondary schools developed under auspices of the 1902 Act were in fact 'grammar' schools in which the great majority of places were fee-paying. Terminologically the words 'secondary' and 'grammar' remained officially synonymous during the lifetime of the Board of Education 1900–44, and the purchase of places in State secondary schools was not abolished until the passage of the 1944 Education Act. Obviously this was a situation increasingly out of tune with the changing social context and it was gradually overcome by a process of erosion during the first half of the century. This process can be most easily considered and understood in terms of a number of major influences and developments underlying and composing it.

(a) Growth of the Scholarship System

First mentioned by the Taunton Commission, reiterated by the Bryce Report and embodied in the provision of the 1902 Act which permitted the Part II authorities to grant scholarships, this idea was crystallised in the 1907 free-place regulations requiring State secondary schools (i.e. all those in receipt of grant) to make at least 25 per cent of their intake available to elementary pupils of proven ability. The free-place system was to be operated on the basis of a qualifying examination to establish suitability for grammar schooling, but growing demand and limited supply was soon to ensure that this became an increasingly competitive affair. Between 1906 and 1914 the new departure was responsible for trebling the number of scholarships provided for elementary pupils to transfer to secondary education. Thus, whilst the traditional distinction between elementary and secondary schooling continued, the gulf between the separate and parallel systems was now narrowly bridged by a minority of very able elementary pupils passing into the largely fee-paying secondary schools. On the eve of the First World War only 2½ per cent of the appropriate age group actually in the elementary schools obtained free places; but by 1939, as a result of the growth in the number and size of the State grammar schools and the tendency to raise the proportion of scholarship places provided, there were some 10 per cent of such pupils being transferred. Thus the position improved, but not remarkably so during the inter-war years. Even H.A.L. Fisher, the liberal-minded President of the Board 1916–22, though eager to widen the educational ladder and thus increase the proportion of beneficiaries, was content to accept an arrangement which inevitably limited the majority of children to an elementary education. The 1918 Education Act did not provide for any real change in the concept of secondary education and prosperous middle class parentage remained the best hope of obtaining it.

(b) Attitude of the Organised Labour Movement

The earliest demands for 'secondary education for all' were voiced by the Trades Union and Labour party conferences in the years before the First World War. On behalf of the working class they condemned elementary schooling as inadequate, demanded the raising of the school leaving age to sixteen years and the provision of a secondary education for each and every child. The educational ladder arrangements were likened to a 'greasy pole', calculated to benefit the lower-middle rather than the working class. Reassured by the changing image of the elementary schools, and attracted by the scholarship possibilities, a growing number of lower-middle class parents began to send their children to them, whilst the poverty barrier militated against many able working class children taking advantage of secondary school free places without associated maintenance allowances. Nor was the Labour movement content to accept compulsory part-time continuative education from the age of fourteen to eighteen years for ex-elementary pupils (as provided for by the Fisher Act, 1918) as a satisfactory alternative to secondary education for all. The latter objective became official party policy in 1922 when the Labour spokesman R.H. Tawney issued the publication *Secondary Education for All*. The first short-lived Labour government of 1924 commissioned the Hadow Report on *The Education of the Adolescent* (1926) which examined the condition of post-primary education and pointed the way towards the realisation of Tawney's hopes. In the succeeding years the Labour party not only supported the Hadow reorganisation process and attempted to raise the school leaving age to fifteen, but also used its power and influence at local government level to reduce the proportion of fee-paying places in State secondary grammar schools and to explore the idea of multilateral secondary schools to which all children could go.

(c)   Reassertion of Post-Primary Growth

Following the Cockerton judgement and the abolition of the School Boards, Morant used his decisive influence as Permanent Secretary to the Board of Education 1903–11 in favour of enforcing a clear and rigid distinction between elementary and secondary education. The existing higher-grade schools and pupil-teacher centres were forcibly reconstituted as secondary grammar or ordinary elementary schools. The only permissible variant was the new higher elementary school provided for by special regulations which not only placed it very firmly in the non-secondary sector but also ensured, because of the onerous conditions and limitations to be observed, that LEAs showed very little interest in its development. In 1906 Morant's policy received the backing of the Consultative Committee in its Report on *Higher Elementary Schools*; the need to prevent any post-primary outgrowth which might threaten to compete, however marginally, with the grammar schools and once again blur the distinction between elementary and secondary education was stoutly reaffirmed. But in face of the developing needs of industry and commerce and the changing social context such a simplistic and class-ridden approach by the Board of Education could not last for long. The mounting opposition of the National Union of Teachers and the organised Labour movement to the influence and policy of Morant, leading to his final downfall in 1911, prepared the ground for new developments. In 1911–12 the London and Manchester LEAs launched their selective central schools for abler elementary pupils not transferring to secondary grammar schools; these central schools were to provide post-primary instruction with some industrial or commercial bias for the eleven to fifteen years age group.

By the outbreak of the First World War the Board of Education had not only recognised but had approved this development. Impressed by the problem of 'marking time' (i.e. occupying the senior pupils by repetitive exercises rather than by the breaking of new ground) in ordinary elementary schools, the Lewis Report on *Juvenile Education in Relation to Employment after the War* (1917) insisted on the need to reconsider the organisation and curricula of the upper forms of elementary schools. The Lewis Committee felt that such action was essential if its recommendation for raising the school-leaving age nationally to fourteen years was to produce real educational benefits. H.A.L. Fisher clinched the issue when he told Parliament that one of the vital post-war tasks facing the Board of Education would be 'to develop upon sound lines what may be called higher-grade elementary education'(*Hansard*, vol. 108, 16 July 1918). To this end the 1918 Education Act required the LEAs to make adequate provision for both advanced and practical instruction for senior elementary pupils 'by means of central schools, central or special classes, or otherwise'. The Act raised the school-leaving age to fourteen years, provided for its further extension to fifteen years on the basis of local option and allowed individual elementary pupils to continue in school to the age of sixteen. The result was that a growing number of authorities joined London and Manchester in the development of both selective and non-selective central schools for elementary pupils over eleven. The seeds of the future secondary modern schools were already being sown. Meanwhile the emergence of full-time day junior trade and technical schools had introduced another dimension to post-primary growth. The trade schools were pioneered by the London LEA and received recognition for grant purposes in 1905; they aimed at giving ex-elementary pupils specialised training in the manual skills and scientific principles associated with a particular skilled trade. The junior technical schools developed in the north of England somewhat later and became eligible for grant in 1913; they combined a continued general education with preparation for apprenticeship in such group industries as engineering, building and construction, or shipbuilding. Both types of school provided two- or three-year-courses for abler senior elementary pupils who would transfer into them at thirteen or fourteen. A much smaller number of junior commercial and art schools also emerged as part of this new development. By the mid-1920s these schools, operated under the Board's separate regulations for technical institutions, were forming an intermediate sector distinct from both the elementary and secondary grammar systems. In any move towards secondary education for all their existence would now have to be taken into account.

(d) Hadow Report on *The Education of the Adolescent* (1926)

Once it had become official policy to consider the particular needs of senior elementary pupils, the logical extension of this was to end the separation of elementary and secondary education and to think in terms of one continuous process of schooling composed of a primary and a secondary stage through which all children would pass. Such was the main thesis of the report submitted by the Consultative Committee to the government in 1926. Under the chairmanship of Sir W.H. Hadow the Committee had been commissioned by the first Labour government two years earlier to investigate the existing provision of non-secondary post-primary education and to make suggestions for its improvement. Its subsequent consideration of the organisation and substance of the education received by the ninety-odd per cent of adolescents not attending secondary grammar schools resulted in a report full of far-reaching *recommendations*:

(i)   the provision of secondary education for all through the abandonment of the old parallel and separate systems of elementary and secondary schooling in favour of a single and continuous educative process divided into primary and secondary stages at the age of eleven plus.

(ii)   the raising of the school leaving age to fifteen years nationally (with effect from September 1932) so as to allow every child at least three years of secondary schooling and to make such provision a viable curricula proposition.

(iii) the organisation of secondary education on a selective basis in order to relate it to the different abilities and interests of the children and their prospective age of school leaving and career possibilities. Accordingly the report suggested two main types of post-primary education, each to be associated with a particular type of institution. Firstly, there would be the secondary grammar schools to serve the needs of the ablest ex-primary pupils aiming at professional employment or university entrance; such schools would maintain their strong academic orientation and all pupils would continue in attendance until at least sixteen years of age. Secondly, there should be secondary modern schools developed from the existing central schools and senior elementary classes;

although a secondary modern education would initially often have to be provided within the existing framework of senior elementary classes, the ultimate objective was to be its provision in 'another institution, with a distinctive staff, and organised definitely for post-primary education'(page 80). The modern school would serve the needs of the great majority of adolescents between eleven and fifteen years; in common with the grammar school the curriculum during the first two years was to concentrate on providing a sound general education, but thereafter it was to be differentiated by a more practical and realistic bias without ever becoming strictly vocational. The Report also acknowledged the valuable contribution being made to post-primary education by the junior technical schools and recommended that the development of this third element should be encouraged. But it was insisted that because of their vocational orientation the normal age of entry should continue to be thirteen years rather than eleven. The junior technical schools were not visualised as an integral part of the new secondary arrangements; rather they were seen as appendages of the technical colleges to which a small number of suitable pupils could make late transfers from the modern or grammar schools. Thus the Hadow strategy was really bipartite rather than tripartite in basis.

(iv) the acceptance of responsibility by the LEAs for the mounting of suitable selection examinations for channelling pupils to the appropriate type of school; such arrangements were to include provision for the transfer of late developers from the modern to the grammar and junior technical schools. It was further suggested that the LEAs and other interested parties should combine to frame a new leaving examination and certificate for the benefit of the modern schools and their pupils.

(v) the accordance of parity of support and esteem to the different types of post-primary school. The Committee was particularly insistent upon the need to ensure that the modern schools were seen as different from rather than inferior to the grammar schools, and underlined the importance of accommodation, equipment and staffing in this respect.

(vi) the promotion of administrative efficiency by devolving the responsibility for both primary and secondary education upon a single type of LEA. Quite rightly the Committee saw the continued existence of Part II and Part III LEAs with their different roles as a serious obstacle to the satisfactory implementation of its other proposals.

The 1926 Hadow Report has been widely regarded as a major watershed in English educational development, yet it can also be seen as merely the purveyor of 'old wine in new bottles'. Radical in its intent and flavour, the report was certainly less than progressive in its substance and outcome.

Although the report demanded and secured an end to the existing element-ary/secondary dichotomy, its selective strategy for the provision of secondary education for all allowed the continuance of the old distinctions in a new form. Its plea for parity of esteem was extremely naive; having itself provided the secondary modern schools with inferior specifications (e.g. lower ability, a less demanding course for less rewarding occupations, and a lower leaving age) it was impossible for them to attain any real standing in the public eye. Thus the cause of educational equality was not seriously advanced and real opportunity remained tied to grammar school entry. In the event, the Hadow Report proved relatively easy meat for 'conservative' manipulation. After long consideration the Baldwin government accepted the report in principle and the Hadow reorganisation process was officially launched by the issue of *The New Prospect in Education* (1928). But the raising of the school leaving age was rejected and the Committee's intention to provide the modern schools with their own leaving examination and certificate was also turned aside. Meanwhile, the progress of reorganisation was slowed down by the financial stringencies of the world economic depression and by the particular difficulties associated with the decapitation of denominational elementary schools and the problem of sparsely populated areas. But on the credit side, as the process gradually advanced, not only did a separate and more wholesome primary stage of education emerge, but many senior pupils found themselves in secondary modern schools, some newly built, which were relatively better equipped and staffed than their typical elementary forbears.

(e) Education Act 1936

This measure attempted to facilitate and expedite the Hadow reorganisation process by raising the school leaving age to fifteen years (with effect from September 1939) and by authorising the LEAs to pay specially favourable grants for the establishment of denominational secondary modern schools. Although the outbreak of war postponed the raising of the school leaving age, the latter provision enabled the Anglican and Roman Catholic Churches to enter into special agreements with particular LEAs for the furtherance of reorganisation. By 1939 over one-half of pupils over eleven were in reorganised schools although the proportion for the denominational and the rural school children was much lower than this.

(f) Spens Report on *Secondary Education* (1938)

Although the terms of reference related to this report did not include the new modern schools, the Consultative Committee, whilst concentrating its attention on the grammar and technical schools, found it impossible to ignore the wider context of post-primary education as a whole. Will Spens and his colleagues began by confirming the basic Hadow strategy and thereby encouraged the emergence of secondary education for all along selective lines; very impressed by the recent work of educational psychologists on the nature and importance of mental differences they felt it 'evident that different children from the age of eleven, if justice is to be done to their varying capacities, require types of education varying in certain important respects' (page 358), and that this was best provided in separate post-primary schools. However, the report also proposed a number of significant refinements to the existing policy:

(i) the abolition of all fee-paying places in State secondary education; this would mean that all grammar school places would be tied to eleven-plus examination success.

(ii) the conversion of a number of the existing junior technical schools into technical high schools which were to be accorded equality of status with the selective grammar schools. This newly conceived institution was to provide a liberal education with science and its applications as the curriculum core for abler children. The age range was to be eleven to sixteen years and the schools were to be developed under the auspices of local technical colleges. Thus the technical school was to be drawn into the main stream of secondary education beginning at eleven plus; the basically bipartite strategy of Hadow was superseded by the clearly tripartite approach of Spens.

(iii) the improvement of the inter-relations of the post-primary schools by selection at eleven plus for all three types of secondary education supplemented by open-ended thirteen-plus transfer arrangements. It was stressed that the satisfactory handling of the latter concern depended on the pursuance of a comparable curricula in all secondary schools during the first two years.

(iv) the realisation of parity of esteem for the different types of secondary school through administrative action. The report suggested a new code of regulations to cover the new and wider secondary field with the different schools being treated alike in relation to staffing, salary scales, buildings and facilities except where special considerations justified otherwise.

It is also noteworthy that the Spens Committee considered the possibilities of multilateral and bilateral secondary schools, only to reject them on grounds of size and other problems. However, it was admitted that some benefits (e.g. ease of internal transfer) accrued from all secondary pupils being taught together in the same school and the Committee was happy to see such experiments in areas of new or sparse population.

The Spens Report had a mixed reception. Chamberlain's Conservative government welcomed the tripartite strategy but was ill-disposed towards the abolition of fee-paying places and the introduction of a single Code of Regulations to cover all types of post-primary school. The Labour movement was unimpressed and the Trades Union Congress persuasively argued that the Committee's concern for parity of esteem pointed to the multilateral recipe for future development – yet the report had backed the continuance of eleven-plus selection with its restrictive effects upon educational opportunity. And so the war began without the report being acted upon.

(g) Norwood Report on *Curriculum and Examinations in Secondary Schools* (1943)

The criticisms of secondary curricula and examinations by the Spens Report led to a wider and more intensive investigation of this particular field by the Secondary School Examinations Council under its chairman Sir Cyril Norwood. But the Council went well beyond its terms of reference to consider the organisation of post-primary education as a whole and the resultant report acquired enhanced significance because it crystallised the case for secondary education for all and its provision along tripartite lines. Its basic thesis was that all secondary pupils fall into one of three psychological categories, namely the academically-minded, the technically-minded and the practically-minded, and that each group is best served by a distinctive curriculum developed in an appropriate type of school. The Norwood analysis, though naïvely ill-founded in its basis, was welcomed in official circles for it equated most conveniently with the three types of secondary school thrown up by the Hadow reorganisation. In common with Spens, the Norwood Report did not favour the multilateral alternative but emphasised the importance of the different types of school pursuing a comparable curricula during the first two years of secondary education to facilitate a satisfactory system of late transfers. Having thus received further confirmation of the efficacy of the Hadow strategy, the Board of Education and many LEAs could rest happy that recent developments in post-primary education were along the right lines.

(h) White Paper on *Educational Reconstruction* (1943)

The coming of war finally provided the necessary impetus for major educational advance. In 1943 Churchill's Coalition government (1940–45) produced its White Paper on *Educational Reconstruction* which provided a basis for legislative action and, more generally, mapped out the intended course of future development. With regard to secondary education the White Paper

very largely reflected the received wisdom of the Hadow, Spens and .
wood Reports. In particular, it gave unequivocal support to eleven-pₓ
selection and the tripartite organisation of secondary education for all.

(i) Education Act 1944

This wartime measure was certainly a landmark in that it provided a statutory basis for secondary education for all, raised the school leaving age to
fifteen years and abolished fee-paying places in State grammar schools. But
significantly, whilst the LEAs were required to provide secondary education
for all appropriate to 'their different ages, abilities and aptitudes', the Act
did not make any mention of selective or tripartite organisation. Thus,
although the 1944 Act finally secured secondary education for all between
eleven and fifteen years, the discretion afforded to the LEAs left the way
open for a reconsideration of the organisational pattern and set the stage for
the long post-war struggle between the selective and comprehensive
approaches.

As the education of the adolescent emerged as the main centre of reformist
concern during the period 1902–44 it is important to assess the nature and
extent of the progress made. Creditably enough the minimum school-leaving age was raised from only twelve years under the 1899 Act to fifteen years
under the 1944 Act. The system of State grammar schools grew from
nothing to afford nearly half a million places by 1939; scholarship entry ulti-·
mately accounted for 50% of these places and access by fee-paying was
finally abolished in 1944. Secondary education for all was accepted as policy
from 1928 and became a statutory requirement under the 1944 Act. The
Hadow reorganisation process produced a growing number of secondary
modern schools in which many senior pupils enjoyed superior accommodation, better facilities, improved staffing arrangements and more imaginative
teaching than had characterised the old elementary schools. Yet, for all this,
the advancement of adolescent schooling and opportunity was limited and
superficial. For the great majority of working class pupils the educational
ladder to the State grammar schools had proved a 'greasy pole'. The emergent framework for providing secondary education for all was one in which
old distinctions and inequalities could be perpetuated; the modern schools
had the stamp of inferiority from the start and lacked any distinctive or positive role in the new order. 'Parity of esteem' for the different types of secondary school always was and would remain a pipe-dream. At the close of the
Second World War secondary schooling in England and Wales was composed of three distinct tiers which were clearly differentiated in terms of educational opportunity and occupational hopes. The top tier consisted of the
fee-paying independent schools operating outside the State system; accounting for about 6 per cent of the age group, these schools afforded the best

prospect of a university education and high position. The second tier was made up of the State grammar and technical high schools covering one-sixth of the age group; whilst their products might aspire to a university or college education, they would normally leave at sixteen to fill intermediate positions of various sorts. The bottom tier was filled by the secondary modern and unreorganised elementary schools which provided over three-quarters of the age group with a diluted general education which inevitably restricted their prospects to the lower rungs of the occupational ladder. Needless to say, the main determinant of which tier an individual child found himself ascribed to was the social class factor.

3   Educational Welfare and Special Services

The critical bearing of physical health and normality upon the capacity of children to take full advantage of the developing educational system was only gradually recognised. By the turn of the century, however, pioneers like the McMillan sisters were able to play on the public conscience with increasing effect and thereby stimulate measures designed to reduce the serious educational handicap faced by children suffering from poor health, undernourishment and other disorders. The long-term result was greatly to widen the responsibilities of the State in the educational field through the introduction and expansion of special services and other associated developments.

(a)   School Medical Service

Military recruitment during the Boer War (1899–1902) and the Departmental Committee report on *Physical Deterioration* (1904) having revealed the parlous state of health of the younger generation, the Education (Administrative Provisions) Act of 1907 founded the School Medical Service for the benefit of elementary school pupils. Initially the LEAs were simply required to provide medical inspection, but many took it upon themselves to provide facilities for treatment as well; the latter function was therefore made mandatory by the Education Act of 1921 and before long every LEA was equipped with at least one school clinic. The successful establishment of the service owed much to the initial enthusiasm of Sir Robert Morant who immediately established a new Medical Branch of the Board of Education, and to the sterling work of Sir George Newman who served as its head from its inception until his retirement in 1935. In 1918 the Fisher Act provided for the mandatory extension of medical inspection to State secondary pupils and also empowered the LEAs to provide such pupils with treatment. Throughout the inter-war years treatment, where provided, for elementary or for secondary pupils, was to be charged to the parents if they could possibly afford to pay; but given the economic climate and social distress of that time many children received their treatment free of charge. In this formative period the main concern was to deal with lice, rickets, dental caries and defects of the eyes, ears, nose and throat. But during the 1930s some LEAs established child guidance clinics to help with difficult pupils and this provision became part of the service. Overall the School Medical Service was gradually expanded and strengthened until the 1944 Education Act gave it responsibility for both the free inspection and treatment of all pupils encompassed by the State system of education. Winston Churchill described the service as the greatest piece of preventive medicine undertaken in our history; certainly within Newman's period of office the health of the nation's younger generation had improved beyond recognition.

(b) School Meals and Milk Service

The efforts of voluntary charity organisations to meet the needs of under-nourished children attending elementary schools had become clearly inadequate by the beginning of the century. Accordingly the Labour-inspired 1906 Education (Provision of Meals) Act authorised any LEA to spend up to a ½d rate on the support of a school meals service, although it was stipulated that only necessitous children should benefit from such provision and that even then their parents should be required to contribute to the cost if at all possible. Thus the Act was merely permissive and hedged with limitations. Consequently the school meals service developed very slowly and, prior to the Second World War, except in times of massive unemployment, the proportion of elementary schoolchildren benefiting from it never rose above 3 per cent of the total. It was the exigencies of war after 1939 which brought about a rapid expansion of the service and within five years no less than one-third of the children were staying for school dinners. The 1944 Act made it compulsory for all LEAs to provide school meals for all pupils in State schools desiring them: thus the provision of school dinners became a social service and an integral part of the educational system, affecting both the primary and secondary stages. Meanwhile subsidised school milk had been introduced into maintained schools in 1934, with provision for making it free to necessitous children. By 1939 about half the pupils were taking advantage of the scheme and the proportion rose further in the war years. The 1944 Act made the supply of school milk a statutory duty and the subsequent Family Allowances Act (1946) made it free for all pupils.

(c)   Provision for Handicapped Pupils

The State first assumed responsibility for making provision for handicapped children in 1893 when the Elementary Education (Blind and Deaf Children) Act empowered the School Boards to support schools for blind and deaf children under sixteen years of age. This was followed in 1899 by the Elementary Education (Defective and Epileptic Children) Act which permitted them to make similar provision for mentally defective and epileptic children. The 1902 Education Act transferred these powers to the new LEAs and by the outbreak of the First World War they had been translated into positive duties. Thus this new type of concern developed gradually and in piecemeal fashion until the Education Act of 1921 consolidated and strengthened previous legislation by making the LEAs responsible for providing suitable education in special schools for blind, deaf, physically handicapped, mentally deficient and epileptic children. During the inter-war period the provision was consequently limited to children with overt disabilities and it was related to composite groupings (e.g. the totally blind and the partially blind were not distinguished). And in line with the 1913 Mental Deficiency Act LEA responsibility for feeble-minded children was limited to those capable of being educated in special schools; the more severe cases were placed in the charge of separate mental deficiency bodies. Although the child guidance service began to emerge the associated need to provide special schools for maladjusted pupils was not met. Before the Second World War provision for the handicapped was still looked upon as an 'extra' or a sideline; it took the 1944 Act to make such provision an integral part of the educational system by underlining and elaborating the responsibilities of the LEAs in this field.

The medical, meals and milk services and the special provision for the handicapped were certainly the foremost expressions of the growing recognition of the importance of physical health and well-being to a child's progress at school. But they were supplemented by the enhanced position of physical education and organised games in the school curriculum, by the interest in nursery education and open-air schools, by progressive changes in school architecture and facilities, and by the spread of school camping and recreational activity. The 1918 Education Act, which recognised the potentially harmful effects of premature employment, also helped to improve matters. It raised the school leaving age nationally to fourteen years and abolished the half-time system which still afflicted senior pupils in certain areas. It further prohibited the employment of children under twelve and regulated the time that could be worked by twelve- to thirteen-year-olds outside school hours.

7 The 1944 Education Act and the State System of Schooling in the Post War Years

The legislative foundations of the present system of education in England and Wales are still basically dependent upon the 1944 Act passed towards the close of the Second World War. Its origins lay in the educational debates and developments of the inter-war period and, more immediately and urgently, in the much sharpened wartime interest in educational reform. In 1941 R.A. Butler, a rising and liberally-minded Conservative politician, became President of the Board of Education and energetically spent the next two years securing the agreement of all the main interested parties to an actual programme of reform. Once the thorny question of the future of the voluntary schools had been finally settled with the churches, such a programme was submitted to Parliament as the 1943 White Paper on *Educational Reconstruction*. Churchill's Coalition government was to secure major advance by two means. Legislative action was to be taken and in this regard the White Paper provided the basis for the 1944 Education Act – although, in the event, to maintain inter-party unity within the Coalition, the White Paper's support for the tripartite organisation of secondary schooling did not receive direct expression in the Act. In certain directions, however, it was felt that administrative action would suffice to bring about improvement. The betterment of primary school premises and facilities and the reduction of the size of primary classes attracted priority for such action. The abolition of the free-place examination in its existing form and the remodelling of the curriculum for secondary schools could also be achieved without legislation. And finally, advances in the field of teacher recruitment and training and in the widening of opportunities for university education could be similarly effected.

1   Provisions of the 1944 Act

Butler's measure received the royal assent in August 1944 after a slow but smooth passage through Parliament. It consisted of five main parts.

(a)   Part I: Central Administration

This provided for:

(i) the replacement of the Board of Education, with its mere superintendence role, by a new Ministry of Education responsible for promoting national educational policy and development and for securing their effective execution by LEAs placed under its 'control and direction'.

(ii) the replacement of the Consultative Committee by two Central Advisory Councils (for England and for Wales) authorised to investigate and report upon any educational matter they thought fit or upon any question referred to them. Subject to the inclusion of members of suitable professional experience, the constitution and composition of the Councils was left to the discretion of the Minister.

(iii) the requirement that the Minister present to Parliament an annual report upon the work of the Ministry and the Central Advisory Councils.

(b)   Part II: The Statutory System of Education

This provided for:

(i) the reorganisation of local educational administration. The Part III LEAs were abolished, leaving the County and County Borough Councils (146 of them) as the only LEAs and as such they were to undertake responsibility in respect of all stages of education in their areas. Provision was made, however, for divisional administration (via divisional executives and excepted districts) in the larger county areas; by this means county LEAs could delegate their functions (the borrowing of money and the raising of rates excepted) to subordinate bodies better acquainted with the local circumstances affecting different parts of their areas.

(ii) the extension and stricter definition of the responsibilities of the LEAs. They were required to make sufficient and satisfactory provision for primary and secondary education and to secure adequate facilities for further education in respect of persons over compulsory school age. The latter requirement included the duty to establish and maintain county colleges for the provision of compulsory part-time continuative education to the equivalent of 330 hours instruction per annum for the fifteen to eighteen years age group. It now became a duty for the LEAs to provide medical inspection and treatment and meals and milk for pupils in maintained schools and for county college students. Furthermore, in carrying out their duties they were to show particular regard for the needs of nursery education and the education of handicapped children. To ensure that all these responsibilities were being satisfactorily met the Act required the LEAs to submit development plans, which would be subject to amendment, to the Ministry.

(iii) the organisation of the statutory system of education as a continuum made up of primary, secondary and further stages. Primary and secondary schooling was to be provided separately with transfer between schools at eleven plus. The education given was to be appropriate to the children's different ages, abilities and aptitudes and to the different ages at which they might be expected to leave school. Some may regard this stipulation as favourable to the provision of distinct types of secondary education in separate schools, but there was no mention of tripartite or selective arrangements and the provision was open to interpretation by the LEAs.

(iv) the raising of the school leaving age to fifteen years and its extension to sixteen years once the Ministry was satisfied that it had become a practical proposition. Provision was made for effecting the extension by Order in Council so as to avoid the need for later legislation.

(v) the abolition of all fees for admission to State maintained schools. This meant that places in selective schools (grammar and technical) maintained by the LEAs would henceforth have to be obtained on scholastic merit.

(vi) the introduction of standard requirements for school management and governance. Henceforth all schools within the statutory system were to have a body of managers (primary) or governors (secondary). Such bodies were to be appointed by the LEAs in the case of County schools; voluntary schools were to include representatives of the LEA on their managing or governing bodies, but the arrangements in all respects were subject in their case to Ministry approval.

(vii) the modification of the dual system. Whilst it was retained and even extended to the secondary field, the detailed provisions forced the denominational schools to choose between their desire for more independence and their desire for greater financial support. Those schools established and maintained by the State (named 'provided' schools since 1902) were now to be called County schools. The schools founded by the churches (called 'non-provided' schools since

1902) were renamed voluntary schools and were to be divided into three categories according to the particular balance of privileges received and obligations accepted. The first category was the voluntary special agreement school which emanated from the 1936 Education Act. Under this measure the churches entered into over five hundred special agreements with LEAs for the establishment of denominational secondary modern schools on the basis of 50–75 per cent of the capital cost being borne by public funds. Because of the war only thirty-seven of these projects had materialised; the Act provided for the revival and implementation of any of the unfulfilled agreements on the original terms offered. The voluntary special agreement schools which emerged were allowed to provide denominational religious worship and instruction and their governing bodies were to enjoy a two-thirds majority of foundation trustees. But the appointment and dismissal of staff ('reserved' teachers for denominational religious teaching purposes excepted) was in the hands of the LEA and the governors were committed to meeting one half of the capital cost of alterations and repairs to the school's exterior. Current costs were met by the LEA , as they had been since 1902 for voluntary schools. The second category was that of the voluntary controlled school and involved the surrender of their denominational independence and character in exchange for complete financial support from public funds. Two-thirds of the managers or governors of these schools were to be representatives of the LEA. They were committed to undenominational religious worship and instruction (the latter according to an Agreed Syllabus), although special arrangements could be made for individual pupils in response to parental application for the provision of religious teaching according to the school's trust deed. Thus this category was not far removed from the ordinary County schools. The third category consisted of voluntary aided schools which retained the most favourable denominational position, though at a considerable price. Having provided the premises of these schools the churches undertook to meet half the cost of external alterations and repairs to the premises and in return received certain privileges. The denominational atmosphere remained completely intact and the church nominated two-thirds of the managers or governors. Indeed the school managing or governing body was given the responsibility for the appointment and dismissal of all (not just religious) teachers, though subject to the approval of the LEA.

The Act allowed the churches a period of six months to determine the category into which each of their voluntary schools should fall.

Whilst more than half of the Anglican schools chose 'controlled' status, the Roman Catholic schools strongly preferred but reluctantly accepted the other more expensive possibilities.

(viii) the introduction of compulsory religious worship and instruction into all schools within the statutory system. In County and voluntary controlled schools (subject in the latter case to the special arrangements already mentioned) the religious education was to be undenominational and in accordance with an Agreed Syllabus drawn up by the Anglican and Free Churches in association with the teachers' organisations and the LEAs. In both County and voluntary schools religious worship and instruction would continue to be subject to the right of parents to withdraw their children from it. Moreover, the Act provided that, except in the case of voluntary aided schools or 'reserved' teachers, no teacher could be required to give religious instruction or should be penalised for not doing so. The provision for compulsory religious teaching in the schools was justified in terms of Christian heritage and the wishes of the majority of parents, but it was also expedient as a sop to the churches which had given ground over the reform of the dual system.

(ix) the execution of responsibility for the training and supply of teachers by the central authority. To fulfil this vital duty the Ministry was empowered to direct LEAs to contribute in various ways to the support of the system of teacher training. One calculated result of this was the proper and equitable financing of teacher training. Hitherto all LEAs had employed teachers, whilst a minority were left with the burden of training them. New arrangements now emerged which divided the cost between central and local government on a 60:40 basis and required all LEAs to contribute to a pool according to the number of teachers they employed.

(x) the redefinition of parental duty in respect of the child's education. Previously parents had been required to ensure 'efficient elementary instruction in reading, writing and arithmetic'; now they were made responsible for ensuring their child received 'efficient full-time education suitable to (his) age, ability and aptitude, either by regular attendance at school or otherwise' (section 36). This requirement could be met by satisfactory home tuition or attendance at a registered independent school as well as through the statutory system.

(c) Part III: Independent Schools

This provided for:

(i) the registration of all independent schools with the Ministry as a statutory requirement for their continued operation or initiation.

(ii) the inspection of all independent schools by the Ministry, involving the possibility of removal from the register where standards of provision were judged inadequate. In this respect the nature of the premises, accommodation, instruction and proprietor were specified to be of particular importance. The Act provided for appeal to an Independent Schools Tribunal where the proprietor was aggrieved by an unfavourable decision of the Ministry.

(iii) the introduction of Part III of the Act on 'an appointed day'. Thereafter, anyone conducting an unregistered independent school would be criminally liable.

In 1944 the private sector consisted of some ten thousand schools of various sorts and sizes, encompassing about one-twentieth of school pupils. The need was to protect the public from fee-paying schools providing an unsatisfactory education and thus the Act provided for a closer oversight of the private sector by the State. It was not, however, until 1957 that the Ministry found enough breathing space to apply this part of the Act.

(d) Part IV: General

This provided for:

(i) the reorganisation of central grants for education by means of Ministry regulations to place them on a more generous and equitable basis. Although the specific and percentage grant system introduced by the Fisher Act (1918) was retained, the actual grant formula was revised to raise the proportion of total expenditure met by the Treasury from the pre-war figure of 48 per cent to a new level of 55 per cent. The amount of aid received by any individual LEA would vary according to its rateable wealth and size of school population and special additional assistance was made available for the poorest authorities. Thus a real attempt was made to shift more of the financial burden on to the shoulders of the central government as a necessary pre-condition of effecting the progress envisaged by the Act.

(ii) the grant of scholarships, exhibitions, bursaries and other allowances for further and advanced educational study by both the LEAs and the Ministry. This was calculated to widen opportunities for undertaking full-time courses in teacher training and higher education.

  (iii) the statutory recognition of the Burnham Committees and the salary scales for teachers agreed by them. This meant that henceforth all LEAs were legally committed to paying Burnham scales (primary/secondary or further) once they had been agreed and approved by the Minister.

  (iv) the consideration of parental wishes in relation to the education of their children within the context of the statutory system. But this general principle enunciated in section 76 of the Act was subject to serious qualifications; parental wishes were to be met only 'so far as is compatible with the provision of efficient instruction and training and the avoidance of unreasonable public expenditure', and in practice this put the LEAs in a pretty strong position.

(e) Part V: Supplemental

This provided for:

  (i) safeguards against the danger of government by regulation. All regulations made under the Act or thereafter modified by the Ministry were to be laid before Parliament for forty days (with the possibility of being annulled) to acquire the force of law.

  (ii) a proper interpretation of the Act by giving definitions of various terms used (e.g. Agreed Syllabus, independent school, young person) and by clarifying the limits of the Act (e.g. inapplicable to Scotland and Northern Ireland).

Although the broad framework laid down by the 1944 Act has been basically maintained, many of its provisions have been subject since to the modifying effects of some twenty amending Acts, various other Parliamentary enactments, the odd Order in Council and – even – tacit agreement to ignore certain of its requirements. These changes are most easily considered in parallel with the preceding analysis of the original provisions.

(Part I) In 1964 the functions of the Ministry of Education were transferred to the new Department of Education and Science (DES) which also assumed responsibilities connected with the universities and civil science. Since 1968 the two Central Advisory Councils have been in abeyance and the Secretary of State has used other means for mounting important inquiries.

(Part II) The pattern of local educational administration has been modified by the 1963 London Government Act and the 1972 Local Government Act. And whilst the duties of LEAs in respect of the provision of primary, secondary and further education remain unchanged, the position in respect of other providing duties requires detailed comment. Firstly, the

duty to provide compulsory part-time continuative education for early
school leavers to the age of eighteen years has never been met as originally
intended. Secondly, the duty of LEAs to provide medical inspection and
treatment, which was not significantly changed by the advent of the
National Health Service (1947), ceased in 1974 when the National Health
Service Reorganisation Act transferred this responsibility to the new Area
Health Authorities. Thirdly, the duty to supply free milk to pupils was
curtailed from 1968 and the 1980 Education Act made the provision of both
school milk and meals, except for children deemed in special need, a discretionary matter for each LEA. Fourthly, the 1980 Education Act has now
clearly established that the provision of nursery education is a permissive
power and not a mandatory duty. Fifthly, the duty of LEAs to have particular regard for securing special educational provision for various categories of
handicapped children has been modified. The 1970 Act widened this duty
by transferring the responsibility for the education of severely sub-normal
children from the Department of Health and Social Security to the DES.
And the 1976 and 1981 Education Acts provided for the integration of as
many handicapped pupils as possible into the ordinary school system,
abolishing the separate categories of handicap and replacing same with a
general concept of 'special educational needs'. Meanwhile the original
requirement that compulsory schooling be organised in two separate stages
with transfer from primary to secondary at eleven plus was modified by the
1964 Education Act which facilitated the introduction of middle schools.
For a short spell, 1976–9, the law was also amended to require the comprehensive organisation of secondary education. The 1962 Education Act
terminated Christmas leaving and ten years later the minimum school-
leaving age was finally raised to sixteen years. The post-1944 arrangements
for school management and governance were modified in various ways by
the 1980 Education Act. And the financial position of voluntary aided and
special agreement schools was improved by the 1959, 1967 and 1975 Education Acts which progressively reduced their capital cost obligation from 50
to 15 per cent.

(Part III) Although the law related to independent schools has remained
unchanged since 1944, their position has been affected recently by the introduction of the 'assisted places scheme' via the 1980 Act. This State-sub-
sidised scheme is designed to provide several thousand independent school
places each year for able pupils from maintained schools; as such it does
something to fill the gap left by the phasing out of the direct-grant grammar
schools in 1975–6.

(Part IV) Under the original provisions of the 1944 Act the Ministry of
Education was responsible for making specific grants on a percentage basis
to cover over half of the total expenditure of the LEAs. But in 1958 the Local

Government Act of that year introduced a general fixed grant (later called the 'Rate Support Grant') which substituted an annual block payment to each local authority to help finance all its services. And in 1980 another Local Government Act gave central government the power to rule upon the annual level of a local authority's overall expenditure and to penalise any overspending. Latterly, the 1984 Rates Act has armed the government with even stronger (rate-capping) powers for the containment of local authority budgets. For State education these various changes in the system of central-local funding have been distinctly unfavourable.

On the distinct matter of student grants the discretionary powers given to LEAs by the 1944 Act were modified by amending Acts in 1962 and 1975; the result was to introduce and extend the application of mandatory awards to students accepted for first degree, teacher training and comparable full-time or sandwich courses. The Burnham arrangements for the negotiation of teachers' salaries, to which the 1944 Act had given a belated statutory foundation, were modified by the 1965 Remuneration of Teachers Act; this amending measure provided for direct government representation on the management panel and for arbitration in case of disagreement. Finally, over many years section 76 of the 1944 Act proved an unsatisfactory means of affording parents a significant influence upon the choice of schools for their offspring; accordingly the 1980 Education Act attempted to improve matters by requiring the LEAs to provide parents with a choice, with more information upon the schools available and with a new local appeals procedure.

2 An Assessment

The 1944 Act was probably the greatest single advance in English educational history, its provisions showing real breadth of outlook and considerable educational vision. Borne on the tide of wartime hopes and goodwill it even instrumented, in the interests of educational progress, a major revision of the dual system without engendering the usual acrimony. It did, in fact provide a fairly satisfactory legislative framework for the unprecedented expansion and development of the statutory system of education over the next thirty years. But, like many other measures, time has shown the 1944 Act to be a mixture of strengths and weaknesses.

In the 1943 White Paper Mr Butler readily admitted that 'legislation can do little more than prepare the way for reform' (page 26). Nevertheless, in various ways his measure made a really significant contribution to educational progress after the war.

(a) It wisely retained and purposefully refined the developing partnership in English education between the central and local authorities. The national interest in education received greater emphasis than hitherto, the new Ministry assuming clear responsibility for the control and direction of educational policy and development. The LEAs were faced with many statutory duties which the Ministry was responsible for ensuring they fulfilled: the Minister was equipped with the necessary powers of enforcement and was authorised to administer and interpret the Act through the issue of statutory regulations and orders. Thus the balance of power changed to the disadvantage of the LEAs, but the central authority remained subject to the influence of Parliament and public opinion and was not authorised to initiate any new departures which contravened the letter or spirit of the Act. In a word, the increased power of the Ministry was strictly dependent upon and limited by the Act itself. The result was that Butler's measure allowed the central authority to give much more unity and direction to educational development, without being able to ride rough-shod at the expense of other interested parties. And the trend towards a much greater degree of centralisation over the last decade or so cannot be attributed to the Act. Indeed, in response to demographic, economic and political pressures this process has been carried forward by the administrative actions of the Secretary of State (e.g. in respect of teacher training) and by the amendment of Butler's measure (e.g. in relation to financial control). Some would say that whilst the 1944 Act championed the central-local partnership, very recent developments with other roots constitute a growing threat to it.

(b) It rationalised the system of local educational administration by removing the distinction between Part II and Part III authorities and by giving statutory recognition to a single continuous educative process to be organised in three successive stages (primary, secondary and further) under one type of LEA. Accordingly the County and County Borough Councils were given exclusive ultimate responsibility for the local administration of education, and the resultant diminution in the number and increase in the effective size of LEAs made for improved provision and administration. The situation was further helped by the revision of the dual system in such a way that the voluntary schools were drawn much more firmly under the jurisdiction of the LEAs and received the financial wherewithal to meet the demands of the new Act. Moreover, the experience of the last decade questions whether the 1972–4 reorganisation of local educational administration was really beneficial. The disappearance of some fifty County Boroughs with educational responsibilities under the 1944 Act, including many with a fine record in education, has hardly been offset by any marked improvement in provision and efficiency which justified their absorption by larger units. And, meanwhile, the Act has proved quite compatible with a progressive modification of the financial position of the voluntary schools thus ensuring the continuing viability of the dual system.

(c) It provided free secondary education for all, finally burying the elementary tradition with all its shortcomings and class connotations. The raising of the school-leaving age to fifteen soon provided an extra year's secondary education for each child and the abolition of fee-paying places at State secondary schools met the demand for formal equality of opportunity within the statutory system. In 1972 the school-leaving age was raised to sixteen years as prospectively provided for in Butler's measure. This overall result was considered to be the most outstanding single contribution of the Act to the future of education in England and Wales.

(d) It set the stage for the expansion and improvement of further and higher education. The establishment of secondary education for all obviously had implications for the stages that lay beyond it; once the secondary schools produced an enlarged number of appropriately qualified students, the demand for places in further and higher education would inevitably increase. Moreover, the LEAs were now equally committed to making adequate provision in further education as in the primary and secondary fields. Thus both colleges of further education and teacher training colleges could hope to escape the comparative neglect they had suffered in the inter-war years. Finally, the provision for Ministry and LEA grants for students undertaking further or advanced studies was also calculated to wield a critical and beneficial influence in this field and in the growth of university education.

(e) It reformed the system of educational finance, thereby distributing the cost burden more equitably whilst at the same time encouraging and facilitating more generous provision. From 1944 to 1958 the main grant formula ensured that each LEA received a specific central grant for education expressed as a percentage of its total net expenditure. This meant that the central government was committed to matching an authority's expenditure, thus encouraging the more progressive LEAs to press ahead fast. It is no accident that public expenditure on education grew at an unprecedented rate 1944–58, or that central government finally insisted on the switch to a general and fixed grant system. Since 1958 the system of educational finance has changed markedly and latterly the nature of the central-local partnership has been radically affected by the 1980 Local Government Act with its penalties for local overspending. The particular interests of education have been ill-served by these changes and the arrangements which operated under the original provisions of Butler's Act were certainly preferable.

Nonetheless, given the benefit of hindsight, there are various criticisms that may be levelled at the 1944 Act and it is significant that certain sections of informed educational opinion believe that a new legislative enactment is long overdue.

(a) It was over-ambitious, its provisions ranging over the whole educational field without any clear indication of priorities. Given the limited resources available for education, especially in the immediate post-war decade, the Act was unable to achieve many of its intended purposes within a reasonable time of its passage and meanwhile the relevant context was changing. Part III of the Act did not come into operation until 1957 and the county college scheme was quietly and it seems irretrievably shelved. The intended raising of the school-leaving age to sixteen was progressively postponed and the provision of State nursery education on a widening scale was virtually ignored until the early 1970s and recently made purely permissive. It was not until after 1956 that technical education (within the further and higher stages) began to receive serious attention and the revitalisation of the Youth Service had to wait upon the Albemarle Report (1960). The junior schools for the seven to eleven age group, in respect of premises and accommodation had been represented in the White Paper as the 'Cinderellas' of the statutory system, yet it was not until 1970 that a clear policy of 'priority for primaries' emerged. The vigorous expansion and reform of teacher training was delayed until the 1960s, whereupon too much was attempted too quickly. The Act attempted so much that it can be argued that in the post-war setting an improvised and piecemeal response to its many demands was inevitable as well as unfortunate.

(b) It tolerated certain weaknesses in the reorganisation of local educational administration. Some of the 146 Counties (e.g. Rutland) and County Boroughs (e.g. Hastings) were really too small to operate as viable LEAs, but they undertook the role on grounds of status rather than size. To placate certain municipal boroughs and large urban districts which ceased to be Part III LEAs, the Act made provision for divisional administration in the county areas. As divisional executives were not democratically elected (apart from in excepted districts) and made for more expense and less efficiency in the administration of county education, there was a strong case against their existence. These particular weaknesses were removed by the 1972 Local Government Act which abolished the smaller and minor authorities.

(c) It retained the dual system in a modified form in spite of its having proved such an obstacle to educational progress since 1902, and it introduced compulsory religious worship and instruction for all schools within the statutory system. The new arrangements and their later development have been subject to sharp criticism from secular and humanist sources. The considerable independence accorded to voluntary aided and special agreement schools by the Act was justified in terms of their meeting half of their capital and repair costs. Yet, faced with increasing financial pressure after the war, the churches successfully negotiated a further improvement in the financial arrangements for these schools. As the result of amending Acts 1959–75 the church contribution was reduced to 15 per cent and for the first time since 1870 building grants (of 85 per cent of total cost) were made available for the establishment of new voluntary aided schools. Thus such schools are now able to maintain a denominational atmosphere and a favoured position, whilst the State meets all their running costs and 85 per cent of their other costs. The result would seem to be anomalous in relation to the principles governing the religious settlement of 1944. Indeed, the critics insist that experience has shown that the 1944 Act began an erosive process, the logical extension of which is the final acceptance of a Scottish solution by which denominational schools, whilst retaining their particular identity, will be completely financed from public funds. To some people this would be a betrayal of one of the fundamental principles which has governed educational development in England and Wales since 1870. The provision for compulsory religious worship and instruction has produced more widespread and growing criticism, leading to the recent pressures (especially from the Humanist Association) for the repeal of this particular requirement. Here the Act gave rise to a new area of controversy where there was not one before.

(d) It afforded no clear definition (via its provisions or derivative regulations) of minimum standards of primary and secondary school provision or of what constituted adequate facilities for further education. Thus, in practice, whether individual LEAs performed satisfactorily in these respects was simply subject to the discretionary judgement of the Minister or (later) the Secretary of State. Whilst education enjoyed high priority and educational expenditure in real terms consistently rose (i.e. to the close of the 1960s), this weakness was of limited import. However, once mounting economic difficulties and changing political attitudes put educational spending under growing pressure this particular chicken came home to roost. Critics of recent central government policies insist that they have led in both the schools and further education sectors to reducing levels of provision which contravene any proper interpretation of the 1944 Act. Yet as central government itself is the ultimate arbiter of what level of provision is reasonable it is no easy matter to challenge and redress the position.

(e) It left the organisation of secondary education for all to local discretion, provision according to 'age, ability and aptitude' being consistent with either selective or comprehensive arrangements. The lack of clear central direction produced a patchwork of local solutions which varied very greatly in the extent to which they afforded the sort of opportunities envisaged by the Act; this in turn left the way open for the organisation of secondary education to become a bitter party political issue. One unfortunate side-effect of the prolonged and continuing controversy over this matter has been the waste of so much time and energy upon the secondary sector to the comparative neglect of other educational problems (e.g. the state of primary education).

(f) It failed to achieve the egalitarian ideal which inspired its passage because of the continued existence of the independent schools, the anomalous position of the direct-grant schools (with their large proportion of fee-paying places) and the favoured treatment accorded by most LEAs to their grammar schools. Given this loaded context the secondary modern schools were unable to realise that parity of status and esteem to which so much official lip-service had been paid, and equality of educational opportunity through secondary education for all became a pious hope rather than the reality intended. Nor could comprehensive reorganisation within the existing framework completely solve this problem, for the Act had left the private sector largely unaffected.

3 Selection Versus Comprehension

Above all else the 1944 Act sought to extend educational opportunity by securing a satisfactory secondary education for each and every child. Thus it provided for the final dismantlement of the old elementary system via the completion of the Hadow reorganisation process. And under its terms the school-leaving age was raised to fifteen (1947) and subsequently to sixteen years (1972). The number of pupils in maintained secondary schools rose almost continuously from one and a half million to over four million during the period 1948–79. A particular feature was the impressive growth in the number of Sixth Formers; the proportion of seventeen-year-olds remaining at school rose from only 5 per cent in the early 1950s to over 18 per cent thirty years later. In 1947 the School Certificate and Higher School Certificate examinations were taken by just over 100,000 and 25,000 candidates respectively: by the early 1980s the corresponding figures for the 'O' and 'A' level GCE examinations were well over one million and 300,000. Moreover the relatively new CSE examinations were attracting some 600,000 separate candidates. But it was not upon these developments that public and political interest tended to focus; increasingly attention was concentrated on the controversial matter of how to organise secondary education for all – in relation to which the 1944 Act had provided no definitive answer.

In 1942 both the Labour Party Conference and the Trades Union Congress gave their official support to the idea of a common school as the basis for secondary education for all. Three years later the Labour government of Clement Attlee was swept into power as a result of the 1945 election. Yet in the immediate post-war years the great majority of LEAs organised secondary education selectively along tripartite or bipartite lines (only half of them bothered to develop secondary technical schools). Some LEAs established bilateral schools, but only a tiny minority established or planned multilateral or comprehensive schools; the Isle of Man, Anglesey, and certain parts of rural Wales embraced the common school for reasons of practicality and economy, but only London and Coventry chose and effected this alternative on grounds of principle. The Ministry, though desisting from any open and bold attempt to push the tripartite approach, refused to recommend multilateral or comprehensive organisation and insisted that such experiments should involve the development of very large schools of about 1,600 pupils to ensure the emergence of an economic Sixth Form. It was not until they were on the verge of electoral defeat in 1951 that the Labour leadership produced *A Policy for Secondary Education* and came out strongly in favour of comprehensive education. Meanwhile innumerable Labour-controlled LEAs had done little or nothing to advance the cause of the common school in spite of the room for manoeuvre allowed under the 1944 Act. When Churchill's Conservative government took office, six years of Labour rule had resulted in the actual establishment of some thirteen comprehensive schools which accounted for less than 0.5 per cent of the secondary school population. This curious fact has a number of explanations:

(a) a lack of real enthusiasm for the comprehensive school on the part of the Labour leadership, which saw the State grammar school (now at last opened completely to talent) as the best answer to the competition of the independent public schools. Many Labour leaders, both central and local, were themselves grammar school products and their loyalty to the traditional institution inevitably died hard; throughout the inter-war years they had fought to secure open competition for all State grammar school places and this had limited their horizons.

(b) a deep distrust of multilateral and comprehensive schools on the part of the professional civil servants at the Ministry and professional administrators serving the LEAs. The majority of these professionals had received a grammar school and university education and their sympathies lay with an elitist approach to educational opportunity. The Labour party, long starved of office, did not find it easy to challenge their advice.

(c) the process of conditioning and associated developments related to the organisation of secondary education going back to the early 1920s. Convinced of the overriding importance of individual ability differences and secure in their belief in the efficacy of intelligence testing, the Hadow, Spens and Norwood Committees had sanctified the selective approach to secondary education. Given the pre-war development of grammar, technical and modern schools the line of least resistance after 1944 was the selective solution, and the many other problems faced by the LEAs at this time ensured that the temptation to take it was very great.

(d) the serious doubts about comprehensives, and even outright hostility towards them, amongst the teaching profession. Secondary modern teachers quickly became jealous of the independence of their own growing empire with its particular character and opportunities for nongraduates, whilst selective school teachers remained fearful of academic traditions being lost in a common school and of having to cope with the whole ability range. Even the National Union of Teachers (NUT), which had resolved to support comprehensive experiments at its 1943 Conference, became distinctly lukewarm in its attitude.

Thus by 1951 comprehensives had made only insignificant headway at the expense of the selective system. For the next thirteen years of Conservative rule Ministry policy was to use its influence (especially financial) to limit comprehensive advance to new purpose-built schools which did not injure the fortunes of existing grammar schools. The Conservative government was happy that the tripartite or bipartite approach should continue, although Sir Edward Boyle ultimately began to educate some of his party colleagues to see properly developed comprehensives as an acceptable alternative. But meanwhile the selective system and the associated elevenplus examination were having to face growing criticism and mounting challenge; this was the result of a number of influences and developments:

(a) the gradual recognition that tripartite approach rested on palpably false premises and highly questionable procedures. Norwood's three psychological categories with their different qualitative minds were naïve and unacceptable as basic propositions. Professional educationists such as Brian Simon, John Daniels and Philip Vernon went on to undermine the long-standing reputation of intelligence tests as a reliable predictor and means of eleven-plus selection. In 1957 a high-powered investigation on behalf of the National Foundation for Educational Research revealed a 12 per cent margin of error in the existing selection procedures; translated into national terms this meant that some 70,000 children were being mis-selected at eleven-plus every year. It was also shown that, in a context which cried out for the later reassessment of the initial selection, less than 1.5 per cent of eleven-plus failures were subsequently transferred from modern to selective schools. Finally, the psychological ill-effects of eleven-plus failure on pupil motivation and progress, especially in the case of borderline candidates, were also investigated and to some extent substantiated. If eleven-plus selection was already unpopular with a growing number of parents and teachers, it was now shown to be unreliable and unfair as well.

(b) the organisational and geographical anomalies which emerged and could not be defended. The selective system conformed to no generally accepted pattern; indeed many LEAs chose to ignore the technical school and organised along simple bipartite lines. The result was a hotch-potch of arrangements which differed in detail and were the result of local option rather than any clear national policy. The proportion of eleven-plus pupils awarded selective school places varied from about 10 per cent to over 40 per cent with wide variations often occurring between adjacent authorities. Unofficially there was a 'black list' of LEAs with low selective entry percentages: for a child to be brought up in such an area meant only a slim chance of a grammar school education. Yet the Ministry made no real attempt, and perhaps did not have the inclination or the power, to equalise selective entry proportions throughout the country at a reasonable and considered level.

(c) the successful development of GCE 'O' level courses by some secondary modern schools after 1952, when they were freed from the previous ban on their entering their pupils for external examinations. The subsequent results showed that many eleven-plus failures had academic potential which could be capitalised upon; by the end of the decade a few such pupils had even found their way through to the universities. But only a minority of secondary modern schools were adequately staffed or equipped to run such courses effectively. The consequent waste of talent was bemoaned as well as demonstrated by both the Crowther (1959) and Newsom (1963) Reports, although their recommended solution was the improvement of the secondary modern schools rather than the abandonment of selection.

(d) the mounting concern over the sociological dimensions of the eleven-plus examination and the selective system. Because of the social distribution of intelligence and educational attainment it was inevitable, in spite of the formal equality of opportunity vested in the eleven-plus examination, that the middle class should continue to dominate the grammar schools whilst the secondary modern schools became the preserve of the working class. Evidence was produced to show that many working class children, selected for a grammar school education either failed to meet requirements or in doing so became alienated from their own home background. Thus it was argued that eleven-plus selection tied the organisation of secondary education very strongly to differences in social class background and accordingly the selective system was castigated as an intolerably divisive influence in a democratic community. The recommended solution to this social problem was the comprehensive school.

Although forceful and considered counter-arguments were presented in defence of the grammar school and the retention of selection by Eric James, Harry Ree, G.H. Bantock and the Joint Four (a committee representing teachers in selective schools), the opposition to the continuance of the eleven-plus grew visibly stronger and was reinforced by the increasing objection to its backlash effect upon the work of the primary schools. In 1953, its reorganisation along comprehensive lines now complete, Anglesey achieved the distinction of being the first LEA completely to abandon the eleven-plus examination. The Labour party now closed its ranks and fully embraced the comprehensive cause; in 1955 comprehensive schools appeared in a Labour party election manifesto for the first time. In 1957 the Leicestershire Plan was launched, with the Conservative government's approval, to demonstrate the viability of a two-tier comprehensive system as an alternative to the very large all-through comprehensives pioneered by the London County Council. As a two-tier arrangement was much more compatible with the use of existing secondary school buildings and avoided the disadvantage of overpowering size, this experiment was a significant departure calculated to ease the way forward. In 1964 the Conservative government amended the 1944 Act to allow the West Riding LEA to introduce the new middle school for the nine to thirteen years age group as another means of comprehensive reorganisation. Almost simultaneously the forward planning of several other LEAs presented yet another possible pattern – that of the comprehensive school from eleven to sixteen, followed by the Sixth Form college. Resistance was visibly weakening and the comprehensive tide was beginning to swell in Labour-controlled areas: by the time the Conservatives fell from power in 1964 the number of comprehensive schools had risen to well over two hundred and now accounted for 8 per cent of secondary school pupils.

Given the developing context just described it was not long before the new

Labour government of Harold Wilson decided the time was ripe to move from local option to a national policy in relation to secondary education. The result was Circular 10/65 on *The Organisation of Secondary Education* by which Anthony Crosland, the Secretary of State for Education, exhorted all LEAs to submit plans within a year for the comprehensive reorganisation of secondary education. This critical Circular identified four organisational patterns deemed acceptable for long-term comprehensive secondary provision. These were:

(i) the orthodox eleven to eighteen 'all-through' pattern involving the retention of pupils in one comprehensive school throughout their secondary education.

(ii) the two-tier pattern covering the eleven to eighteen age range and involving separate junior and senior comprehensives with transfer at thirteen or fourteen. The official preference was for a thirteen-plus transfer wherever possible.

(iii) the middle school pattern involving the transfer of young pupils to a comprehensive middle school at eight or nine and later to a senior comprehensive at twelve or thirteen. The resultant three-tier arrangements would accordingly be *either* five to eight, eight to twelve, twelve to eighteen *or* five to nine, nine to thirteen, thirteen to eighteen.

(iv) the Sixth Form college pattern involving eleven to sixteen comprehensive schools linked to distinct Sixth Form or 'tertiary' colleges or units.

The Circular intimated that the latter two options would be available only for 'limited experiment' but this restrictive attitude soon disappeared. It was emphasised that no additional funds would be made available for comprehensive reorganisation and therefore the maximum use and improvisation of existing school premises was vital. The Circular also underlined the need for care over the demarcation of catchment areas for individual comprehensive schools to ensure that they would be 'as socially and intellectually comprehensive as is practicable'. And, optimistically, it was suggested that LEAs should consult with the governing bodies of voluntary aided, voluntary special agreement and direct-grant grammar schools in their area and thereby try to secure their incorporation in the overall reorganisation plan. A year later Circular 10/66 applied financial pressure by announcing that future secondary building programmes would only be approved so far as they were compatible with comprehensive reorganisation. In 1967 the Labour government's policy was bolstered by the Plowden report which condemned the distortive effects of the eleven-plus examination upon the work of the primary schools and recommended the end of selection. In the same year the government amended the financial arrangements for the voluntary schools to facilitate the co-operation of the churches in the reorganisation process. Meanwhile some 80 per cent of the LEAs made satisfactory responses to Circular 10/65 and only eighteen failed to respond in any shape or form. In 1970 the government determined to overcome the resistance of unco-operative Conservative-controlled authorities through new legislation and a bill was introduced to Parliament to accomplish this; at the same time the government received the Donnison Report which recommended that the direct-grant schools be given a straight choice between incorporation within the comprehensive system or independence and loss of State financial aid. The stage seemed set for a final showdown when the unexpected Conservative electoral victory later in the year suddenly changed the situation.

One of the first acts of Mrs Thatcher, the new Conservative Secretary of State for Education, was to withdraw Circular 10/65. It was replaced by Circular 10/70, the declared purpose of which was to restore the LEAs' freedom of choice and action; to this end they were removed from any obligation to submit schemes of comprehensive reorganisation or to proceed with schemes already approved. This secured the position of those Conservative-controlled authorities which had previously responded to Circular 10/65 with delaying tactics or open resistance. But in practice it did not secure similar freedom for those LEAs (a number of which were in fact Conservative-held) intent upon the completion or initiation of comprehensive reorganisation plans. Such plans were now subject to a number of developments calculated to slow down the change from selection to comprehension.

Firstly, the DES began to examine all plans school by school; this resulted in decisions being long delayed and to the partial approval of schemes. The latter result was particularly associated with Mrs Thatcher's refusal to approve the disappearance of some two hundred grammar schools; such refusal punctured the total scheme, required the retention of some selection and resulted in new comprehensives being little more than misnamed secondary modern schools.

Secondly, and most significantly, the Conservative government combined its 'priority for primaries' policy with a determined attempt to deny capital funds to the secondary sector. Expenditure on secondary school building, beyond the separately financed programme for raising the school leaving age, was made strictly dependent upon establishing a need for 'roofs over heads', thereby gravely limiting the room for manoeuvre available for the promotion of satisfactory reorganisation. However, the tide continued to run in favour of comprehensive reorganisation, the advent of the Heath Conservative government simply stiffening resistance to it. The proportion of secondary pupils in comprehensive schools increased from 8 per cent to 62 per cent between 1964 and 1974. But after 1970 the continued rise owed much more to the impetus derived from the previous period of Labour rule than to the actions of the Conservative government. By this time the Labour opposition was firmly committed to ending selection by legislative action and won the official support of the NUT for this policy.

In 1974 the comprehensive cause gained renewed impetus from another Labour victory at the polls. The Labour government 1974–9, successively led by Wilson and Callaghan, resumed the attack on the selective system through several initiatives. Almost immediately Circular 4/74 was issued to induce reluctant LEAs to submit plans for comprehensive reorganisation. When this failed to produce the desired result the 1976 Education Act was passed to require such plans and to force the governing bodies of voluntary secondary schools to co-operate. Additionally the Act disallowed the taking up of places at independent schools by LEAs. Within two years legal action was being taken or prepared against the few LEAs still holding out. By the time the Labour government fell, over 88 per cent of secondary school pupils were attending comprehensive schools. Meanwhile, the Donnison Report had been acted upon and 1975–6 saw the phasing out of the ultra-selective direct-grant grammar schools. Ironically, some two-thirds of the 174 schools involved chose to go independent rather than be incorporated in the State comprehensive system – so adding considerably to the strength of the private sector.

When the Thatcher Conservative government assumed office the position was difficult to retrieve and by 1982–3 the pipeline effect of pre-1979 developments had pushed the proportion of secondary pupils in comprehensive schools beyond the 90 per cent mark. Over the period 1965–81 the number of State grammar and secondary modern schools had fallen by 83 per cent and 89 per cent respectively. Nevertheless the government chose to defend the shrinking perimeter of secondary selection. The 1979 Education Act was quickly passed to annul the legislative requirement for comprehensive reorganisation. And where schools of 'proven worth' (generally equated with academic success) were put at risk the Secretary of State was commissioned to reject or hold up any further plans for secondary reorganisation. On a wider front the government's critical attitude towards mixed ability teaching in secondary schools, its rearguard action over the introduction of a common system of sixteen-plus examining and its new technical and vocational education initiative (TVEI) for the fourteen to eighteen age group have all been seen in some quarters as symptomatic of the Conservative party's desire to preserve or re-introduce selection in one form or another. Finally, to offset the demise of the direct-grant grammar schools and to bolster the private sector, the 1980 Education Act introduced the 'assisted places scheme' allowing able pupils to be transferred from maintained to independent schools at eleven, thirteen and sixteen. Initially some

220 independent schools (over half of them previously direct-grant) participated in the scheme and were committed to providing about 5,500 subsidised places each year.

However, appearances can be deceptive and certainly the comprehensive 'victory' is not as complete as the official statistics would suggest. There are various reasons for this:

(a) the private sector continues to support a form and degree of socio-academic selection of the utmost significance; accounting for only 6 per cent of the total secondary school population its products acquire about 28 per cent of the available university places. The elimination of the direct-grant grammar schools is now being offset by the growth of the assisted places scheme.

(b) over one-quarter of the LEAs still operate selection in some part or parts of their areas. Such co-existence and the right of parents to seek a grammar place for their children in any individual LEA area subjects some comprehensive schools to a creaming process which distorts the nature of their intake.

(c) the criteria used by the DES to distinguish a school as comprehensive have always been less than exacting, especially in terms of it having the sort of ability spread and social mix called for in Circular 10/65. Many neighbourhood comprehensives have drawn their pupils from areas which are distinctly more *or* less salubrious and this has given rise to so-called 'academic' and 'sink' comprehensives respectively. Mobile, well-to-do parents make their homes in the former areas and avoid the latter. Given the strong link between housing and socio-economic grouping this poses a serious problem for the comprehensive school; attempts by some LEAs to overcome it by banding, zoning and busing have proved most unpopular. Another difficulty is that the efforts to provide for parental choice have also favoured 'hidden selection'. Former secondary modern schools with no Sixth Form have been eschewed for those comprehensives developed from grammar school roots. And voluntary aided schools, especially Anglican, with their special entry arrangements have also attracted more than the normal distribution of pupils of above average ability and socio-economic grouping. Thus some comprehensives are seen as little more than glorified secondary modern schools whilst others can aspire to much higher repute, and all this becomes self-reinforcing.

(d) the operation of selective devices inside the comprehensive school remains widespread and crucial. In their internal organisation such schools vary from the progressively egalitarian to the traditionally meritocratic but with a marked leaning towards the latter. Although the comprehensive principle points to the need for mixed ability classes and groupings, this is rarely the practice beyond thirteen-plus. Streaming, banding or setting usually supervene as a preliminary to the even more critical selection for GCE, CSE or non-examination courses. And beyond the age of sixteen comprehensive Sixth Form units operate entry arrangements varying from the completely open to the judiciously restricted, in this case leaning heavily towards the former. Thus within the comprehensive system pupils and parents face a sorting-out process which some critics find comparable with the original eleven-plus.

Although socio-political forces have done most to sustain the drive to end the selective system, the ongoing development of comprehensive schools has been significantly affected by educational considerations, economic constraints and demographic pressures. Initially the official comprehensive 'model' was the purpose-built eleven to eighteen 'all-through' school with a minimum ten-form entry to ensure Sixth Form viability. With well over a thousand pupils such schools made special and elaborate arrangements for 'pastoral care', a distinguishing feature of the comprehensive scene. But this approach was costly and experience showed that the problems of sheer size usually outweighed the benefits. By the early 1970s a marked reaction had set in with many LEAs turning to other variants as a means of reorganisation; other LEAs, helped by the prior rise in the proportion of pupils staying on beyond sixteen, decided that much smaller (even six-form entry) eleven to eighteen comprehensives were viable as well as preferable. Both of these shifts in direction were compatible with the use of existing school premises for reorganisation purposes and tended to reduce the average size of comprehensive schools. Latterly shortage of money and falling school rolls have forced some LEAs to think again and a second wave of reorganisation plans has resulted. The changing circumstances have strengthened the case for those comprehensive patterns which provide for eleven to sixteen schools feeding into separate post-sixteen units. Indeed there are now well over one hundred Sixth Form or 'tertiary' colleges in existence with many more planned for the future. Conversely, in some areas the two-tier system, the middle school pattern and smaller eleven to eighteen comprehensives are being phased out or face an uncertain future. Yet the DES has refused to give a clear lead in favour of the Sixth Form/tertiary college solution lest this should pre-empt the Secretary of State's right to exercise his discretion upon reorganisation plans that might threaten existing schools of 'proven worth' – including well-established eleven to eighteen comprehensives with a good academic record. Combined with the decentralised system of school provision in England and Wales, this sort of policy ensures the continuance of a veritable patchwork of different patterns of secondary schooling both between and within individual LEA areas.

4   Primary Education and Other Concerns

A feature of the post-war period has been the tendency for the secondary and higher stages of education to attract more than their fair share of attention and resources. An unhappy outcome of this has been to deny the primary schools, special education and the educational welfare services the sort of support and priority they deserve.

(a)   Primary Education

Apart from the curricula matters dealt with in the next chapter, post-war developments in the primary field may be considered in terms of three related areas.

(i)   *Nursery Schooling*

After 1945 the changing social context produced a growing need and demand for nursery schooling. The advance of the nuclear family unit, slum problems and ill-judged new housing developments, the growth of immigrant communities and the rising proportion of under-fives with working mothers combined to ensure this. Initially, with the 1944 Act requiring LEAs to give regard to the need for securing nursery provision for the under-fives, the prospect of this need being met seemed good. But in the event the post-war birth rate and other economic constraints decided successive governments to concentrate on the needs of compulsory schooling. In 1954 the Ministry instructed the LEAs that the reduction of over-size primary classes must take precedence over nursery provision or the early admission of under-fives. Six years later Circular 8/60 expressly forbade any further increase in nursery places and this general instruction remained in force until 1973. In this unfavourable climate the expansion of nursery schools and classes in 1945–70 was severely curtailed; however, a rise in early admissions to infant classes increased the proportion of three- and four-year-olds receiving some maintained schooling from 11 per cent to 17 per cent.

From the late 1960s the fortunes of maintained nursery schooling improved considerably. It received strong backing from the Plowden Report (1967) which recommended a ten-year drive to provide 90 per cent of four-year-olds and 50 per cent of three-year-olds with nursery schooling. For 15 per cent this was to be full-time provision, with priority for children in deprived areas. In the following year this met with some response in the new Urban Aid Programme which tied in with Plowden's 'educational priority area' recommendations. The 1972 White Paper *Education: A Framework for*

Expansion gave a special place to nursery provision; the Plowden plan was accepted and Circular 8/60 subsequently withdrawn. With primary rolls about to fall most of the expansion was to take the form of new nursery classes housed in converted units. Although economic difficulties ensured that the Plowden 'target' was not approached, the period 1970–82 witnessed considerable advance. Maintained nursery provision almost trebled to some 260,000 places (albeit 80 per cent part-time) and the proportion of three- and four-year-olds receiving some early schooling rose from 17 per cent to 40 per cent. However, the main gains were made before 1980, since when the original momentum has been lost; and the 1980 Education Act, by making nursery provision a permissive power rather than a mandatory duty for LEAs, is not calculated to help matters.

With the Department of Health's day nurseries affording even more restricted admission to the under-fives, post-war pre-school provision has relied very considerably upon private and voluntary effort. Most important in this regard has been the growth of the national movement inspired by the Pre-School Playgroups Association (1962); by the late 1970s it was claimed that 46 per cent of three- and four-year-old children attended a play-group provided by local voluntary iniative. But, whilst extending the available provision and involving mothers in their children's activities, the play-group movement has had two untoward effects. Its success has weakened the case for universal maintained nursery provision and its social pattern has reinforced the pre-school advantage of middle class children.

(ii) *Infant and Junior Schooling*

To allow all five- to eleven-year-olds to undertake the first phase of compulsory schooling in separate primary schools the 1944 Act provided for the completion of the Hadow reorganisation process. But it is not generally realised that it took more than twenty years to get rid of all the remaining pre-war 'all-age' elementary schools; and very often the older pupils were removed to leave a 'new' primary school housed in the old premises and dependent upon 'minor works' for improvement. In this developing context the post-war system of primary schooling generally was organised in two parts – the infant stage from five to seven-plus followed by the junior stage to eleven. About half the primary schools catered for the whole five to eleven age-range with the rest operating as separate infant or junior schools. Nationally the average primary school had rather less than two hundred pupils, although the figure was significantly lower for Wales. Many of the schools were voluntary aided and featured an Anglican or Roman Catholic 'denominational atmosphere'; in 1980 almost 20 per cent of primary pupils attended such schools compared with only 12 per cent in the secondary sector.

Since 1945 the primary schools have been almost permanently beset by demographic pressures. For a quarter of a century the problem was to keep pace with the expanding primary population which rose by over one-third to exceed five million in the early 1970s. Unable to secure equal priority for staffing and other resources, the primary schools faced a long uphill struggle. In the inter-war years the average number of pupils per teacher in the elementary schools had gradually improved to reach 27.2 in 1938. Twenty years after the 1944 Act the corresponding primary school ratio was 28.7 and almost one-fifth of the pupils were in classes of over forty! Not until after 1970 did the primary sector begin to improve upon the pre-war elementary ratio. However, with the sharp fall in the birth rate 1964–77 one problem was now giving way to another. The size of the five to eleven age-group peaked in 1973 and thereafter the primary schools were faced with falling rolls until the mid-1980s.

Increasingly this new trend produced a number of adverse effects. In the inner city and rural areas some primary school rolls ceased to be viable, necessitating individual closures or even complete reorganisation. Some staff suffered redeployment and newly qualified primary teachers found appointments hard to secure. From 1977, with financial constraints now compounding the situation, the primary teaching force began to decline. The only consolation was that staff numbers did not reduce as fast as pupil rolls; consequently during the period 1970–82 over-size classes were virtually eliminated and the ratio of pupils to teachers improved from 27.4 to a record 22.3 figure.

The post-war 'Cinderella' position of the primary schools was reflected in the fact that for many years the new Central Advisory Council devoted almost all its energies to reporting upon matters related to the secondary stage of education. However, in 1963 the Ministry finally commissioned the Council to inquire into 'primary education in all its aspects and the transition to secondary education'. The outcome was the Plowden Report on *Children and their Primary Schools* (1967). Its particular significance in relation to the retreat of the eleven-plus examination and to changes in the curriculum and internal organisation of primary schools is considered in the next chapter. But the report raised other issues which may be dealt with here. Firstly, it underlined the stark link between educational attainments and socio-environmental influences. Attention was focused on the deprived urban areas, encompassing 10 per cent of the population, where old school buildings, decaying housing, parental indifference and high staff turnover condemned thousands of children to social and educational handicap. The Plowden solution was a policy of 'positive discrimination' in the shape of 'educational priority areas' which would receive preferential treatment in terms of nursery provision, staffing and other resources. This recipe for compensatory education was well received by the Wilson Labour government and helped to promote the Urban Aid Programme launched in 1968. Over four years special allocations of some £34 millions were made for school building projects in educational priority areas. To stabilise staffing in priority schools an above-scale allowance of £75 per annum was introduced. The government also commissioned the Halsey Project (1968–72) to explore the best means of effecting positive discrimination in deprived areas with four pilot schemes being undertaken to this end. But as time passed the compensatory education approach received more lip-service than resources, especially as the educational service faced growing financial constraints. The 1972 White Paper on expansion virtually ignored the special needs of deprived areas and the 1974–79 Labour government did little to revive the dwindling interest. Symbolically, perhaps, the five-year-old Centre for Information and Advice on Educational Disadvantage was closed down in 1980. Secondly, the Report made a most justifiable plea for equality of status and treatment for primary schools, especially in relation to class sizes, buildings and equipment, per capita allowances and the Burnham points system. This included the idea of teacher aides to assist qualified infant and junior teachers both inside and outside the classroom. Although the latter recommendation fell foul of the inevitable professional opposition, some progress resulted in other directions. The Burnham points system was modified to give less advantage to secondary schools. Mrs Thatcher's 'priority for primaries' policy 1970–74 included a £112 million building programme to rid the primary sector of its worst accommodation; but in 1976 one-fifth of primary pupils were still in pre-1903 school premises. And, in the decade following the Report the teacher-pupil ratio in the primary sector improved much more substantially than in the secondary schools.

(iii) *Middle Schools*

Middle schools form the second stage of a three-tier system of first, middle and senior schools developed by some LEAs since the late 1960s. By 1980 they were attended by half a million pupils and accounted for one-seventh of the eight to thirteen age-group. They were pioneered by the West Riding LEA which in 1964 procured the amendment of the 1944 Act to allow for their introduction. Soon afterwards the concept of middle schools received strong support from the Plowden Report (1967). Thereafter a growing number of West Riding type nine to thirteen (deemed 'secondary') and Plowden type eight to twelve (deemed 'primary') middle schools were established. Various educational justifications were produced for such schools: it was claimed that they would provide new interest and motivation at the age of eight or nine and that they would ease the transition from more informal junior teaching to the more formal subject teaching of later years. But for most LEAs turning to middle school arrangements the main attraction was simply pragmatic – the new system afforded a means of comprehensive reorganisation based on existing school premises and avoided the need for large secondary establishments. This was reflected in the appearance of some 'mongrel' ten to thirteen and ten to fourteen middle school systems.

Whilst the eight to twelve and nine to thirteen middle schools acquired roughly equal importance in terms of the number of pupils attending them, they tended to differ considerably in their character. The eight to twelve middle schools tended to provide an extension for the more informal junior schooling approved of by the Plowden Report. The somewhat larger nine to thirteen middle schools had an average roll of some 420 pupils and were more distinctive. For the first two years they normally operated on a class teacher and mixed ability basis. Then, to a varying degree, the last two years saw the introduction of specialist teaching and of streaming or setting at least for certain studies. But the specialist provision would be broadly based (e.g. Humanities, Crafts) rather than subject specific in the traditional secondary fashion. In some areas of activity mixed ability grouping might continue and team-teaching arrangements appear. In both types of middle school the aim has been to provide a broad, balanced and common curriculum with no place for optional choices.

However, the middle schools now seem to be under serious threat from the general fall in school rolls and the associated interest in Sixth Form or tertiary college arrangements. And a less than favourable report on *9–13 Middle Schools* (1983) by HM Inspectorate is not calculated to help either. Indeed, since middle schools numbers peaked in 1980, a growing number of LEAs have decided to abandon them in favour of more viable alternatives. Most ominous is the fact that whereas falling rolls have led to the future of individual primary or secondary schools being put at risk, in the case of middle schools the tendency is to consider the abolition of the whole system. The cynics would say that the middle schools arose from expediency and that their fate is now being similarly determined.

(b) Special Educational Provision

Before the Second World War all legislation upon and arrangements for the education of handicapped children had treated them as a class apart. But during the years 1929–38 three separate reports upon various areas of special provision deplored this approach and advised the Board of Education to draw special schools firmly into the general framework. Happily the terms of the 1944 Act both accepted and reinforced this new outlook. Special educational provision now became simply part of the LEA's general duty to afford all children an education appropriate to their ages, abilities and aptitudes. Such provision was to relate to all pupils suffering from any disability of mind or body instead of being restricted to the five specified categories previously laid down. Most wisely the need for certification, with its unacceptable stigma, to qualify for special educational treatment was removed. And henceforth appropriate provision was not confined to special schools as the Act allowed for it to be 'otherwise' secured; this meant that where possible special education could be provided within ordinary schools. LEAs were required to ascertain which children needed special education and to that end could require parents to submit their child to examination from the age of two. Although the Act did not specify the categories of pupils likely to require special educational treatment, it did require the Minister to issue regulations for this purpose. Accordingly *The Handicapped Pupils and Special Schools Regulations* (1945) named eleven such categories. These were the blind, partially sighted, deaf, partially hearing, educationally subnormal, maladjusted, epileptic, physically handicapped, delicate, diabetic and speech-defective; diabetics soon disappeared in the broader delicate category but later on autistic children came to form a new category.

The 1944 Act paved the way for a considerable expansion and extension of special educational provision. During the period 1947–77 the number of pupils in special schools rose from 40,000 to 135,000 and latterly comprised nearly 2 per cent of the total school population. The main means of providing special education were boarding special schools, day special schools, hospital special schools, special hostels with ordinary day school units, special classes in ordinary day schools and individual tuition in hospital or at home. One in six of special school places were in boarding establishments. LEAs came to provide over 90 per cent of special school places but voluntary effort accounted for one-third of boarding places. Throughout the period the educationally subnormal remained by far the largest category with some 60 per cent of total numbers in the 1970s. This was a function of two influences. Firstly, this category was broadly conceived and potentially embraced slow-learning pupils who were of low ability or were simply retarded for reasons other than intelligence. The Ministry felt that any child whose attainments were more than 20 per cent below average might be considered for transfer to a special school. In these terms some 10–15 per cent of pupils could be eligible and there was a tendency for some LEAs to operate on that basis. Secondly, the 1970 Education (Handicapped Children) Act brought into the educational system those severely subnormal children who had hitherto been regarded as ineducable. Many of the 35,000 involved entered the educationally subnormal category which was thereupon sub-divided into ESN(M) for moderate and ESN(S) for severe handicap. This Act resulted from the growing conviction that many of the children concerned could benefit from special educational treatment and that the complete isolation of them and their teachers was no longer acceptable.

Although the post-war period was one of general advance there was a persistent shortage of special places for educationally subnormal and maladjusted pupils. And, despite the opportunity afforded by the 1944 Act, LEAs were disinclined to provide for special education within the ordinary school setting. Meanwhile informed opinion was gradually moving in favour of the abandonment of the categorised approach to special needs and the fullest possible integration of handicapped pupils into the ordinary school system. The 1976 Education Act provided for such integration subject to it being practicable, compatible with efficient instruction and financially supportable. In 1978 following a four-year inquiry the Warnock Committee published its report on *Special Educational Needs*. The category arrangements were condemned as both divisive and restrictive and it was recommended that the scope of special education should be greatly extended to include even short-term remedial provision in its milder forms. Thus the Warnock concept of special educational needs would relate to about 20 per cent of pupils at some time during their schooling. Remedial work was already an integral part of ordinary schooling; the need now was to integrate much more of the hitherto categorised special provision into the normal school situation. To sustain the Warnock approach the Report identified four future priorities: the early introduction of a new legislative and regulative framework, the expansion of nursery schooling for children with special needs, the improvement of sixteen-plus provision for young people with special needs and the reform of teacher training to meet the new challenge.

So far action on the Warnock Report has been less than full-blooded. The 1981 Education Act and its associated Regulations (1983) gave much weight to the bureaucratic requirements of ascertaining, assessing and recording children's special needs and parental rights in relation to this process. Beyond that the tendency was to be content with a statement of general principles. Thus the old categories were replaced by the wider concept of 'special educational needs' and the LEAs were constrained (as far as possible and still subject to the 1976 provisos) to educate pupils with special needs in ordinary schools. But the Warnock priorities on nursery schooling, post-sixteen provision and teacher training were not squarely faced and the Conservative government provided very little extra money to encourage and sustain the new policy. Although falling rolls have provided an added incentive to look closely at special educational provision, recent surveys indicate that many LEAs and teachers have little real commitment to the policy of integration. The danger is that of an under-funded and cosmetic operation involving considerable disruption to ordinary schools and little real benefit to children who would previously have entered special schools. Nor does the fact that some children are now being referred to as 'SEN' augur well for the future of the Warnock strategy.

(c) Educational Welfare Services

Until the 1970s the general trend was to strengthen and extend the educational welfare services pioneered before the Second World War. However, in more recent years various developments have combined to weaken their position.

(i) *School Health Service*

Under the 1944 Act the renamed School Health Service was to provide free medical and dental inspection and treatment for all pupils in the State system. On a discretionary basis similar provision could be extended to independent schools. Such was the pre-war reputation of the School Medical Service that the advent of the National Health Service (1948) did not occasion its disappearance; instead the LEAs were simply empowered to turn to the new service for free specialist and hospital treatment for pupils in need. In the years that followed the School Health Service undertook routine medical inspections which sometimes exceeded two million per annum and dental inspections of twice that proportion. In terms of treatment provided the main beneficiaries were pupils with impaired vision or squints, ear, nose and throat conditions, orthopaedic and postural defects, speech impediments and behavioural problems. Overall the School Dental Service treated one-third of the pupils inspected. However, in 1974 the School Health Service was drawn firmly into the reconstituted National Health Service when responsibility for it was vested in the new Area Health Authorities. Whilst LEAs still have the duty to ascertain and provide for children in special educational need and to make arrangements for the continuance of health inspections in school, they have lost their central position in Newman's original field.

(ii) *School Meals and Milk*

After the Second World War the provision of school meals and milk was regarded as an important social service and the 1944 Act made it an integral part of the educational system. Ministry Regulations committed teachers to school meals' supervision and by the 1960s an average of two-thirds of the school population were taking advantage of the much expanded service. There is little doubt that such provision made a significant contribution to the health of the post-war generation. But the original hope that the service would become free for all children rather than merely for those deemed necessitous was not realised. Since 1968 the supervision of school meals by teachers has been voluntary and the unsatisfactory situation which resulted has become a serious bone of contention for headteachers left with the overall responsibility. Gradually the original commitment to the service has waned and the 1980 Education Act has now relieved the LEAs of their general obligation to sustain it. However, they are still required to provide for those entitled to free meals (which had risen to almost one in five by the late 1970s) and to provide facilities for children bringing their own lunch-time food. Already some 50,000 women have lost their jobs in the school meals service and many more have had their hours and wages cut. The proportion of pupils taking school dinners has fallen below one-half; over one-third of them now bring their own sandwiches. And some LEAs are saving money by contracting the service out to private caterers. Clearly the service has seen its best days and faces a bleak future.

During the years 1946–68 at least 80 per cent of pupils in maintained schools took advantage of the free milk service. But in 1968 economic difficulties persuaded the Labour government to withdraw the privilege from secondary pupils; three years later the succeeding Conservative government terminated free milk provision for healthy junior children. This left the infants, pupils in special schools and other special cases as the only recipients of free milk. The 1980 Education Act has made the provision of school milk a totally discretionary matter upon which each LEA may decide. This whittling away of a service considered vital after the war has been justified in terms of the lesser need of older pupils, the improved standards of home consumption and the prior financial claims of other needs.

Although changes affecting the school health, meals and milk services have weakened the welfare dimension within the educational system, to some extent this may have been offset by other developments. A product of comprehensive secondary reorganisation has been the more conscious concern for providing effective pastoral-care arrangements for school pupils. All LEAs have come to employ Education Welfare Officers whose chief function is to help schoolchildren in trouble or difficulty and where necessary to co-operate with social workers and parents to that end. And since 1974 all LEAs have had a duty to provide a Careers Service for all those attending its schools and other institutions; a particular benefit has been that secondary schools now devote more staff time and energy to careers information and counselling.

8 Schools' Curricula and Examinations

In the last analysis the real substance of education resides in the curriculum, by means of which the educational system is finally brought face to face with its numerous charges in the school setting. The nature of the curriculum wields a decisive influence upon what and how a child learns in school, and thereby goes a long way towards determining the benefits or otherwise of a formal education. The curriculum has its basis in a more or less conscious appreciation of the aims of the educational process; these are subject to both institutional differentiation and marked chronological change. In terms of subjects and syllabuses to be studied, learning activities or experiences to be engaged in and the methods of teaching to be used, the curriculum formulates the knowledge, skills, attitudes and values with which the school equips its pupils. The maintenance of a proper standard and pattern of work in relation to the curriculum may be secured by means of inspection or examinations or both. External examinations for schools have, over the last century or so, enjoyed great prominence; they have been used to raise or maintain standards of work in the schools, to solve administrative problems related to finance or selection and to promote or retard upward social mobility in the emerging meritocracy of the twentieth century. Whilst wielding a beneficial influence in certain respects, they gave rise to the serious and continuing danger of an externally controlled and standardised curriculum rendered insensitive to the needs of the pupil and the changing demands of society. To explore all these related matters in greater detail it is advisable to consider the curricula traditions of the public elementary and the secondary grammar schools separately, before passing on to an analysis of the modern developments which have gathered momentum and force over the last half-century.

1   The Elementary Tradition

Rooted in the class consciousness of Victorian society, the cheap and inferior traditions of the public elementary school were not seriously challenged until the early twentieth century, or officially and finally abandoned until 1944. This tradition, given clear expression in the curricula and examinations associated with the elementary school, is explicable in terms of a variety of nineteenth-century influences which only began to give ground in Edwardian times. It was in relation to the schooling of working class children aged seven to twelve years that the tradition of meanness established itself and became entrenched. From an early date the tradition was, however, diluted by the richer and more liberal heritage which shaped the development of infant education. Later on, the growth of post-primary schooling added another more wholesome and promising dimension to the original tradition, thereby contributing to its gradual modification.

(a)   Basic Influences

The development of the elementary school curriculum was conditioned by a number of critical influences which bore upon it during the nineteenth and early twentieth centuries.

(i)   *Social*

The narrow, utilitarian curriculum of the Victorian elementary school, with its strong emphasis on the basic skills and social conditioning, reflected the determination of the propertied classes to deny the children of the poor and their teachers more than the minimal learning required to equip them for their humble station in life and to encourage an acceptance of the existing social fabric. The elementary school was a charitable institution designed to provide a very limited education for the children of those parents who could not afford to secure it independently; the middle classes were increasingly prepared to bear the cost as they recognised the contribution which such schools could make to the 'gentling of the masses' and the production of a more effective labour force. But cheapness and cost efficiency were the hallmarks demanded of these schools which had their roots in the charity schools and the schools of industry of the eighteenth century. At a time when all parents of any substance were expected to pay in full for any education received by their children, it was thought quite intolerable that philanthropic or public effort should secure anything but a markedly inferior schooling for the less fortunate or industrious sections of the community. Because they met these essential requirements, the monitorial and 'payment by results' systems were welcomed by those paying for the development of elementary education. Hence the Victorian elementary schools were inevitably characterised by large classes, spartan accommodation and facilities, a narrow and rudimentary curricula and a strict and repressive discipline. Even the teachers, with their working class background and restricted education and training, were successfully conditioned to accept the limits of their role. Indeed their long compliance with the stern requirements of the Revised Code gravely inhibited their capacity to take advantage of the more favourable climate which emerged at the turn of the century. By this time some of the basic assumptions which had differentiated the elementary school on purely social grounds were being challenged; in 1904 the elementary schools were officially recognised as a vital public service to the community at large rather than a charitable provision for working class children. As egalitarian influences wrought a gradual change in social attitudes and the collectivist philosophy wormed its way into political life, the image and work of the elementary school began to take on a more wholesome character. With the Hadow Reports of 1926–33 the process of finally abandoning the narrow social traditions of the elementary school for the developmental rationale of the modern primary school began in earnest. The curriculum was at the very centre of the changes which ensued, although more publicity has been given to the associated reorganisation of institutional forms.

(ii) *Economic*

Initially the needs of the Victorian economy reinforced the bare and narrow outlook upon elementary schooling. Employers were interested in securing the early employment of young persons who had acquired pronounced habits of industry and a working knowledge of the three Rs. Even in the later nineteenth century the nature of the economy was such that this was enough for the great bulk of the labour force. But meanwhile, amidst this economic context, there were those who were determined to protect the youngest children from the rigours of both industrialism and the typical elementary school; the result was the growth of a separate and much more enlightened native tradition of infant education. Much later the developing demands of both industry and commerce promoted the growth of post-primary education, first provided by the large School Boards in their higher-grade elementary schools and subsequently by the LEAs in their central and junior technical schools. From 1880, in spite of much official indifference to or disapproval of such outgrowths, the national system of elementary education persistently developed various forms of post-primary schooling. This is explicable in terms of an increasingly industrialised society drawing into existence a type of school geared to providing a vocationally oriented secondary education fitted to the needs of more able young persons entering responsible employment at the age of fifteen or thereabouts. The quest was for an alternative to the secondary grammar school with its traditionally academic curricula. Such post-primary experiments involved the provision of much advanced instruction and a considerable broadening of the curriculum; both these developments were calculated to modify the original elementary tradition for the better.

(iii) *Institutional*

The basic elementary tradition was also conditioned by a number of unfavourable institutional limitations and influences. The duration of elementary schooling operated as a critical limiting factor upon the curriculum. In the middle of the nineteenth century the average school life was only two years; at its close it was still only six years. Even the benefits of the Hadow reorganisation process for senior elementary pupils after 1928 were undermined by the maintenance of a minimum school leaving age of fourteen throughout the inter-war period. HM Inspectorate, with its literary background, wielded its early influence in favour of non-manual instruction on a limited front. The teaching of practical skills, formerly associated with the schools of industry, were squeezed out and the claims of physical and aesthetic education almost completely ignored. The die was finally cast by the Revised Code and the institution of the 'payment by results' system; designed to simplify the problem of dispensing central funds to grant-aided elementary schools and to raise the level of proficiency in the three Rs, this system placed a curricula strait-jacket upon the elementary schools which lasted for over thirty years. It was not until the turn of the century, with the abandonment of 'payment by results', the official encouragement of practical subjects and physical activity and the issue of the enlightened 1904 Elementary Code, that the institutional context became distinctly more favourable. Even then there were important residual limitations. The provision of a significant number of scholarships after 1907 for the transfer of able elementary pupils to secondary grammar schools was double-edged; whilst the preparatory tradition (hitherto centred in the private sector) was preferable to the original elementary one, it encouraged the teachers to concentrate on the needs of those pupils with scholarship potential. From the outset the demands of the emergent eleven-plus examination had a distorting effect upon the curriculum of the junior classes and also became associated with the tendency to treat many senior elementary pupils as a rump, to be occupied by simply re-treading ground already covered. Happily, this latter phenomenon, officially described as 'marking time', underlined the need to give much fuller consideration to the curricula needs of the senior elementary pupil. Herein lies one of the seeds of the Hadow reorganisation and the abandonment of the elementary tradition. But, in spite of the Hadow Reports, the Board of Education continued to maintain separate sets of Elementary and Secondary (Grammar) Regulations; this helped to ensure that the secondary modern schools inherited part of the old and inferior elementary tradition.

(iv) *Pedagogic*

What passed for educational theory in the nineteenth century was also largely disposed to reinforce the aridity of the elementary tradition. The Lockian philosophy and associationist psychology of the time combined to justify an exclusively teacher-centred approach to education in which the child mind was conceived as an empty receptacle to be filled with the essentials of knowledge and the basic moral precepts. Effective learning was held to depend upon the teacher's capacity to curb children's presumed predilections toward indolence and mischief and to present their lesson material in a systematically organised form conducive to initial assimilation and subsequent 'stamping in'. Thus the ideal teacher was the strict disciplinarian who demanded the children's constant attention and who built up their knowledge in associationist fashion by moving step by step from the simple to the complex. The question of motivation was completely ignored (apart from the sanction of fear) and the child was expected to learn by passive reception and response. The resultant regime was inevitably characterised by an unimaginative reliance on sequential rote-learning and drill methods; initially applied to the three Rs, this barren approach was later applied to other subjects of the developing elementary curriculum. Pioneered by the monitorial system, encouraged by the Revised Code and propagated by the denominational training colleges, such a pedagogy was peculiarly illdesigned to stimulate the pupils' interest in their own education.

However, by the early twentieth century various progressive influences in the field of educational theory were combining to challenge and erode the insensitive and misguided pedagogy of Victorian times. Indeed, infant education had developed a separate tradition from the early nineteenth century, based on the child-centred naturalism of Rousseau and Froebel, but adjusted to native conditions. This liberalising influence was cut off from the elementary school by the Revised Code; but after 1900, enriched by the work of the McMillan sisters and the influence of Maria Montessori, the infant tradition was able to infect the schooling of older children to some degree. Meanwhile, the ideas of Herbart, as interpreted by Sir John Adams in his *Herbartian Psychology as Applied to Education* (1897), began to wield a beneficial influence upon the elementary tradition itself. Although the Herbartian approach remained basically impressionist, the teacher was exhorted to know the child as well as the subject and to recognise the importance of sound psychology as a basis for effective teaching. The teaching of all subjects, even science, in an exclusively verbal and mechanical way was condemned; conversely the need to capitalise on the child's interest and experience and to relate one subject to another was underlined. By the time of the First World War the forces making for curricula and pedagogic change had been reinforced by the influence of Dewey and the pragmatic school of educational thought from across the Atlantic. The followers of Dewey stressed the social purposes of education; bookish learning was rejected in favour of practical pursuits, vocational studies and co-operative activities within a democratic school community. The emphasis was placed on learning by doing, based on a problem or project approach to the accumulation of useful experience. Traditional teaching methods were frowned upon and experiments involving a much more positive role for the learner were encouraged. By the inter-war period the 'New Education' movement was, in eclectic fashion, affecting practice in the elementary schools. The influences described made their mark on the tone and the recommendations of the Hadow Reports 1926–33 and thus received a degree of official blessing.

(b)   The Core of the Elementary Tradition

This centred itself on the education of the seven- to ten-year-old children, who suffered most from the restricted curriculum and teaching methods of the elementary school. The monitorial system was not designed to cope with infants or to provide the individual tuition and training in practical skills which had been features of the earlier and smaller charity schools and schools of industry. Thus the monitorial school's stock in trade was mechanically to impart the rudiments of reading, writing and cyphering to children of over six who were unlikely to attend for more than two years. State involvement initially worked in favour of better provision, especially after 1846 when the aided schools began to benefit from specific grants and the pupil-teacher system. A decade later inspectors' reports were able to point to a small number of elementary schools with a comparatively liberal curricula, where the three Rs were supplemented by such subjects as grammar, history, geography, drawing, needlework and the inevitable religious instruction. However, the benefits of this were limited to the tiny minority who stayed until the age of twelve, and most elementary schools were much more restricted in their scope. In 1861 the Newcastle Report publicised the fact that even the three Rs were being inefficiently taught to those pupils whose schooling was typically short in duration. The need, it seemed, was to cut out the curricula frills and concentrate exclusively on the basics.

From the Revised Code of 1862 until the end of the century, the curriculum of the elementary school was largely determined by grant earning considerations. What subjects were taught, to which children and by what means was decided by close reference to the regulations of successive

Codes. Lowe's original design was to focus attention on instruction in the three Rs (together with needlework for girls) by tying two-thirds of the possible grant earnings to the results of annual examinations in these subjects. Pupils aged six to twelve years were to be assessed on the basis of Standards I-VI and the Code laid down a schedule of examinable work for each standard. The immediate result was to stimulate the drilling of the younger and less proficient pupils to a satisfactory mastery of the three Rs and to destroy interest in more ambitious designs. Infants were exempt from the system, whilst no grants were payable for pupils over twelve. It was only gradually that Lowe's system was relaxed and it was the younger children who gained least from the changes. The study of 'specific' subjects, first introduced in 1867, was reserved for the older pupils. In 1875 grants were offered for 'class' subjects undertaken by the whole school from Standard II upwards. Thereafter the younger children were taught grammar, geography, history and elementary science; however, any particular school was limited to two 'class' subjects and there was a strong tendency to apply the established drill methods to their teaching. As the 'payment by results' system was being phased out at the close of the century, HM Inspectorate identified the lower standards as the least satisfactory part of the elementary system.

The institution of the block grant for elementary schools (1900) opened the way to a more liberal approach. Furthermore the Board of Education was now happy to place the responsibility for the curriculum squarely on the teachers, convinced that the oversight of the Inspectorate and the prevailing consensus of professional opinion was sufficient insurance against any bizarre developments. Accordingly the Elementary Code of 1904 recast the aims of the elementary school to embrace the physical, mental and character development of its pupils and the associated *Handbook of Suggestions* (1905) officially disavowed any need for uniformity of practice in relation to curricula or teaching methods. Although the consensus curriculum was identified as English, arithmetic, history, geography, nature study, music, drawing, handwriting, handicrafts, needlework, housecraft, gardening and physical exercise, the breadth of outlook was such as to provide much opportunity for practical activity, aesthetic education and individual teacher initiative. Unfortunately the conservatism of teachers and the distraction of the scholarship examinations after 1907 militated against full and rapid advantage being taken of the Board's new policy. Significant improvements in the education of younger children had to wait upon the diffusion of new educational ideas and a change in organisational forms. The free-place examinations, the rise of central schools and the 1918 Act's requirements in respect of senior elementary pupils all encouraged the establishment of distinct junior departments. It was then a short step to the Hadow arrangement of a separate primary stage of education, in relation to which the particular needs of junior children aged seven to eleven years would at last receive real consideration.

(c) Infant Development

Prior to 1870 many small children were sent to the largely inefficient and squalid dame schools inherited from the eighteenth century. But at the same time a growing number were able to attend new infant schools pioneered by such progressive spirits as Robert Owen, Samuel Wilderspin, David Stow and the Reverend Charles Mayo. To some extent indebted to the continental ideas of Rousseau and Pestalozzi, they shared an appreciation of the importance of understanding the nature of the infant as a basis for providing appropriate care and attention. Their schools combined sound habit training with open-air play activity, simple nature study, singing and rhymes and the learning of letters by such means as 'picturing out'. Thus in the first half of the nineteenth century the developmental tradition, based on a prior concern for the needs and interests of the child at a particular stage in its natural development, took root in the field of infant education and from the outset contrasted very favourably with its austere elementary counterpart. As the aided elementary schools accepted more infants they tended to treat them separately and this policy was encouraged by the Inspectorate. Accordingly they were exempt from the operation of Lowe's examinations, which allowed the infant teachers much more freedom than their colleagues and left the door open for the markedly child-centred ideas of Froebel further to develop the existing infant tradition. The 1870 Act, in specifying the age of five years as the starting point for compulsory attendance purposes, made the infant schools and departments an integral part of the national system of elementary education. This was of great potential importance, for the rich infant tradition, though held at bay for nearly forty years by the 'payment by results' system, was ultimately and inevitably able to infect the rest of the elementary school in an upward direction. Strengthened by the accession of Montessori's ideas and the nursery school movement in the early twentieth century, the infant tradition clearly influenced the reports of the Hadow Committee. Here lay the main source of the principle that education should be seen in terms of activity and experience rather than of knowledge to be acquired and facts to be stored. In 1931 Hadow recommended that henceforth it should underpin the approach to curricula and teaching methods in the reorganised junior schools for the seven-to eleven-year-olds.

(d) Post-Primary Development

The tendency for the elementary system to produce post-primary outgrowths of a pseudo-secondary character was another development which helped to leaven the basic tradition. From the middle of the nineteenth century there were always some certificated elementary teachers who were interested in and capable of carrying their pupils well beyond a mere mastery of the three Rs. The beginnings of such development were cut short by the Revised Code (1862), but its later modification allowed for a rising amount of post-primary instruction. Grants were offered for a growing range of specific subjects, including algebra, geometry, English literature, French, German, botany, mechanics, physical geography and commercial studies, for pupils in Standard IV and above. In 1882 a new Standard VII was added for the twelve- to thirteen-year-olds. Out of these developments emerged the higher tops and higher-grade schools designed to provide more advanced schooling for those older pupils who were prepared to stay on. Most higher-grade schools catered for pupils of twelve and over, combining Standards VI and VII work with advanced science courses financed by the Science and Art Department. The majority of them registered as organised science schools and developed a marked vocational orientation based on the study of mathematics, practical geometry, physics, chemistry, machine construction and drawing. Pupils in the upper standards of ordinary elementary schools certainly benefited from the downward influence of the higher-grade movement: in the 1890s the Education Department introduced special grants for teaching the older pupils such practical subjects as manual instruction, cookery, laundrywork, household management, dairywork and gardening. The Inspectorate was also encouraged to take an increasingly critical view of the use of rote-learning methods in relation to the widening curricula of the upper standards.

The abolition of the School Boards and Morant's determination to enforce a rigid distinction between elementary and secondary education administered a temporary check to post-primary growth during the Edwardian period. But the development soon reasserted itself in the form of the new central and junior technical schools which had begun to emerge by the onset of the First World War. The central schools, although developed under the Elementary Code, were for pupils between eleven and fourteen or fifteen and provided an improved general education along practical lines, with an industrial or commercial bias that was never directly vocational. Their purpose was to prepare fairly able senior elementary pupils for immediate employment in workshops, warehouses and offices without the need for special intermediate training. The 1918 Act, which raised the minimum school-leaving age to fourteen and required the LEAs to provide both advanced and practical instruction for senior elementary pupils, encouraged the rise of the central schools. In 1926 their rationale and curriculum was recommended as the basis for the development of Hadow's 'new' secondary modern schools. The curricula of the junior trade, technical, commercial and art schools had a much stronger vocational flavour, although the continuance of the pupil's general education was not neglected. The junior technical school for thirteen- to sixteen-year-olds emphasised the manual skills and scientific principles related to a particular group of industries; accordingly much time was given to mathematics, science, drawing and practical instruction. Thus, under the regulations for technical institutions, there developed a post-primary dimension that was strongly vocational. The Hadow Report (1926) also accepted this as a worthwhile development and recommended its close association with the reconstituted secondary system of education.

2   The Secondary Grammar Tradition

Originally based on the Classics and later upon a liberal education rooted in the humanities, this tradition dominated the English conception of secondary education until well into the twentieth century. Indeed, until 1944 the terms 'secondary' and 'grammar' were officially regarded as synonymous. From the early nineteenth century the grammar tradition was questioned and refined, but also perpetuated, by a variety of influences that bore upon it. Its development was characterised by considerable curricula change and an associated growth of external examinations. These matters must now be considered in some detail.

(a)   Operative Influences

These may be analysed on the same four-fold basis previously applied to the elementary tradition.

(i)   *Social*

The grammar school has always drawn great strength from the fact that the education provided has been accepted as socially prestigious. In the nineteenth century a grammar education was largely restricted to those of considerable means and social standing; its links with the ancient universities, medicine, law and the Church reinforced its pretensions in the public eye. Appropriately, the curricula of the public and endowed grammar schools were calculated to differentiate their products clearly from others who might have managed to obtain some sort of elementary, technical or private education. Hence the grammar tradition centred on the provision of a liberal education of lengthy duration which emphasised learning for its own sake rather than a vulgar concern for vocational knowledge and skills. Because the Classics fitted so well into this class-conscious framework, they were able to muster much support for their retention; later on the concept of a liberal education found expression in the provision of a sound general education with a marked literary bias. The latter development, facilitated by the Secondary Regulations of 1904 and reinforced by the School Certificate examination (1917), was in accord with certain social forces at play in early twentieth century English society. As the State system of secondary education developed after 1902, the influence of graduate teachers and aspiring parents worked in favour of an academic curriculum with its social prestige and economic benefits. As a sound general education was the minimum requirement for entry into the professions and other white-collar occupations, the State secondary schools were under considerable pressure to ignore technical and vocational education of a practical character. Once the free-place system began to widen secondary opportunity, the Labour movement was insistent that able working class children should receive a proper grammar education rather than any vocationally oriented alternative.

The rise of the middle classes and the emancipation of women were two other important social factors wielding considerable influence upon the development of the secondary grammar tradition. In the early nineteenth century the middle class, with its largely utilitarian and modern frame of mind, criticised the Classical curriculum of the public and endowed grammar schools and gave support to the more progressive private academies and schools. The subsequent broadening of the grammar school curriculum was partly attributable to middle class pressure, although the claims of a thoroughly vocational approach were successfully resisted. Meanwhile, the growth of higher education for women and secondary schooling for girls reinforced the process of broadening the curriculum. Unfettered by tradition and prejudice, the girls' high schools, which grew markedly in number after 1868, were responsive to new ideas from the outset and readily accepted reforms in curricula and methods of teaching. They showed an early recognition of the need to allow older pupils a choice of curricula pattern and of the importance of aesthetic and practical subjects. The early growth of professional training for secondary teachers rested upon the interest and support of their headmistresses.

(ii) *Economic*

The changing nature and needs of the economy exerted an influence upon the development of secondary provision, but the impact on the grammar

tradition was limited rather than marked. In economic terms the quasi-vocational type of secondary schooling pioneered by the higher-grade schools
and other post-primary developments offered the most direct benefits, but
down to 1944 the grammar tradition successfully resisted serious incursions
of this sort. Of course, the economic factor helped slowly to undermine the
position of the Classics in favour of a more broadly based general education.
Indeed, the increasingly important tertiary occupations found such a general education a most suitable basis for the further training of their employees
and therefore supported the academically oriented School Certificate examinations of the inter-war period. In contrast to commerce and the
professions, manufacturing industry was largely content to rely on early
recruitment and on-the-job training, even for those destined to hold responsible positions; the result was that the grammar tradition was not put under
any great pressure to change its face from this source. The late nineteenth-
century tendency, emanating from the work of the Science and Art Department and the Technical Instruction Committees, for technical instruction to
infiltrate the grammar tradition was checked after 1900 and the two developments went their separate ways. But the economic factor embraced a concern for the claims of scientific education as well as technical instruction and
in this respect helped to bring about real change. Under the direct pressure
of the 'scientific movement', drawing strength from the growth of foreign
competition, the grammar curriculum granted a significant place to the
study of pure science subjects. This development was facilitated by the fact
that such studies of a non-vocational nature could be fairly easily incorporated into the basic conception of a liberal education. Similarly, the study
of modern languages, albeit with their prospective commercial utility, could
be absorbed without difficulty.

(iii)   *Institutional*

The largely static and unsatisfactory condition of the grammar school curriculum in the first half of the nineteenth century was partly the result of
founders' statutes determining both the studies undertaken and the methods
of instruction used. The advantage of endowments made the grammar
schools less susceptible to outside pressures than private establishments
wholly dependent on paying custom. However, from the 1860s various
institutional pressures combined to produce piecemeal and limited curricula
reform. The influence of the Clarendon (1864) and Taunton (1868) Reports
and the subsequent work of the Schools Commissioners appointed to reform
both governing bodies and trust deeds, slowly served to widen the curriculum and raise standards of staffing and attainment during the last quarter
of the century. But it was not until after 1902 that the grammar tradition
became subject to the strong influence of a single central institution. With

the launching of the State system of secondary education, the new Board of Education opted for the 'grammar' model and determined to regulate the curriculum to ensure the provision of a sound general education. Morant's decision to abandon the pupil-teacher system and use the new secondary schools as a preparation ground for teacher training certainly put a premium on the mounting of academic courses compatible with the basic grammar tradition. The Secondary Schools Regulations of 1904 were drawn up accordingly and throughout the inter-war period the Board was content to secure the situation by supporting the development of a School Certificate examination calculated to ensure the neglect of practical and vocational subjects in the grammar school curriculum. In spite of the Hadow reorganisation, the Board continued to issue separate and distinctive regulations for the State grammar schools; this also helped to insulate them from quasi-vocational and other non-academic influences.

But the main single institutional influence to affect the development of the grammar tradition was that of external examinations. From the middle of the nineteenth century public examinations developed rapidly as a means of countering patronage and influence, of raising standards of competence, of controlling entry to various occupations and of searching out the sort of talent upon which the nation's future was increasingly recognised to depend. A major aspect of this development was the growth of external examinations for secondary schools. The basic trend was towards such examinations exerting a quite decisive influence upon the nature of secondary grammar curricula and teaching styles; this culminated in the inter-war School Certificate arrangements which were generally supportive of traditional forms rather than progressive change.

(iv) *Pedagogic*

A critical influence which supported the maintenance of a grammar curriculum at once both academic and common to all pupils was the faculty psychology of the nineteenth century. This held the human mind to be composed of separate faculties, all of which could be trained to a high level of efficiency as the result of sustained and appropriate mental exercise. The ultimate product was the trained mind which could then turn itself successfully to any activity. The proponents of faculty psychology further believed that there were certain forms of study which were eminently suitable for the training of the various faculties. Initially they emphasised the prior position of the Classics (especially Latin) for developing the powers of memory and verbal accuracy; later on mathematics was enthusiastically approved for its potential in developing reasoning powers and the sciences were accepted for their capacity to develop the power of observation. Conversely, practical and vocational subjects were rejected as narrow and incapable of supporting the sort of mental training that was transferable to other areas. It was not until the turn of the century, when educational psychology began to assume a scientific basis and the transfer of training theory was upset, that faculty psychology began to suffer a decline in influence. By the inter-war period the ideas of Dewey were challenging the notion of a hierarchy of secondary subjects and pressing the claims of non-academic activities. But as late as 1938 the Spens Report, in so many ways progressively disposed, strongly supported Latin as the second language for any respectable grammar school and even bemoaned the serious decline in the study of Greek.

Reforming headmasters made a growing impact on the development of curricula and methods. Outstanding in this respect were Thring of Uppingham and Sanderson of Oundle whose combined headships spanned the years 1853 to 1922. Edward Thring pioneered the development of English and aesthetic subjects such as music and art as integral parts of the grammar tradition; his influence was also responsible for the acceptance of a wide range of extra-mural activities as an essential part of a healthy school life. His book *The Theory and Practice of Teaching* (1883) helped to stimulate the beginnings of interest in matters of technique and professional training among the reluctant schoolmasters. Sanderson was an opponent of sedentary classroom studies who stressed the importance of pupil interests and motivation. His school developed both science and workshop practice, whilst a more creative approach was applied to the teaching of English, history and geography. By the early twentieth century the University Departments of Education (UDEs) were emerging to add their weight in favour of greater enlightenment. To the prospect of professional training for secondary teachers they gave a new respectability. Whilst supporting the provision of a sound general education as the grammar school's basic role, they contributed to a considerable improvement of teaching methods in the various academic subject areas.

(b) Changes in Curricula and Method

In the mid-nineteenth century the Classics and associated elements of history and geography dominated the secular curriculum of the public and endowed grammar schools. In 1937 the majority of grammar school pupils entered for the School Certificate examinations offered English, French, mathematics, history, geography and at least one science subject; half of the entrants offered Latin or art which completed the basic curriculum designed to afford a sound general education. Thus a century of development simply broadened the essentially academic basis of the grammar tradition. Although the position of Classics was irreparably damaged by the virtual disappearance of Greek, the influence of official policy and university matriculation requirements ensured the widespread retention of Latin. Meanwhile, the study of English, both language and literature, secured a prime place in the curriculum; initially the emphasis was on formal grammar and philology, but gradually the literary and creative dimensions received more attention. History won early recognition as a subject worth adding to the original Classical core, but for many years its teaching suffered from too much rote-memory work at the intermediate stage. However, Dr Keatinge's source method and the professional influence of the Historical Association helped to improve the situation in the early twentieth century. Geography slowly established itself as a basic subject, although it was not until after 1900 that a major transformation of substance and method made it a worthwhile field of study. By the time of the First World War, English, history and geography had clearly emerged as the new 'humanities' core of the grammar curriculum. In complementary fashion, mathematics emerged as a vital subject and developed its several distinct branches; the abandonment of Euclid, which had supported a highly abstract and syllogistic approach to mathematical study, opened the way to beneficial changes of substance and method pioneered in the Edwardian period. It was not until the 1880s that the natural sciences began to make rapid headway in the grammar schools. At first their teaching suffered from a verbal approach encouraged by the written examinations of the day; the result was a sharp reaction in favour of H.E. Armstrong's 'heuristic method' which expected the pupil to assume the position of the scientific discoverer. Of course, whilst emphasising the practical nature of the sciences, this proved too ambitious and finally led to a more reasonable compromise in the inter-war years. The study of science was developed through its separate disciplines, with chemistry, physics and biology enjoying widespread support. Modern languages, especially French and to a much lesser extent German, became the third essential element in the developing curriculum. In this field the introduction of the direct method after the turn of the century was double-edged; it stimulated the first serious interest in the question of how best to teach foreign languages, but generally proved too demanding for all but the best teachers and ablest pupils. Yet here were the seeds of the modern audio-visual technique of language teaching. In the late nineteenth century drawing forced its way into the curriculum of some grammar schools: subsequently and predictably it was creative art rather than linear drawing that won a significant place in a general education. Other subjects to establish their presence in the broadened curriculum were religious knowledge and music. Of the various practical subjects, which later laid claim to inclusion, only domestic science for girls assumed any importance before the Second World War.

(c)   The Development of Secondary Examinations

The growing influence of external examinations on the grammar school curriculum, initiated in the late nineteenth century, finally crystallised itself in the shape of the School Certificate after the First World War. The process may be considered in terms of three successive developments:

(i)   *The Emergence of the University Examining Boards*

It was the Oxford and Cambridge Local and the University of London Matriculation examinations, dating from 1858, which first affected the secondary schools. Half a century later there were eight University Examining Boards, the most important addition being that of the Northern Universities' joint body in 1903. The attraction of qualifications and certificates enjoying wide public esteem, and the policy of the Charity Commissioners to make external examinations obligatory for the reformed grammar schools, ensured an expanding custom. Initially the university bodies set their examinations without reference to the schools, with a particular interest in establishing their own matriculation requirements. Later on they developed school leaving certificate examinations that took account of the school context and were associated with a system of inspection. Their reputation was such that the competition of such bodies as the College of Preceptors, founded and controlled by teachers, ultimately proved unavailing. Their influence both raised the standards of work and widened the curriculum of the schools concerned. But the fact that each university body worked independently without provision for any sort of equivalence combined with the growth of Civil Service and professional entrance examinations to produce a jungle of alternatives for the schools to face. This posed serious difficulties for the organisation of viable courses to suit different needs.

(ii)   *The Incursion of the Board of Education*

Once the State began to develop its own system of secondary schools, the University Examining Boards were forced to take account of the policy of the Board of Education which immediately exercised its right to control the curriculum in aided schools. The 1904 Secondary Schools Regulations required the grammar school to provide a general education based on a minimum four-year course of graded instruction commencing at about twelve years of age. The course was to provide for the study of English language and literature, history, geography, mathematics, science, at least one foreign language, physical exercises and either manual work or housewifery. The initial three humanities subjects were to receive a combined total of not less than 4½ hours per week. Mathematics and science were allocated a minimum of 7½ hours, of which at least 3 hours were to be devoted to the latter.

A single foreign language received 3½ hours, whilst two obtained 6 hours; where a second language was studied, the omission of Latin needed the Board's express approval. No pupil was to be presented for external examinations below the age of fifteen years and the whole framework was guaranteed by general inspections. Although the University Examining bodies had to work within the set context, the Board's rejection of the quasi-vocational curricula of the higher-grade schools in favour of a strongly academic orientation was most acceptable. But the problem of so many unco-ordinated examinations for secondary schools remained; this the Board referred to the Consultative Committee for a solution and a far-reaching report was submitted in 1911. The report's main recommendations underlined the pressing need for rationalisation and identified the existing University Examining Boards as the best available means for the establishment of a State-sponsored system of secondary examinations. This set the stage for prolonged negotiations between the Board of Education, the universities and certain other interested parties.

(iii)   *The Establishment of the School Certificate (1917)*

Once the majority of professional bodies accepted the principle of equivalence and the University Examining Boards agreed to co-ordinate their activities, the Board of Education was able to launch the School Certificate and Higher School Certificate examinations. The former was designed for pupils of sixteen years and was underpinned by the ideal of a sound general education. Accordingly the award of the certificate was tied to success in a minimum of five subjects, including at least one from each of three groups – the humanities, foreign languages and mathematics/science. A fourth group, including art, music, domestic science and other practical subjects, was recognised by the Board, but was accepted for certification purposes only slowly and reluctantly. In the 1930s it became possible to secure a School Certificate which included two Group IV subjects; but as many pupils found success in a foreign language beyond them, the group system itself came under growing criticism. Meanwhile, the situation was exacerbated by the fact that the examination was from the outset used for matriculation as well as school-leaving purposes. The strictly academic subjects, if passed at credit level (at least 50 per cent mark), counted for university entrance requirements. As matriculation was a well known level of attainment before 1917, many employers demanded it from secondary schoolleavers and head teachers were under considerable parental pressure to organise the curriculum so as to present this possibility to the pupils. Thus the School Certificate, the basic pattern of which conformed to the desires of the universities, came to exert a dominant and over-academic influence upon the curriculum of schools whose range of ability was now widening.

Thus in 1938 the Spens Report recommended the severance of the School Certificate from the question of matriculation and more freedom of subject choice for entrants. The Secondary School Examinations Council, set up in 1917 to oversee and co-ordinate the work of the eight examining bodies on behalf of the Board, instrumented these changes on the eve of the Second World War. At last the long preoccupation with a rigidly academic and general education was under serious challenge.

The Higher School Certificate was designed for pupils of eighteen and involved specialised work in Classics, modern studies or science and mathematics. During the inter-war period it contributed much to the steady growth of grammar school Sixth Forms and to their developing concern for high academic standards. But it also produced other less happy effects. The Arts–Science dichotomy within the English Sixth Form became firmly entrenched and the curriculum conflict between those aiming at university entrance and other Sixth Formers began to develop.

3   Progressive Change and Professional Autonomy

From the 1930s, and especially in the post-war years, the whole question of curriculum and examinations moved to the centre of the educational stage. The issues involved enjoyed more attention and concern than ever before and the result was a large number of new and quite major developments in the field concerned. Amidst the ensuing changes the increasingly accepted wisdom – until the 1970s – was that the teachers could and should be left to control such matters as the school curriculum, teaching methods, internal organisation and pupil discipline. This respect for their professional autonomy extended to secondary examinations in regard to which the teachers came to exert much greater and more direct influence.

(a)   Changing Context

Social, economic, institutional and pedagogic factors now came to exert a growing influence in favour of progressive change. Curriculum and examinations could not be unaffected by the introduction of secondary education for all, the raising of the school-leaving age to fifteen and then sixteen, the substantial increase in voluntary staying on and the impressive growth of Sixth Forms. The constraints of the selective system and the eleven-plus examination were of critical importance for many years; the rise of the comprehensive tide and the retreat of the eleven-plus were even more significant. Equality of educational opportunity was increasingly seen in terms of an open system of education providing a broad and varied curriculum which would encourage and enable the individual pupil fully to extend himself without the constriction of premature examinations or rigid curricula patterns. The ideal was to subordinate both curricula and examinations to the needs and interests of the pupil; such an outlook inevitably challenged the traditional academicism of the grammar schools and the dominant influence of the universities on secondary examinations. Educational theory widened its dimensions and increased its stature. The developmental approach to learning, essentially child-centred in its basis, drew much of its growing strength from educational psychology. Philosophy of education showed much more interest in the social aims of education and their curricula implications. Sociology of education and curriculum development gradually emerged as new and influential disciplines. The three-year Certificate course ultimately gave the training colleges the time to infect many of their students with progressive ideas related to curricula and method. At a higher level many official reports, notably those of Hadow, Spens, Norwood, Crowther, Beloe, Newsom and Plowden, gave considerable attention to curriculum and examination matters. The results were various and important. For younger pupils the old elementary tradition finally gave way to the rise of modern primary education. At the secondary level the School Certificate was displaced by the General Certificate of Education (GCE) and the Certificate of Secondary Education (CSE) was developed for less able pupils. Finally, the new found concern for curricula reappraisal found expression in the establishment of the Schools Council for the Curriculum and Examinations.

(b)   Rise of Modern Primary Education

The primary school for five- to eleven-year-old children, institutionally the product of the Hadow reorganisation process, inherited the mixed legacy of three different traditions. The elementary tradition emphasised a narrow and formal approach based on the three Rs, the preparatory tradition associated with the educational ladder stressed academic preparation for the subsequent secondary stage, whilst the developmental tradition of the infant schools rested upon a child-centred concern for the nature and needs of the child at particular stages of growth. The rise of modern primary education is, to a large extent, the story of the gradual advance of the latter tradition at the expense of its less wholesome counterparts. The Hadow Report on *The Primary School* (1931) struck a futuristic and progressive note when it insisted that junior schooling should be seen in terms of activity and experience rather than of knowledge to be acquired and facts to be stored. A recognition of the educational needs and interests of childhood and a prior concern for general all-round development were to underpin the curriculum. The report stressed the need for much more creative and expressive activity; simple craftwork, drawing, painting, poetry, music, dance and drama were identified as areas of outstanding potential in this respect. The efficacy of subject-centred teaching was brought into question and qualified support was given to the topic or project approach. But it was emphasised that the mastery of the three Rs remained indispensable and should be secured by regular and systematic practice. The importance of adequate space, equipment, library facilities, audio-visual aids, playing fields and outside visits to the prospective success of the 'new' junior school was also made plain. Six years later a revised *Handbook of Suggestions* (1937) included a new and separate section on the junior stage of education which was said to deserve and require 'its own life, identity and technique'. The nature of junior schooling should be conceived in terms of the nature of the pupils concerned rather than simply in terms of subjects and standards; its organisation should provide for a judicious mixture of class, group and individual instruction and activity. The disciplinary need was for teachers to provide order and guidance without any resort to harmful repression. The Board also reiterated the need for 'personal resourcefulness and enterprise' on the part of the individual teacher rather than a slavish commitment to any established pattern. But there were important qualifications to this generally progressive stance. Activity and experience in the junior school were expected to contribute to the development of knowlege and skills; indeed some knowledge and skills were deemed so crucial as to require 'regular drill or constant practice' – with number tables cited as an example. This sort of balance was calculated to promote a more child-centred approach without endangering the broad consensus on curricula forms and teaching styles.

After the 1944 Act the broadening and humanising process in primary education made slow but sure headway. For many years, however, it faced serious obstacles. Hadow reorganisation dragged on interminably and the last all-age schools did not disappear until the late 1960s. The influence of the eleven-plus examination and the logistical priority given to the later stages of education were both unfavourable. The widespread adoption of streaming in junior schools and the constraints of large classes housed in old buildings encouraged the continuance of traditional forms. But gradually a number of factors combined to quicken the pace and extent of change. The child-centred rationale was now generally accepted as the pedagogic orthodoxy by teacher training tutors, HM Inspectors and LEA advisers concerned with primary education. The new post-war generation of Certificated teachers were increasingly imbued with a child-centred outlook and by the 1960s some of them were securing headships. Of critical importance was the retreat of the eleven-plus examination; once under way this began to dissolve the still widespread attachment to streaming, subject-centredness and formal class teaching. Meanwhile the number of new or modernised primary school buildings with better facilities and more flexible accommodation increased; latterly some LEAs began to switch from traditional to open-plan styles in the design of new schools. The NUT and the newly established Schools Council (1964) gave their influential support to the progressive approach. Thus the tide of change was already growing strong when it received the official and enthusiastic blessing of the Plowden Report (1967).

The Plowden Report, with its child-centred title *Children and their Primary Schools*, gave its eager and full endorsement to progressive change. It attempted its own definition of a 'good' primary school – one concerned with values and attitudes rather than mere instruction, where pupils are treated as children rather than future adults and are allowed 'to be themselves', where stress is laid on learning by individual discovery, direct experience and creative activity, where traditional subject divisions are not allowed to fragment the growth of knowledge and where work and play are seen as complementary elements in the child's development. The Committee estimated that about one in three primary pupils were fortunate enough to be placed in schools which approximated to the Plowden 'model', with the implication that many primary schools needed to improve by changing their ways. Accordingly in its section on school curricula and internal organisation the report emphasised:

(i)   the need for an end to secondary selection to free the primary schools from the tyranny of the eleven-plus examination. This recommendation had already been anticipated by the Labour government's issue of Circular 10/65.

(ii) the need for a broad, child-centred approach to primary education at the junior as well as the infant level. The report backed unstreaming, vertical grouping, interactive group activity, individualised learning procedures, open-plan arrangements, the integrated day, project and topic work, discovery learning and creative activity.

(iii) the need to cultivate a friendly atmosphere in the primary school, with sound discipline being founded on the satisfactions of learning experiences rather than upon 'outdated sanctions and incentives'. In particular, the Report condemned outright the use of corporal punishment in primary schools and recommended its abandonment.

Thus the Plowden position on primary school curricula, organisation and teaching methods clearly lacked the balance and caution of Hadow (1931) or the pre-war *Handbook* (1937). The social and preparatory roles of the primary school were discounted by the concern to treat all primary pupils as children and to let them 'be themselves'. The time-consuming and schematic limitations of discovery learning were largely ignored. The rejection of traditional subject divisions opened the way to a 'magpie' curriculum. And to expect ordinary teachers to secure routine order and discipline largely through the satisfactions of learning experiences was simply naive. Moreover, the massive expansion of the training system and the teaching force after 1960 spelt danger for the Plowden approach; less able students, inexperienced teachers and college tutors lacking satisfactory primary experience were unlikely to make it work effectively.

However, the report was generally well-received and for some time its influence gave considerably greater strength to the progressive tide. One outcome was the formation of an unofficial 'Plowden Club' dedicated to the task of promoting and defending the Plowden position. But the Report also focused much attention on the primary schools and made them vulnerable to increasing scrutiny. In 1969 the first of the polemical Black Papers identified progressive primary and comprehensive secondary schooling as the twin cancers of the time. Three years later a National Foundation for Educational Research report suggested that reading standards were on the decline and the subsequent Bullock Report (1975) on the teaching of language in schools reinforced the anxieties regarding such basic skills. Significantly, in 1974 the government set up the Assessment of Performance Unit (APU) to develop methods for the long-term monitoring, on a national scale, of standards of pupil performance in school. Clearly the swing of the progressive primary pendulum had reached its limit and a reaction was beginning to set in. This augured ill for for the professional freedom of teachers.

(c) Secondary Curricula and the GCE Examinations

The principle that secondary examinations should grow out of the curriculum, which the Board of Education had subscribed to as early as 1918, remained an unrealised ideal throughout the inter-war years. The group-based School Certificate came to determine the grammar school curriculum in a very rigid way; the outcome was a strongly academic stereotype, favoured by the University Examining Boards with their matriculation interests, but far too demanding and unsuitable for the majority of pupils. It was the gradual recognition of the serious defects and distorting influence of the School Certificate which paved the way for the introduction of the much more flexible, subject-based GCE. But the new examinations did not prove ideal and wielded an adverse influence upon the curriculum in other directions. For the abler pupil the former rigidity of secondary courses gave way to a developing and disturbing imbalance. This broad course of change may be illuminated by reference to a number of developments.

(i) *Spens Report on Secondary Education (1938)*

This accepted the Hadow principle that the purpose of secondary education is to provide for the needs of pupils entering and passing through the stage of adolescence. The idea that the grammar school curriculum should be designed to give a foundation course for Sixth Form work and perhaps university entry was firmly rejected. The relegation or neglect of creative, practical and vocational subjects was severely criticised. The recommended curriculum strategy was that of a wide-ranging common core of subjects for the eleven- to thirteen-year-old pupils, followed by differentiation through options according to pupil interests and strengths. Inevitably the report underlined the need to alter the shape of the School Certificate and to detach it from the question of matriculation requirements. This set the stage for a more intensive investigation of the whole area by the Secondary School Examinations Council.

(ii) *Norwood Report on Curriculum and Examinations in Secondary Schools (1943)*

This gave clear and almost unqualified expression to the principle that examinations should follow the curriculum and not determine it. On the curriculum it echoed the views of Spens: although strongly in favour of tripartite arrangements, the Norwood Report insisted upon the need for each type of secondary school to provide a variety of courses within it. But its recommendations for the future of secondary examinations were much more radical than Spens. Firstly, it was suggested that there should be a planned move to a system of internal examinations for sixteen-year-old secondary pupils. Such examinations would be conducted by the teachers themselves on the basis of syllabuses and papers designed by them; the main guarantee of standards would be the oversight of an enlarged Inspectorate. Secondly, it was recommended that for an interim period the School Certificate should continue in a much modified form. The University Examining Boards were to operate through sub-committees containing a strong contingent of teachers and pupils were to be allowed to offer any number and combination of subjects. Finally, the existing Higher School Certificate was to be abolished in favour of a new dual arrangement. An eighteen-plus qualifying external examination would be provided for the majority of Sixth Formers; a separate selective examination would be mounted for scholarship purposes. Both would be based on a narrow range of chosen subjects studied in depth. Thus in the Norwood Report lay the seeds of a more flexible and teacher-controlled examination system, but also of a secondary curriculum weakened by lack of balance and too much specialisation.

(iii) *Adoption of the General Certificate of Education*

In the event, however, the Norwood policy was seriously compromised because neither the Ministry nor the teachers were prepared to support an internal system of examinations for the grammar schools. The need to maintain standards and the external currency of any certificate offered finally won the day; in this respect their inhibitions simply reflected the attitudes of employers, parents and pupils. In 1947 the die was cast. A new General Certificate of Education based on external examinations was to replace the old School Certificate. Although the University Examining Boards were to administer the examinations at Ordinary, Advanced and Scholarship levels, they were to be bound by much more flexible arrangements designed to benefit the pupil and free the curriculum. The GCE was to be a subject examination with no conditions laid down in respect of the number or nature of the subjects to be taken. But the removal of the restrictions formerly associated with the group-system was to some extent offset by the raising of the qualifying standard from 33 per cent to 45 per cent. The new examinations were first held in 1951; whilst they bestowed considerable benefits and enjoyed a rapidly growing custom, they were soon beset by their own problems and shortcomings in relation to the curriculum.

Before long the GCE had developed something of the character of the School Certificate. The universities adjusted their matriculation requirements to five Ordinary levels, including English language and mathematics or an approved science and a foreign language, and two Advanced levels. For the ablest pupils this became the minimum target and inevitably affected the approach to the curriculum. The less academic grammar pupils were once again the main sufferers. With the rise of the comprehensive school there was also the temptation to resort to a restrictive system of third- or fourth-year subject options in the interests of examination success. Indeed growing competition for university places encouraged many grammar schools to follow this path; able pupils were rushed through Ordinary level on a restricted front to allow three years' intensive study in the Sixth Form. Thus the ideal of a sound general education gave way to the competitive advantages of an imbalanced curriculum. And as the Advanced level qualifying examination became an instrument of eighteen-plus selection the needs of the non-university Sixth Former were largely neglected. Although the Crowther Report *15 to 18* (1959) drew attention to the deteriorating situation it was unprepared to make any radical attack upon Sixth Form specialisation as such. To suggest the introduction of General Studies and the better use of minority time was a palliative rather than a solution and so the problem of the Sixth Form curriculum was left for the Schools Council to grapple with later on.

(d) Secondary Curricula and the CSE Examinations

For many years the central authority and the teachers concerned concurred in the view that the secondary modern schools should remain free of external examinations so as to ensure the unrestricted development of their curriculum. The Hadow Report (1926) recommended that this curriculum should afford a general education, characterised during the final two years by a practical and realistic bias. However, the secondary modern school was not to concern itself with any directly vocational work. Thus from the outset it lacked the academic prestige of the grammar school or the utilitarian appeal of the technical school. Unable to find a distinctive and meaningful curriculum for itself, the modern school began to content itself with a diluted and truncated version of grammar school courses. In search of a clear goal and determined to earn some measure of public esteem, a growing number of modern schools began to enter their pupils for external examinations and by the 1950s this tide was running strong. In 1955 the Ministry abandoned its policy of discouraging GCE entries from the secondary modern schools. But as only a few modern pupils were able to reach the standard required, others were entered for external examinations run by such bodies as the College of Preceptors, the Royal Society of Arts and the Union of Lancashire and Cheshire Institutes. Alarmed by the growing influence of examining bodies over which it had no control, the Ministry was forced to consider the prospect of an officially sponsored system of external examinations. The Crowther Report (1959) supported such an idea and meanwhile the Secondary School Examinations Council considered the possibility. The resultant Beloe Report on *Secondary School Examinations other than GCE* (1960) provided the basis for the development of the Certificate of Secondary Education. Designed for pupils of average ability completing a five-year course in secondary modern and comprehensive schools, the CSE system of examinations was characterised by a number of radical features.

(i) From the outset the new system was teacher-controlled. Although the governing bodies of the fourteen Regional Examining Boards included representatives of LEAs, Area Training Organisations, further education and employers, the actual conduct of the examinations was delegated to committees of serving teachers.

(ii) The Regional Examining Boards adopted a flexible approach by offering the schools and their teachers three major options. Under Mode 1 pupils could simply be entered for external examinations based on syllabuses set and published by the Boards. Under Mode 2 the Boards set examinations on syllabuses devised by the schools, either individually or on a group basis. Under Mode 3 the syllabuses were determined and the examinations set and marked internally by the schools, subject only to the external moderation of the Board.

(iii) To allow and encourage pupils of less than average ability to take isolated papers, the CSE examinations were run on a subject rather than a
group basis. The growing range of practical and vocational subjects
offered and the development of course assessment, project work, objective and oral testing as part of the examining procedures ensured that
the CSE did not become a pale replica of the GCE. Even the traditional
pass/fail concept was abandoned; a five-point scale (Grades 1–5) was
used to categorise results, with those falling below the minimal standard being ungraded. For comparability purposes the CSE Grade I was
soon equated with a GCE pass at Ordinary level.

Responsibility for admission requirements and for the maintenance and co-
ordination of standards was vested in the Secondary School Examinations
Council. The comparability of results between the different Regional
Boards was safeguarded by statistical means and by inter-regional liaison.
Launched in 1965, the CSE examinations were well received and the raising
of the school-leaving age in 1972–3 drew mounting support. As a radical
departure designed to provide less able pupils with a worthwhile examination goal and teachers with more professional autonomy the CSE deserved
and obtained an enthusiastic response from the schools. During the period
1965–77 the annual number of candidates grew from 65,000 to 625,000 and
the proportion of Mode 3 entries rose from 8 per cent to 25 per cent.
However, the growth of public interest and confidence in a system which
implies that teachers can be left to assess the quality of their own examination work was tardy rather than really encouraging.

(e) The Schools Council for the Curriculum and Examinations

Until the 1950s a large measure of consensus existed upon what should be
taught in schools, allowing the central authority to accord considerable curricula freedom to the profession. But as the consensus began to give way
before progressive developments in the primary sector and innovation in
non-selective secondary schools a Curriculum Study Group (1962) was set
up within the Ministry of Education to keep matters under review. Seen as a
threat to their professional autonomy, this unilateral initiative aroused
strong opposition from the teachers. The outcome of this conflict was a
general agreement to establish the Schools Council for the Curriculum and
Examinations; from 1964 this new body took over the functions of the
Secondary School Examinations Council and the Curriculum Study Group.
The nature and role of the Council may be considered in terms of its constitution and actual work in the related fields of curricula and examinations.

(i) *Constitution*

The Schools Council was an independent body equally financed by the DES and LEAs. To secure full professional acceptance and support the constitution required its main working committees to include a majority of teachers nominated by their associations. Whilst a Programme Committee determined priorities, three Steering Committees addressed themselves to the school curriculum and its development in respect of different but overlapping age ranges. Two Examinations Committees were concerned with sixteen-plus and eighteen-plus examinations respectively. And some fifteen Subject Committees worked on both curriculum and examination matters related to their particular fields.

(ii) *Curriculum Development*

The Schools Council's main interest was in the review and reform of the curriculum but in accordance with the principle that each school should retain both freedom and responsibility for its own work. Thus the danger of a central body with a vested interest in change was offset by it having to proceed by persuasion. The Council's work gradually straddled the whole field of curriculum development with a spate of enquiries and sponsored projects. The latter were most numerous in relation to the teaching of English, the humanities, science and mathematics; many emerged from the Council's programme of response to the raising of the school-leaving age. An official Curriculum Development Project (e.g. Nuffield Secondary Science or History 13–16 Project) consumed much time and effort. New strategies and materials for a particular area of the curriculum were produced, tested in pilot schools, readjusted according to experience, duly launched and finally evaluated and modified again in the light of feedback from ordinary users. LEAs were encouraged to establish teachers' centres to help diffuse the Council's work and to promote local initiatives in the field of curriculum development.

(iii) *Examinations*

Apart from presiding over the introduction of the CSE examinations and securing their regional comparability and national currency during the early years of development, the Schools Council concerned itself with the other needs and possibilities associated with secondary examinations.

A high priority was given to the reform of Sixth Form curricula and examinations. Convinced of the need to broaden the curriculum and make it more suitable to the widening range of Sixth Form abilities and aspirations the Council forged close links with the Standing Conference on University Entrance to tackle the problem. But vested interests inside and outside the schools ensured that the various reform proposals floated by the Council from 1969 failed to win acceptance. With the entrenched GCE Advanced level arrangements stifling overall change, the Council then pursued the more limited idea of a separate seventeen-plus Certificate of Extended Education (CEE) mounted by the CSE Boards and aimed at less academic Sixth Formers.

A common examining system at sixteen-plus gradually emerged as the Council's other main concern. The co-existence of the GCE Ordinary level and CSE examinations had its drawbacks: pupils were forced to make an early choice of course, separate teaching groups were often required and much time was lost through the long examination season. In 1970 the Council accepted in principle that there should be a single system but it took another six years to produce definitive proposals. The welter of opposition they aroused was such as to make their future both protracted and uncertain.

By the mid-1970s the Schools Council faced growing disrepute. The response of serving teachers to its countless and expensive projects had proved meagre; over a dozen years its piecemeal approach left the question of the whole five to sixteen curriculum still untackled. All its efforts in the field of examination reform had borne virtually no fruit. The majority representation of teachers had inhibited the rightful influence of other parties in a field where ultimate legal responsibility lay with the DES and LEAs. In 1976 the DES openly expressed its dissatisfaction with the Council and declared the quality of its work to be 'generally mediocre'. Suddenly, with all its adverse implications for professional autonomy, the future of the teacher-dominated Schools Council became insecure.

4   The Reassertion of Central Influence

Unhappily the professional autonomy extended to teachers in the post-war years had become associated with a disruptive drift from consensus to conflict in the field of school curricula and related matters. By the mid-1970s the dispute between the progressive and traditional camps had become both polarised and politicised. In 1975 ultra-progressive influence at William Tyndale Junior School, Islington, produced a national scandal and a public inquiry which raised the whole question of responsibility for control of curricula content and method. A year later Bennett's research into the relative effectiveness of formal and informal junior schooling found in favour of the traditional approach. The anti-progressive lobby eagerly capitalised on these events, reinforcing the myth of a Plowdenite primary take-over and a resultant fall in standards. By this time the whole school system was subject to growing public criticism, a situation which the DES felt called upon to deal with both swiftly and positively. Indeed, October 1976 saw the beginnings of a major change of course. In a blaze of secrecy the DES issued its 'Yellow Book' as a prelude to the Prime Minister's seminal speech on education at Ruskin College: the main thrust of both was the need for a return to consensus and control as a means of restoring public confidence. A national debate called for by Mr Callaghan was mounted in 1977 within the context of a consultative Green Paper on *Education in Schools* which directed attention to four leading questions: the school curriculum for five to sixteen-year-olds, the assessment of standards, the training of teachers, and the inter-relating of school and working life. Subsequently, in the new climate engendered by public concern, the central government became increasingly disposed to assert its prior influence in a number of important directions.

(a)   School Curriculum 5–16

At Ruskin College the Prime Minister pressed the idea that the years of compulsory schooling should centre upon a 'core curriculum of basic knowledge'. Thereafter the DES addressed itself to the formulation of an agreed framework for the five to sixteen curriculum. Initially it favoured a firm blueprint to lay down the subjects or areas to be taught, the ground to be covered and even the time to be devoted to the various elements. However, Inspectorial advice and wider consultations diluted this original intent and the ultimate outcome was a much more amorphous recipe for change. In *The School Curriculum* (1981) the DES asserted its new-found responsibility and right to exercise much more influence; in particular it was to see that all schools provided an adequate grounding in literacy, numeracy and other essential skills for a technological society. The need for LEAs, with whom legal responsibility for the curriculum still rested, to have clear and effective policies in the field was emphasised. Whilst recognising that the details must be left to the schools, they were henceforth to set down their curricula aims in writing and recurrently assess how far they were being met. And HM Inspectorate was to keep a close eye on the developing scene.

Whilst all this confirmed the fact that the school curriculum was no longer to be left to the overriding influence of teachers, the document's detailed recommendations were much less definitive than had been feared. Innocuously it stated that the five to sixteen curriculum should offer pupils a broad and balanced programme of work and should place emphasis upon personal development as well as academic achievement. The primary school's crucial responsibility to teach reading, writing and calculating was underlined, but this was to be met within the context of a broad curriculum which should include history, geography, religious education, elementary science, practical and aesthetic activity. But topic work, art and craft, science and junior French were identified as areas of concern and the primary schools were constrained to improve matters in various ways. At the secondary level the main concern was to ensure that all pupils of eleven to sixteen shared a balanced and broadly common curriculum rather than fall victim to a proliferated and incoherent system of third-year options. Although the level, content and emphasis of work needed to be related to ability and aspirations, all pupils should undertake English, mathematics, science, religious education, physical education, some study of the humanities, and some practical and some aesthetic activity. Most pupils should study a foreign language, many of them for the whole five years. In terms of schools preparing pupils more adequately for working life particular importance was attached to craft, design and technology courses and to the systematic provision of careers advice.

Thus in broad terms *The School Curriculum* (1981) bears much resemblance to the 1937 *Handbook of Suggestions* in that it provides common guidelines without specifying curricula content too closely. Of course, given the shortage of well-qualified teachers in certain subjects, to have been more prescriptive would have involved financial implications. Indeed, the document did not lay down the principle of curriculum-led staffing which is essential to a full and balanced secondary curriculum at a time of falling rolls. Rather weakly, in a follow-up Circular, the DES simply exhorted the LEAs and governing bodies to ensure that schools do as much as they can to comply 'within the resources available'.

Within the five to sixteen curriculum the performance of pupils in mathematics had attracted particularly sharp criticism. In response the DES commissioned a special inquiry which finally produced the Cockcroft Report on *Mathematics Counts* (1982). Many changes were recommended in mathematics teaching and examining. But the 'back to the basics' recipe was rejected in favour of a broader approach encompassing computational skills and a wider mathematical understanding. The vital need is for pupils to cover less and understand more; accordingly the schools should provide a common core of 'foundation' topics and skills but with appropriate differentiation according to pupils' level of attainment and rate of learning. Mental arithmetic should be restored to a position of importance. Mathematics co-ordinators and heads of departments should take more overall responsibility for the subject. And, critically, the widespread lack of proper qualifications and expertise amongst those undertaking mathematics teaching must be remedied by recruitment and in-service training. The DES welcomed the report and quickly presented each primary school with a special booklet summarising their role in meeting the Cockcroft recommendations.

Meanwhile in certain quarters it was felt that *The School Curriculum* (1981) did too little to induce a more functional approach to secondary school learning and thereby meet the needs of older pupils who were bored by the traditional 'liberal' fare. In late 1982, like a bolt from the blue, a new Technical and Vocational Education Initiative (TVEI) was launched by the MSC. Aimed at the fourteen to eighteen age-group it involved a five-year pilot scheme designed to prepare some ten thousand students for 'particular aspects of employment and for adult life in a society liable to rapid change'. General education would be combined with strong technical and vocational elements unashamedly related to potential employment opportunities. The courses would lead to qualifications outside the normal ambit of secondary schools. Over half the LEAs applied for inclusion in this separately funded scheme and fourteen were selected. Faced with this *fait accompli* the DES assured its partners that the scheme would develop within the existing system of secondary schooling and would simply provide a wider range and better balance of courses. But the inherent conflict between *The School Curriculum* (1981) and the new initiative and the prospect of the scheme leading to a return of secondary selection were ignored. Meanwhile, the indecent haste with which the LEAs involved were required to prepare for a 1983-4 start augured ill for the success of the whole scheme.

(b) Standards of School Work

Since 1976 the DES has been very concerned to develop ways and means of improving standards of pupil performance. The APU has begun to provide annual information upon general levels of performance of eleven to fifteen-year-olds in mathematics, English, science and foreign languages; but its work provides a long-term yardstick for monitoring national standards rather than an instrument for early improvements. In the latter regard much reliance has been placed upon strengthening and sharpening the role of HM Inspectorate. Thoroughgoing national surveys of primary schooling (1978) and secondary education (1979) were produced; whilst they did not substantiate the claims of the 'back to basics' brigade, areas of weakness were winkled out in a tough-minded but fair manner. In 1983 the new 'watchdog' image of the Inspectorate was further reinforced by the decision that henceforth its reports on individual schools should be made public. The DES also encouraged a more critical view of open-plan and mixed ability teaching; where such arrangements were thrust upon teachers it felt that a lowering of standards could result. Finally, the question of school standards attracted its own White Paper on *Teaching Quality* (1983). Its main pronouncements on initial training, induction and in-service needs are covered in the next chapter. But the White Paper also emphasised the responsibility of each LEA to provide local inspection and advice to schools, to ensure a better match between staff qualifications and teaching tasks and to secure the dismissal of incompetent teachers.

(c)   Secondary School Examinations

Inevitably the central authority's new interventionist role made its sharpest impact in the field of external school examinations for sixteen to eighteen-year-olds where the DES became directly involved in the details of decision-making in three important areas.

(i)   *Common Sixteen-Plus Examining System*

One bulwark of educational standards which enjoyed widespread public confidence was the GCE 'O' level examinations. Yet the logic of compre-hensive reorganisation demanded that they should be subsumed alongside the CSE in a common sixteen-plus examining system and in 1975-6 the Schools Council produced firm proposals for such a change. Whilst agreeing in principle the Labour government cautiously mounted a special inquiry into the matter; the resultant Waddell Report (1978) concluded it was 'edu-cationally feasible' and plans for the new examination were then quickly endorsed. At this stage a 'common system' was seen in terms of a single com-prehensive examination rather than two examinations with a common grad-ing system designed to protect existing 'O' level standards. Thus, although the new Conservative government accepted a single sixteen-plus examina-tion as 'desirable' (1980) its introduction was to be strictly conditional upon the formulation of acceptable 'national criteria' for subject syllabuses and assessment procedures. Significantly a Joint Council of the GCE and CSE Boards (rather than the Schools Council) undertook this exercise, the results of which were subject to the final and detailed approval of the Secretary of State. In 1984, at long last, Sir Keith Joseph decided in favour of merging GCE 'O' level and CSE into a single sixteen-plus examining system with a single scale of seven (A to G) pass grades. For all successful candidates the new examinations will lead to the award of a new General Certificate of Secondary Education (GCSE). To operate the new system the existing GCE and CSE examination boards will combine into five groups – four for England and one for Wales. In a determined effort to safeguard the main-tenance of GCE 'O' level standards and to introduce more rigour generally, the new arrangements include a number of special requirements or features. Subject syllabuses are to be drastically curtailed in number and are to be developed in accordance with the agreed national criteria; grade-related cri-teria for each subject are to be incorporated into the system as it develops. To cope with the wide GCSE ability spectrum each subject is to provide for dif-ferentiated papers or questions as appropriate. But within each examining group the existing GCE boards are to assume responsibility for securing standards in respect of grades A-C by ensuring that they are more demand-ing than the present 'O' level equivalents. Finally, 'distinction' certificates are to be awarded to candidates obtaining good grades in a 'broad range of subjects'; conversely, candidates whose performance falls below the G grade level will simply 'fail'. The new courses are due to begin in 1986 – with the first GCSE awards being made two years later.

Certainly the new system should produce more clarity, cohesion and consistency in the sixteen-plus examinations field than has previously been the case. It will also give more weight to the testing of understanding and practical ability as distinct from the recall and organisation of facts. And the provision for a significant element of school-based assessment will give an important role to many teachers in the working of the new system. But clearly the GCSE is not going to provide for the 'new start' envisaged in the early 1970s; subject-specificity and differentiated forms of examining are to be major features of the combined offering. In a real sense 'O' levels will live on in the shape of the crucial A-C grades of the GCSE. The new examination is likely to dominate the secondary curriculum to an even greater extent than its forbears. It is aimed at the whole ability range rather than the top 60 per cent target group officially served by the displaced GCE/CSE examinations. It is to be underpinned both by national criteria for subject syllabuses and assessment procedures and by the development of grade-related criteria as well. The proffered 'distinction' certificate smacks of a return to the old group-based 'matriculation' arrangements of pre-war days – at least for the abler pupils – and inevitably will wield a strong curricula influence. Progressive critics reject such a formalised system of sixteen-plus assessment which no other European country seems to need; in Norwood fashion they believe that assessment responsibility at that stage should be devolved to the LEAs and the schools in the interests of curricula flexibility and change.

(ii) *Seventeen-Plus Examinations*

In 1976, to meet the needs of the changing Sixth Form, the Schools Council proposed a new Certificate of Extended Education (CEE). Designed for less able seventeen-year-old pupils for whom 'A' level studies were inappropriate, the new examination was to be mounted by the existing CSE Boards. Pilot schemes were undertaken and in 1979 the independent Keohane Committee Report recommended that the CEE should receive official approval and national status. Simultaneously, the Mansell Report, with its focus on the same age group in further education, proposed a new range of pre-employment courses involving a basic core of general education combined with vocational studies. The Conservative government felt that for the students concerned the Mansell approach afforded a better bridge between education and working life than did the watered-down academic courses of the CEE. Accordingly the Keohane proposals were rejected and in 1982 plans were announced for a new Certificate of Pre-Vocational Education (CPVE) for use in both schools and further education. The associated courses were to prepare for entry at seventeen-plus into a wide range of jobs or into more specifically vocational further education courses. Responsibility for the CPVE was vested in a new consortium of examining bodies and interim courses commenced in 1983–4. But simultaneously the government announced a New Training Initiative which provided, in particular, for a Youth Training Scheme (YTS) to give a full year's foundation training to early school leavers without jobs. This scheme involves a weekly payment and may lead on to derived employment; such attractions are likely to deter less able students from continuing in full-time education and could well undermine the future of the new CPVE. Obviously much will depend upon the success or otherwise of the YTS.

(iii) *Academic Sixth Form Examinations*

In principle the need to broaden the curriculum for able Sixth Formers which was recognised in the Crowther Report (1959) continues to attract support. But in practice the dependence of many university first degree courses upon prior specialised studies has prevented any significant change. Whilst General Studies has steadily increased its importance and exerted some unifying influence, Sixth Form work has continued to be dominated by 'A' level combinations in either the Arts or Sciences. After so many years of almost fruitless effort by the Schools Council and other bodies, now the DES has developed its own reform plan (1984) for new advanced supplementary (AS) courses and examinations to be taken alongside existing 'A' levels. Such two-year courses would provide contrasting or complimentary options to broaden the academic Sixth Form curriculum; they would involve about half the normal 'A' level syllabus content whilst demanding similar standards of achievement. If agreed upon, the teaching of AS courses would commence in 1986. But this new central initiative seems to have only a limited chance of success. Firstly, the schools will be expected to mount AS courses without the help of extra resources. Secondly, higher education admission arrangements will have to be markedly changed to give credence to such supplementary courses.

(d) End of the Schools Council (1984)

For the Schools Council the period which followed the Yellow Book's strictures proved terminal. In 1978 the Council was reformed from within to strengthen non-teacher representation and to streamline its working practices; but this only sharpened the internal conflicts without increasing the body's effectiveness. Accordingly the special Trenaman inquiry was mounted; whilst the resultant report (1981) backed the continuance of the semi-independent Council and the retention of its existing functions, the devisiveness of particular interest groups was deplored and some remedies suggested. But, increasingly disinclined to involve the Council in its reform of curriculum and examinations, the Conservative government determined to be rid of it. In 1982 Sir Keith Joseph served notice of his intention to abolish the Schools Council and to replace it with two smaller bodies. A year later a Secondary Examinations Council nominated by the Secretary of State was established to 'co-ordinate and supervise the conduct of examinations'. This was followed by the setting up of a clearly less important School Curriculum Development Committee. Her report ignored, Mrs Trenaman saw the separation of examinations from the curriculum as misguided and the nominated examinations body as a crucial step towards a centralised system of education.

Within a decade the context in which school curricula and examinations were dealt with had radically changed. The teachers who had presumptuously come to regard the 'secret garden' of the curriculum as their own special preserve were put firmly in their place. In the new context the ideal of professional autonomy had to give way to the demand for teacher accountability. The demise of the Schools Council symbolised the serious loss of ground suffered by the teacher associations. Meanwhile the LEAs were cajoled into assuming a more positive role; yet, whilst they retained their legal responsibility for the school curriculum, the exercise of it was now hedged by central directives and guidelines. Cast in its new role of supreme 'watchdog' HM Inspectorate had to steer a difficult course between securing the central authority's quality-control policies and seeing that the resources to sustain them were adequate. And, most critically, at the cost of considerable damage to the tradition of educational partnership, the DES had taken over the centre of the curricula and examinations stage. So far, the outcomes have not exactly inspired confidence in the capacity of government Ministers and senior Civil Servants to do a better job in the field concerned than the professionals they have pushed aside.

9 The Training, Supply and Status of Teachers

It is surely a truism that any system of schooling is only as good as the number and quality of the teachers it employs. In the long run the interests of education and the interests of the teachers are one and the same; the recruitment of well-qualified entrants on a sufficient scale, their satisfactory further education and training, and the provision of salaries and conditions of service calculated to sustain real professional status are all critical to the educational welfare of children as well as to the well-being of teachers. But the practical realisation of this axiomatic principle has involved a long and continuing struggle in relation to which a successful end is not yet in clear sight.

1 The History of Teacher Training Before 1944

It must be recognised that the nineteenth century was an age in which elementary education was not only in short supply, but also the majority of teachers providing it were neither trained nor certificated. Indeed many of the dame, common day and charity schools of the early nineteenth century were staffed by female child-minders and men who had failed at other trades or who treated teaching as a second source of income; most such persons had little or no education themselves and, at best, it was often a matter of the one-eyed leading the blind. It was only very slowly that the concept of a wholly trained and certificated corps of elementary schoolteachers emerged and gained acceptance. In this process a number of phases may be distinguished.

(a) 1805–39 The Monitorial Phase

During this period the National and British Societies established a growing number of 'normal' centres to provide senior pupils and other people with a thorough working knowledge of the monitorial technique before going out to take charge of their own schools. Alas, such training was of very short duration and made little or no attempt to raise the usually low level of personal education of the individuals concerned. However, the monitorial phase was not without considerable influence on later development. The Anglican normal centres in particular provided a diocesan network from which most nineteenth-century teacher training colleges were to emerge. And the subsequent pupil-teacher apprenticeship arrangements, which stressed practical training rather than personal education, owed much to monitorial roots. One long-term result of this was to equate teaching with a craft and restrict its status in the public eye.

(b)   1839–90 The Age of the Pupil-Teacher System

Because of its failure to serve as an effective vehicle for moral and social training, the monitorial system gradually suffered a decline in its popularity. In the 1830s David Stow developed the simultaneous system of class teaching in which an appropriately trained adult teacher directed the learning and moral development of a very large class of children. From his Glasgow Normal Seminary (established 1837) Stow's ideas spread south of the border and were particularly welcomed by Kay-Shuttleworth and the National Society. Encouraged by the new Committee of Council for Education, the National Society began to transform its existing monitorial normal centres and to found new colleges; between 1839 and 1845 over twenty such Anglican establishments emerged for the training of adults along the new lines. The great difficulty was that of obtaining satisfactory entrants of eighteen or over; the attempted solution to this problem was the introduction of the pupil-teacher system by Kay-Shuttleworth in 1846. Initiated by Minutes of the Committee of Council to provide competent teachers for grant-aided elementary schools, the pupil-teacher system incorporated two progressive features:

(i)   the official selection and apprenticeship training of young persons who served as pupil-teachers from thirteen to eighteen years in specially chosen grant-aided schools. Required to teach all day, the pupil-teachers were dependent upon the headteacher for the improvement of their own knowledge and this had to be accomplished outside normal school hours. Periodically they were examined by one of HM Inspectors and were paid a small stipend to help maintain themselves.

(ii)   the provision of Queen's Scholarships for outstanding pupil-teachers to support their attendance at a two-year training college course. With the help of much increased State financial aid, the denominational colleges expanded in size and numbers to train these Queen's Scholars;

by 1859 there were thirty-four such colleges catering for some 2,500 students. The Education Department bestowed official certificates upon those successfully negotiating the final examinations, so giving rise to a growing elite of trained certificated elementary schoolteachers. Those pupil-teachers who successfully completed their apprenticeship, but failed to obtain one of the limited number of Queen's Scholarships, could take the Department's examinations externally and so become an untrained certificated teacher. But many pupil-teachers were content to serve as completely uncertificated teachers and spent their lifetime in the schools in that inferior capacity. Under Kay-Shuttleworth's influence the Committee extended proficiency grants and limited pension rights to certificated teachers.

The pupil-teacher system, backed by the denominational training colleges, formed the base of the developing system of elementary education in the latter half of the nineteenth century, but its operation was gradually modified and even challenged by a number of developments.

(i)   *The Revised Code (1862)*

The 'payment by results' system emphasised the aridity of the pupil-teacher system as the apprentices were increasingly committed to a taxing and narrow concentration upon drilling in the three Rs. The sharp reduction in the number of Queen's Scholarships and the withdrawal of building grants checked the expansion of the denominational training colleges, whilst the associated restriction of their curricula finally scotched any hope of their providing their students with a more liberal education.

(ii)   *1870 Education Act*

Because it resulted in a sudden and impressive rise in the number of elementary school pupils without providing for any means of expanding the supply of teachers, this measure placed the existing pupil-teacher system and training colleges under great strain. The number of pupil-teachers was rapidly increased and training college courses were shortened and certification manipulated in order to get bodies into classrooms. Nevertheless, there was a significant rise in the average size of classes being prepared for the Department's annual examinations.

(iii)   *Development of Pupil-Teacher Centres*

The traditional dependence of pupil-teachers on the knowledge and energy (or otherwise) of their headteacher for raising the level of their personal education was recognised by some of the larger School Boards as a palpable weakness. Led by the Liverpool School Board they began to provide pupil-teacher centres at which, by evening and Saturday attendance, their apprentices could obtain a poor man's secondary education; in 1884 the Education Department authorised half-time attendance by pupil-teachers at such centres. Those able to attend the centres were soon achieving results in the Queen's Scholarship examinations out of all proportion to their numbers.

(iv) *Report of the Cross Commission (1888)*

Whilst the Majority report admitted the need to improve the pupil-teacher system, the Minority report condemned pupil-teachers as persons who were 'badly taught and who taught badly' and called for the abandonment of the system. Furthermore there was general agreement upon the need to expand training college provision, especially on a non-residential and undenominational basis. The continuance of the Kay-Shuttleworth system was now being called into question.

(c) 1890–1914 The Emergence of the Modern System

This was a period of innovation and expansion during which the foundations of the twentieth century system of teacher education and training were laid by a number of critical developments:

(i) the development of day training colleges attached to universities and university colleges. This recommendation of the Cross Commission produced an immediate and full response and by 1900 there were sixteen such new institutions containing about 1,200 students. Apart from making a major contribution to the training of an increased number of certificated teachers, their development had a wider significance. They broke the denominational monopoly of teacher training and successfully challenged the assumption that only residential training was a satisfactory proposition. The development also ended the former complete isolation of the training colleges from the field of higher education. For the first time student teachers were able to undertake degree courses and the universities became interested in the development of educational theory. The new arrangements provided the earliest facilities for the professional training of graduates for secondary school teaching.

(ii) the development of municipal training colleges by Part II LEAs as authorised by the 1902 Education Act. By the outbreak of the First World War there were twenty-two of these colleges helping to swell the number of training places available; some were day institutions, others partly residential, but all were non-denominational. The former

Anglican domination of teacher training thus received a further setback.

(iii) the dismantling of the pupil-teacher system in favour of a full secondary education for all intending elementary teachers. This course of action had been recommended in the Report of the Departmental Committee on *The Pupil-Teacher System* (1898) and had the full support of Robert Morant when he became Permanent Secretary to the Board of Education in 1903. The 1902 Act, which authorised the Part II LEAs to develop State secondary education and an associated system of scholarship places, provided the necessary basis for radical change. In 1903 Morant issued the first self-contained set of regulations for pupil-teachers and training college students; the minimum age for the apprenticeship of pupil-teachers was raised to sixteen for the express purpose of enabling them to obtain at least four years of full-time secondary education. In 1907 further regulations introduced the bursary system by which intending teachers were to continue their secondary education from sixteen to eighteen years pending direct transference to training college. Initially it was possible to serve for one year as a student teacher before going to college and in the remoter rural areas the revised pupil-teacher system continued to operate; but during the inter-war years these anomalies were destined to be gradually phased out.

(iv) the acceptance by the Board of Education in 1911 of a four-year course for graduate certification. Since the 1890s students attending the day training colleges had found it a tall order to combine study for a degree with their professional training even when the time allowed was raised to three years. After lengthy resistance the Board conceded grant for the support of a consecutive three plus one arrangement for such students. Thereafter the UDEs rapidly assumed their modern form, concerning themselves with the provision of a year's professional training for graduates.

Thus by 1914 the basis for the modern pattern of teacher education and training had already emerged, with Morant having been the central figure in its development. And altogether there were now eighty-eight teacher training institutions serving the needs of England and Wales; this total was comprised of fifty voluntary colleges (60 per cent of them Anglican), twenty-two municipal colleges and the sixteen university units.

(d) 1914–44 The Consolidation of the Modern System

The inter-war period was one of consolidation rather than expansion and change in the field of teacher training. Only six new colleges emerged

against the background of fluctuation and stringency in educational expenditure and the recurrent threat of unemployment amongst qualified teachers.
But the Morant system became firmly established and received the approval
of the Report of the Departmental Committee on *The Training of Teachers in
Public Elementary Schools* (1925). Basically the new pattern rested on the
concept of teaching as a professional occupation, entry into which would be
dependent upon the completion of a full secondary education, matriculation
and two years teacher training at a recognised college. Until 1926 the
examination and certification of teachers remained the strict responsibility
of the Board of Education, but in that year, following a recommendation of
the Departmental Committee, the examining function was devolved upon
Joint Examining Boards on which the training colleges and associated
regional universities were represented. Ten such Boards emerged to cover
the country and all were in operation by 1930. This development did
something to bring the universities and the training colleges into closer
association to the benefit of the latter's status. In most cases however the
relationship remained a limited rather than a full-blooded one; the colleges
were still on the fringe of higher education rather than within it. Meanwhile,
having an increasing number of well-qualified ex-Sixth Formers, the
colleges were beginning to move away from the wide and equal coverage of
all the subjects of the elementary curriculum towards the further study in
depth of one or two particular subjects along university pass degree lines.

The foregoing analysis is primarily concerned with the training of
teachers for elementary schools. In the secondary sector the tradition that
the possession of a degree was in itself a qualification to teach died very hard.
But after 1890 there was a slow but steady growth in secondary teacher training, which gradually undermined the dominance of the untrained graduate
in the secondary field. The Board's recognition of four-year courses in 1911
and the consequent shaping of the UDEs is something of an early landmark
in this respect. By 1939 the universities were providing professional training
for some two thousand graduates. But this was largely for entry into secondary grammar teaching, leaving the training colleges to supply non-graduate
teachers for the other schools. This developing role specialisation helped to
ensure the continuance of a divided profession.

2   Teacher Employment, Status and Supply before 1944

It is difficult to appreciate how onerous were the conditions of employment
for elementary teachers, and how low was their status, before the First
World War.

(a) Conditions of Employment

Highly unsatisfactory in the mid-nineteenth century when Kay-Shuttleworth's influence at least extended a pseudo-Civil Service position to the new certificated teachers, conditions of employment became even worse as a result of the Revised Code (1862) and the rapid expansion of elementary education consequent upon the 1870 Act. The deteriorating situation produced the National Union of Elementary Teachers, established in 1870, to fight for an improvement of the teachers' wretched lot. During the ensuing half-century the union campaigned upon control of entry to the profession, the registration of teachers, capricious dismissal, compulsory extraneous duties, admission to HM Inspectorate, the abolition of payment by results, the restitution and improvement of pension rights, better salaries and more favourable staffing ratios. In spite of some limited gains, the pre-war position was still so unsatisfactory that it helped to produce a growing recruitment problem after 1907 which forced the Board temporarily to suspend its attempt to eliminate unqualified persons from the schools.

(b) Status

The status accorded by contemporary society to those who taught in the elementary schools of the early and mid-nineteenth century was inevitably and deservedly low. But even later when the pupil-teacher system, college training and government certification, and the National Union of Elementary Teachers had come to wield a more professional influence, the status of elementary teachers continued to be undermined by a number of factors.

(i) Elementary teachers were drawn almost exclusively from the ranks of the upper working class. No respectable middle class family would allow its sons or daughters to lower themselves by entering elementary teaching. Thus in the highly class-conscious context of Victorian society their social origins proved a severe status handicap to elementary schoolteachers. This contrasted sharply with the much more favourable position of middle class graduates serving in the reformed public and endowed grammar schools.

(ii) The rapid expansion in the demand for elementary teachers following the 1870 Act resulted in a process of dilution. In a quarter of a century there was a five-fold increase in the size of the total teaching force and this was achieved by lowering the standards of the certificate examination and various other expedients. At the turn of the century the staff employed in the nation's elementary schools consisted of the following categories:

> Trained certificated (the elite)   32 per cent
> Untrained certificated (external)   25 per cent
> Uncertificated ex-pupil-teachers   28 per cent
> Article 68-ers   15 per cent

Thus at the close of Victoria's reign, when the number of elementary teachers reached 110,000, over two-fifths of them were still uncertificated; and this ignores the existence of some 30,000 odd pupil-teachers whose services were essential to the manning of the schools. The Article 68-ers were a species of teacher officially recognised by the 1893 Code and employed upon the satisfaction of four conditions: that they were female, that they were over eighteen years of age, that they had been vaccinated and that they had received the (perfunctory) approval of a visiting HM Inspector. They were little more than a source of cheap labour, widely employed by the hard pressed voluntary schools and much resented by the rest of the aspiring profession.

(iii) Elementary schoolteaching became dominated by women, the proportion rising from 53 per cent in 1869 to 75 per cent thirty years later. This trend was strongly associated with the dilution process; at the end of the century less than one-quarter of female elementary teachers were trained and certificated compared with almost three-fifths of their male counterparts. The employment of female teachers was encouraged by the significantly lower cost of hiring their services. Meanwhile other reputable professions remained male preserves in a society still insisting that woman's only place was in the home.

(iv) The conditions of work (described earlier) were associated with low and variable salaries. Promotion prospects were poor as the number of headships was limited and entry to the Inspectorate barred to non-graduates. Since 1862 the elementary teacher had become the hired servant of his employer with his income subject to anxious individual negotiation; even the 1902 Act did not provide for the introduction of machinery for the agreement and payment of a national set of salary scales.

Little wonder that many skilled artisans looked upon the elementary schoolteacher with scant respect, whilst the middle class attitude was one of derision, a derision sharpened by the elementary schoolteachers' aspiration to join that very class.

The period 1916–22, during which H.A.L. Fisher was President of the Board of Education and wartime experience stimulated an unprecedented national interest in educational improvement, may be regarded as a turning point in the fortunes of the teaching profession. Five developments combined then or shortly thereafter immeasurably to improve the position and status of teachers:

(a) the establishment of the Burnham Committee (1920) for the negotiation of national salary scales and the passage of the Teachers' Superannuation Act (1918), which combined to provide elementary schoolteachers with much greater financial security.

(b) the post-war slump and the subsequently depressed economic conditions, which paradoxically benefited the teachers. Reasonably secure in their jobs and having refused to tie the Burnham salary scales to a cost of living index, they were able to improve their real incomes because retail prices fell more heavily than their salaries, even though the latter were subjected to the vicious Geddes (1922) and May (1931) Committee cuts.

(c) the unprecedently low birth-rate of the inter-war period and the surfeit of unmarried female teachers. This situation provided the opportunity for improving the teacher-pupil ratio which had been so unfavourable before the First World War. This situation also facilitated a marked reduction in the employment of uncertificated teachers.

(d) the long-term influence of Fisher upon the LEAs and the public at large. Taking advantage of the widespread interest in post-war reconstruction, he was able to elevate the importance of both education and the teacher in national life. He exhorted the teachers to improve their professional image and did all he could personally to improve their status. Some of the effect of this was lost in the economic troubles that later supervened but it was never completely dissipated.

(e) the rising standard of entrants to the profession once the Morant system became firmly established. By the 1930s it was no longer exceptional to find graduate teachers serving in the elementary sector, especially in the new secondary modern schools which were emerging as part of the Hadow reorganisation process.

But in spite of this welcome advance a serious dichotomy still divided the profession and weakened its claim to full status recognition; this was the distinction between elementary and grammar schoolteachers, reinforced by the Board's separate regulations for the respective sectors. Throughout the inter-war years, in spite of much talk about parity of esteem, they experienced different terms of employment and were allotted separate pay scales; the clear implication was that the elementary teacher was inferior in status to his secondary grammar counterpart. This could not but harm the cause of the profession as a whole, for the great majority of teachers served in the elementary field. Another weakness resulted from the Board's refusal to make an approved course of training and proper certification a strict condition of entry to the teaching profession; neither the exhortations of the NUT nor the recommendations of the 1925 Departmental Committee had prevailed in this respect, and the employment of unqualified staff continued though on a declining scale.

3 Teacher Education, Training and Supply 1944–72

In broad terms this period was one of early improvisation and later major expansion and change in the field of teacher training and supply. Whilst maintaining their connection with the LEAs and the churches, the training colleges strengthened both their association with the universities and their own independence, finally to take their place as a recognised sector of higher education. In relation to this basic context a number of particular developments and problems are worth considering.

(a) 1944 Education Act

This affected the overall situation in several ways:

(i) through associated regulations, it redefined 'qualified' teacher to end the sharp pre-war distinction between elementary and secondary teachers;

(ii) it gave statutory authority to the Burnham negotiating machinery and required a single consolidated scale to cover the salaries of all teachers;

(iii) it secured teachers from dismissal on grounds of religion or marriage;

(iv) it specified the duties of the Ministry of Education and the LEAs as to the training of teachers. Prime responsibility was clearly lodged with the former, but the latter were committed to making a full contribution both financially and otherwise.

(b) McNair Report on *Teachers and Youth Leaders* (1944)

The Departmental Committee set up under the chairmanship of Sir Arnold McNair investigated the supply, recruitment and training of teachers and through its critical recommendations did much to influence the future course of development in the field concerned. The prime concern of the report was the need to establish a truly national and co-ordinated system of teacher training to end the traditional isolation and lack of integration of the various training institutions, and to improve the supply and quality of teachers to match the new demands of the 1944 Act. Out of this concern arose the committee's specific recommendations:

(i) the establishment of a Central Training Council to initiate the new administrative framework for a co-ordinated system of teacher training and to advise the Board on matters concerned with the supply, recruitment and training of teachers. Out of this was to emerge the National Advisory Council on the Training and Supply of Teachers (1949).

(ii) the setting up of Area Training Organisations (ATOs) on a regional basis to integrate the efforts of various colleges and to draw the universities more firmly into the business of teacher education and training. Two alternative schemes were suggested for the actual form which these ATOs should take. Half of the Committee recommended University Schools of Education consisting of an 'organic federation' of training institutions operating in a given area. The other half of the Committee favoured Joint Boards, which would maintain separate institutional identity to a much greater degree and which could be more easily developed from the existing Joint Examining Boards. Happily it was the first arrangement which won official support and came to characterise most of the ATOs and their associated Institutes (or Schools) of Education. By the 1950s twenty such University Institutes were exercising regional responsibility for training courses, standards, examinations and awards as well as the promotion of advanced studies and research in education.

(iii) the adoption of various measures to increase the supply and improve the quality of teachers. The detailed recommendations made were calculated to facilitate the expansion of the teaching force by the minimum 25 per cent deemed necessary and to raise the attractions and status of the teaching profession as a means to that end. They included the consolidation and improvement of teachers' basic salaries (with substantial additions for special qualifications and responsibilities), the recruitment of mature persons and an end to the disqualification of married women teachers, and the lengthening of the teacher training course from two to three years at the earliest possible juncture.

The report obtained immediate acceptance in principle and, with some refinements, was implemented in piecemeal fashion during the period 1945–60. Indeed, it provided the basis for the post-war system of teacher education, training and supply in England and Wales, thus ensuring much greater co-ordination and integration of effort than had been realised hitherto. Apart from the identification of the Ministry's prime responsibility for the training and supply of teachers (section 62, 1944 Act), such an improved national framework was further secured by the establishment of the Association of Teachers in Colleges and Departments of Education

(1943) and the incorporation of the Clearing House and Central Registry (1962) for the co-ordination of college admissions procedure.

(c) Post-War Shortage of Teachers

In spite of a substantial rise in the number of training colleges during the first decade of peace, the raising of the school leaving age, the high post-war birth-rate, the sharp wastage rate amongst women teachers and stiff competition from industry for qualified people combined to produce an acute shortage of teachers. Until the late 1950s the situation was met by a series of improvised and palliative measures:

   (i) the Emergency Training Schemes for ex-servicemen and unqualified serving practitioners which added almost 40,000 to the total teaching force by 1952;

  (ii) the continuance of untrained graduate entry to the profession and the postponement of the introduction of three-year teacher training until 1960;

 (iii) the development of special day training colleges for mature entrants combined with a national campaign to increase the number of married returnees and part-time teachers;

 (iv) the enforcement of a Ministry quota scheme designed to ensure the fair distribution of available qualified staff;

  (v) the reconstitution and progressive improvement of the Burnham salary scales for teachers.

Meanwhile the improving economic situation and the expansion of secondary education was preparing the ground for a more direct and positive assault on the problem.

(d) Expansion of Provision

The period 1945–72 saw the school population of England and Wales grow continuously from 5.0 to 8.4 million – a rise of 68 per cent. To meet this situation, to reduce class sizes and to accommodate the onset of minimum three-year courses from 1960 the training colleges and UDEs increased their total number of places from 12,000 to no less than 114,000 during these years. As a result the annual output of trained teachers shot up from some 6,000 pre-war to over 40,000 by the early 1970s. A concomitant feature of this massive expansion was the major shift in balance between voluntary and provided colleges, with the LEAs increasing their institutional share from under one-third pre-war to over two-thirds at the period's close.

The initial expansion came immediately after the war and was centred upon the Emergency Training Scheme which gave rise to fifty-five new training units. But with the end of the scheme in 1951 only a quarter of these units had been translated into permanent training colleges and the former growth rate was not sustained during the mid-1950s. However, in 1958 a government White Paper announced a crash programme for increasing teacher training facilities which heralded the start of a much bigger and more prolonged second wave of expansion. Various influences underpinned this new drive:

(i) the sharp and continuous 40 per cent rise in the birth-rate 1955–64 which portended growing pressure on the schools and adverse effects upon class sizes well into the 1970s;

(ii) the increase in voluntary staying-on and, following the combined exhortations of the Crowther (1959) and Newsom (1963) Reports, the government's firm commitment to raising the school-leaving age to sixteen;

(iii) the relatively high wastage rate still prevailing amongst women teachers with 70 per cent of them lost to the classroom within five years of qualifying;

(iv) the introduction of minimum three-year courses for initial college training (1960) which required a 50 per cent expansion of provision just to maintain the same annual output of teachers.

These considerations ensured that the government was pressed from various quarters – such as the National Advisory Council, the LEAs and the teachers' organisations – to provide the requisite resources. But it was perhaps the Robbins Committee which did most to sustain the momentum of growth; its report on *Higher Education* (1963) judged existing expansion plans to be inadequate and recommended a new target of 110,000 initial teacher training places for 1973. In the event the Robbins schedule was not only met but surpassed. As a result the post-war shortage of teachers was gradually overcome and the raising of the school-leaving age in 1972 easily accommodated.

(e)   Progressive Change and Mounting Concern

The McNair era featured a number of changes which were calculated to improve the system of teacher training and supply significantly. By the 1950s the ATOs regionally centred upon University Institutes of Education were providing it with a structural framework infinitely better than the looser pre-war arrangements; and the closer association with the universities had favourable implications for the standards and status of the training colleges. Thereafter the position was further improved by a range of other important developments:

(i) the change to minimum three-year courses for the training of non-graduate teachers (1960). The government finally conceded this crucial McNair proposal in the face of determined pressure from the National Advisory Council, the Association of Teachers in Colleges and Departments of Education and the NUT. In anticipation of the event much thought was given to the scope and content of the new three-year Certificate courses. The National Advisory Council stressed the prior need to produce better educated and more mature teachers; HM Inspectorate regarded the extra year as a means to raise academic standards; the NUT saw it as a move towards an all-graduate profession now that pass degree level studies in some areas were a possibility. Thus the emphasis was placed upon the wider education of Certificate students rather than the development of practical competence; the universities were happy to back this strategy and consequently the majority of three-year courses tended to give disproportionate weight to the study of academic subjects and educational theory at the expense of practical training and curricula concerns.

(ii) the initiation of four-year Bachelor of Education degree courses for a minority of college students able to meet university matriculation requirements. This advance followed the Robbins Report on *Higher Education* (1963) which was concerned to further improve the academic standing of the training colleges and resulted in their being renamed Colleges of Education. By 1972 about one in nine teacher trainees were undertaking such degrees and the teaching involved certainly made for greater intellectual rigour in the colleges' work. From 1970 a beginning was made with the provision of BEd degree courses for serving teachers. Unhappily the Robbins report did not provide clear guide lines for the development of the new degree and for a long time regional differences regarding initial entry, course structure and the classification of awards drew bitter criticism. A further bone of contention was the predictable tendency of the validating universities to subject the BEd degree courses to strict control and to insist on a heavy academic and theoretical content irrespective of the age-range the student intended to teach.

(iii) the growth of postgraduate training courses in the Colleges of Education and the termination of untrained graduate entry to teaching. These developments had received the keen support of the Association of Teachers in Colleges and Departments of Education and the NUT for a long time, but the real catalyst was their inclusion in the recommendations of both the Newsom (1963) and Plowden (1967) Reports of the Central Advisory Council. In the late 1960s there was a marked expansion of postgraduate training in the colleges and by 1972 the numbers involved slightly exceeded those of the UDEs. It was during the years 1970–74 that the government finally debarred untrained graduates from entering the profession, albeit subject to any exceptional need to staff 'shortage' subjects. Both these developments were aimed at safeguarding the primary schools and less able secondary pupils from subject-oriented or professionally inept graduate recruits.

Meanwhile a plan to initiate far-reaching structural reform failed to win government acceptance. In 1963 the Robbins Committee recommended that the McNair arrangements should be taken a stage further by making the colleges constituent parts of new University Schools of Education to be established within each existing ATO. The Schools of Education were to exercise not only academic, but also administrative and financial, responsibilities in respect of teacher education and training. Each College of Education would have its own governing body related federally to the School of Education and through it to the university Senate. Moreover, the colleges were to be financed by ear-marked central funds channelled by a new Grants Commission via the Schools of Education. The Robbins Committee felt that only closer attachment to the universities would significantly raise the standing of the colleges and secure their future prospects. Although the response of the colleges to being drawn wholly into the university sphere was enthusiastic, the opposition to this from the LEAs and central government was instant and unqualified. The loss of direct public control over the colleges made the proposed changes quite unacceptable and they were rejected. By way of consolation, however, the subsequent Weaver inquiry (1966) led to some limited reforms which secured more autonomy for the colleges vis-à-vis the LEAs. But, alas, this was a small gain compared with the hopes raised by the ill-fated Robbins plan. Via the DES and the LEAs the colleges remained subject to direct administrative and financial control.

The rejection of the Robbins strategy left the Colleges of Education in their uneasy mid-way position between the universities and the LEAs. But worse still certain developments thereafter combined to pose a longer-term threat to the university link and even to their very survival:

(i) the establishment of the Council for National Academic Awards (1964) with authority to approve degree courses and awards in non-university institutions of higher education. This provided an alternative to university validation and by 1972 this new body was offering its own BEd degree courses.

(ii) the initiation of the binary system for the future provision of higher education (1965). This was to consist of a public sector of non-university institutions and an autonomous sector comprised of the universities. Such a policy was bound to question the continuance of the colleges' mid-way position and almost certainly they would be drawn firmly into the non-university field.

(iii) the rationalisation of public sector higher education following upon the White Paper *A Plan for Polytechnics and Other Colleges* (1966). Some thirty polytechnics developed from existing regional Colleges of Further Education already concerned with a large amount of advanced work now began to emerge and received prior attention from the DES. Within a year the new polytechnics had begun to establish Education Departments. But more worrying than this incursion into teacher training was the danger that certain Colleges of Education might be swallowed up by these favoured and growing institutions. By 1972 the continuing fall in the birth-rate and the prospective need for a sharp contraction of teacher training had considerably increased this threat.

It is also noteworthy that following the resignation of its chairman in 1965 the National Advisory Council on the Training and Supply of Teachers was allowed to lapse; this prevented any serious national debate upon the implications of these new departures for the system of teacher training and supply.

During the 1960s the training colleges had trebled their output, extended the two-year Certificate course to three years and launched the four-year BEd degree. Before the House of Commons in late 1969 Edward Short, then Secretary of State, quite rightly paid tribute to these 'substantial achievements'. Yet, ironically, by this time the prevailing system of training was beset by a welter of criticism that had grown fast over the previous five years. A whole range of complaints emanated from practising teachers, their associations and other sources. It was asserted that the minimum entry requirements for Certificate purposes (i.e. five 'O' levels) were inadequate and involved a serious weakness in respect of maths and science qualifications; that the theoretical weighting of college courses failed to meet the real needs of the schools; that the arrangements for teaching practice denied an equal and proper role to school staff; that too few college tutors had recent primary teaching experience; that too many students reached the schools ill-prepared – especially in regard to class organisation and control, the teaching of reading and remedial work; and that the majority of newly qualified teachers were simply left to sink or swim during their probationary year. Whilst these strictures had real substance, the force with which some of them were pressed was partly consequent upon the schools themselves passing through a difficult time of progressive change in the primary field and comprehensive reorganisation in the secondary sector. Thus the arrival of young recruits embarking upon BEd degrees still unavailable to serving teachers was not calculated to endear the colleges to the schools. But beyond the complaints some deeper issues were also being raised:

(i)   the view was now expressed that the long-established concurrent approach to college courses produced confusion and that a consecutive pattern of personal education followed by professional training made much better sense;

(ii) given the ingrained academic preoccupations of the universities, some critics argued that the breaking of the McNair link was a prerequisite for the provision of teacher training courses with a sufficiently strong professional and practical character;

(iii) with the swift advance of the new polytechnics, the traditional monotechnic arrangements for teacher training came under attack. It was claimed that multi-purpose institutions of higher education offered a broader experience, greater course and job flexibility and superior economies of scale than could be provided by separate Colleges of Education.

The mounting concern gathered such strength that some official action became inevitable. The Plowden Report (1967) recommended 'a full enquiry into the system of training teachers' and a Parliamentary Select Committee which probed the situation 1969–70 found that there was a widespread demand for this. Soon afterwards Margaret Thatcher, the new Secretary of State, set up a special Committee of Inquiry under Lord James of Rusholme (Vice-Chancellor of York University but no friend of the University Institutes of Education) to undertake the task. Asked to complete its work within twelve months the Committee published its report in February 1972.

4   Reorganisation and Contraction

From 1972 the system of teacher training was subjected to a traumatic process of reorganisation and contraction calculated to destroy the McNair-type arrangements so painstakingly developed since the 1930s. As this assault developed it was the Colleges of Education, the chief providers of teacher education and training, which inevitably found themselves placed in the front line.

(a) James Report on *Teacher Education and Training* (1972)

The James Committee's brief was generally 'to inquire into the present arrangements for education, training and probation of teachers'; more specifically to consider the content and organisation of courses, the dominantly monotechnic approach to provision and the prospective roles of the various types of institution in future development; and to make recommendations. In line with the sharp criticism already levelled at the existing position, the Committee condemned the concurrent pattern of education and training applicable to the majority of prospective teachers, the scandal of the probationary year, the inconsistencies and over-academicism of the new BEd courses and the restrictive effects upon college development of the continuing tutelage of the universities and LEAs. Thus the need, asserted the Committee, was for 'a radical solution' which would involve:

(i) a new organisational pattern for teacher education and training. Here the report recommended the abandonment of the concurrent approach in favour of a uniformly consecutive pattern consisting of three 'cycles' or phases.

First cycle: this would provide for students' personal higher education in the shape of three-year academic degree courses or new two-year Diploma in Higher Education (DipHE) courses requiring two 'A' levels for entry. Either a degree or the new diploma would qualify students for selective admission into the second cycle.

Second cycle: this was to be concerned with pre-service professional training and induction. The first year would be spent in a College or Department of Education for instruction and training primarily aimed at meeting the practical demands of classroom teaching; the second year was to be largely school-based with students enjoying the status of 'licensed teachers' but operating under supervision and on a reduced timetable to allow continuing study at a 'professional centre'. Given the satisfactory completion of the second cycle the student would receive a BA (Ed) degree and become a 'registered' teacher. This was the James road to an all-graduate profession.

Third cycle: given top priority by the Committee this was to afford in-service education and training opportunities aimed at ending the prior overdependence on initial preparation. Throughout a teacher's career the third cycle would provide a wide range of relevant courses and activities for which there should be an entitlement to paid secondment for a minimum of one term in every seven years of service.

(ii) a new network of professional tutors and centres. The report recommended that each school should have a professional tutor to help meet the needs of trainees on the second cycle and to organise the in-service release arrangements for colleagues. Further, a variety of appropriate institutions, including large schools and teacher centres, should be designated as professional centres for the provision of courses for both probationary and serving teachers. Such arrangements would forge a closer relationship between the schools and the teacher trainers.

(iii) a new system of government for teacher education and training. The McNair system of ATOs was to be replaced by fifteen Regional Councils topped by a National Council for teacher education and training. Thus the special role of the University Institutes of Education would end. Henceforth the planning and financing functions would be undertaken on a three-tier basis involving the DES, the National Council and the Regional Councils; the latter would include representatives of the LEAs, the teachers, the universities, the CNAA, the central Department and each participant college or polytechnic. These arrangements were deliberately calculated to break the university link and open the way to greater autonomy and higher status for the Colleges of Education. The position of their governing bodies and academic boards would be strengthened further and each college would be directly represented on the Regional Councils responsible for approving courses and validating professional awards. Collectively the Colleges of Education would form a new third force in higher education with its own regional structure and development potential.

The prospect of such fundamental changes naturally aroused the hostility of traditional teacher training interests. The hurried production of the report had inevitably given rise to a range of weaknesses and misjudgements which the opposition capitalised upon. The degree/DipHE dichotomy within the first cycle was seen as a sure means of perpetuating the old professional divisions. The continuance of concurrent courses, especially for the preparation of primary teachers, received surprisingly strong support. The second cycle arrangements, especially the bogus BA (Ed) degree, as the crucial means to securing an all-graduate profession were denounced as weak and unlikely to win public confidence. And the validation of professional awards by new untried bodies would simply underline this weakness. Far better to build on prior experience and develop further the existing and 'proper' BEd degree courses!

Unhappily for the Committee it had worked under an additional disadvantage. Its terms of reference did not embrace teacher supply at a time when the spectre of teacher unemployment was already looming. And Lord

James was unable to exact from the DES any firm statistics on the prospective demand for and supply of teachers. Not only was this topic regarded as politically sensitive but with the falling birth-rate having levelled off (1970–71) the demographic future was uncertain. Thus the report made only passing reference to the likely difficulties ahead and failed to establish the serious threat; ironically, to have done so would have greatly strengthened the James case for a consecutive pattern – so much more flexible in a contracting market for teachers than the traditional concurrent approach.

(b) The Government White Paper (1972) and Circular 7/73

Late in 1972 the government issued its White Paper *Education: A Framework for Expansion* which revealed official policy intentions for the next decade. The section on teacher training and higher education included a response to James. The report's recommendations on in-service training, the reform of the probationary year, the initiation of the DipHE as a general sub-degree qualification and the replacement of the ATOs by a new administrative structure were all accepted. But, explicitly or otherwise, the government set aside the proposed blanket application of a consecutive pattern and the use of new bodies for validation purposes. The bogus BA (Ed) idea was also rejected; three-year Ordinary and four-year Honours BEd degree courses were preferred as a means of moving towards an all-graduate profession.

However, the White Paper's most crucial proposals for the future of teacher education and training sprang from considerations beyond the James Report. Firstly, given the continued rise in demand for higher education and the prevailing Robbins principle of providing places for all qualified applicants, the government was intent upon expansion 1972–81, but with more emphasis on the growth of the cheaper non-university sector. Secondly, with the birth-rate having resumed its downward path in 1972 there was an urgent need to contract the number of teacher training places by about one-third by 1981. The White Paper provided the answer to both these requirements. Like the Robbins' recipe before it, the James strategy for the future development of the Colleges of Education was set aside and the government made clear its intention of drawing them firmly into the public sector of higher education. This would break the university link, reinforce the binary line and make the colleges available for more diversified and flexible use. It was indicated that in such a reorganised framework the Colleges of Education would be faced with a number of possibilities – ranging from free-standing development into major institutions of higher education to outright closure!

Within three months of the White Paper the Secretary of State issued

Circular 7/73 on *The Development of Higher Education in the Non-University Sector* enjoining the LEAs and voluntary bodies to submit plans for the reorganisation of higher education and the contraction of teacher training for which they were responsible. It warned of the need for institutions of over one thousand students if satisfactory economies of scale were to be realised; for the great majority of Colleges of Education this scuppered any hopes of remaining independent institutions and turned their attentions to survival by merger. Interim schemes were to be produced within seven months and final plans five months later (April 1974).

The years 1973–75 witnessed the first major wave of reorganisation and contraction. With political interest focused elsewhere and little effective opposition the DES enforced its will to transform the previous scene. In 1975 ATOs finally disappeared and the separate regulations for teacher training were rescinded; henceforth all public sector institutions were to come under the new Further Education Regulations. Meanwhile some 160 Colleges of Education met various fates. A small minority managed to emerge as free-standing diversified institutions or merged with universities. Well over forty were swallowed up by polytechnics. About sixty entered into negotiations with each other or Colleges of Further Education to form larger diversified colleges. About one in ten faced closure. Only thirty remained monotechnic teacher training institutions – with a mere 15,000 places out of the 114,000 figure for 1971. The logic of the new situation drove the Association of Teachers in Colleges and Departments of Education to amalgamate with the Association of Teachers in Technical Institutions to form the new National Association of Teachers in Further and Higher Education. Finally, a new set of common salary scales was introduced. The inexorable progress of these changes had been virtually unaffected by the switch from a Conservative to a Labour government in 1974.

(c)   Tightening the Screws on Teacher Supply

Circular 7/73 initiated what proved to be merely the first instalment of a protracted process of disruption. By the mid-1970s the demand for teachers was being severely undermined by three factors:

   (i) the continuing sharp fall in the birth-rate which portended a now certain and prolonged decline in the total school population after 1977.

  (ii) the growing economic difficulties which gave rise to a developing squeeze on public expenditure. As the country moved into recession the commitment to the Robbins principle and the expansion of higher education faltered in face of mounting financial pressure. The cost of training and employing teachers became subject to closer scrutiny.

(iii) the overdue Houghton award (1974) which brought about a marked increase in teachers' salaries. This raised the cost of employing teachers and substantially reduced the wastage rate amongst those already in post.

In isolation the demographic factor afforded an opportunity to make the four-year BEd course the standard concurrent arrangement, to further reduce class sizes considerably and to proceed apace with the James' induction and in-service strategy. But the financial factors dictated that the official response to the situation should be in terms of savings rather than improvements. Accordingly the 1972 White Paper's target of 510,000 teachers for the early 1980s was gradually reduced by one-quarter. Its estimate that the existing 114,000 training places would have to fall by one-third was progressively revised to provide for a cut of over two-thirds! Thus in 1977 the Labour government presided over a second bout of reorganisation and contraction during which another twenty-odd colleges were either swallowed-up or phased out. Five years later a further twelve colleges and polytechnic departments of education fell victim to a third operation undertaken by the succeeding Conservative government. By this time about one-sixth of the original 160 Colleges of Education had suffered outright closure and, with the various mergers and re-mergers, the teacher training scene had become unrecognisable inside a single decade. For example, in 1973 the Manchester ATO boasted seven thriving Colleges of Education – five 'provided' and two Catholic; all seven finally succumbed to the recurring onslaught leaving the Manchester UDE and Manchester Polytechnic to monopolise the reduced provision.

Within the context of reorganisation and contraction there were some significant subsidiary developments and shifts. Whilst the voluntary bodies ultimately suffered some diminution of their post-war 'historic share' of teacher training provision, the diversification process gave their surviving colleges access to the wider field of higher education for the first time. By the late 1970s growing unemployment among new teachers was deterring applications for BEd courses and fears arose as to the long-term survival of the vocational BEd degree. Consequently the more flexible consecutive route into teaching (i.e. first degree plus postgraduate training) markedly strengthened its position in the reorganised framework; by 1982 the proportion entering the profession by this route had risen to 60 per cent. An associated shift was the growing share of total admissions for training accounted for by the UDEs – increased from one-tenth to one-third during the years 1972–83. Of course, traditionally one-year postgraduate courses were aimed largely at prospective secondary teachers whose job opportunities continued to expand until 1977. However, until the end of the

1980s falling rolls will hit the secondary sector rather than the primary; as it is generally agreed that concurrent courses are much to be preferred for intending primary teachers the fortunes of the BEd degree may revive and result in some reversal of the recent shifts. However, given the intention to switch some of the postgraduate capacity from secondary to primary training the future balance is uncertain.

(d) Qualitative Reform and Improvement

In quantitative terms the only bright spot in the post-James decade was the continued improvement of the teacher-pupil ratio in maintained schools. The number of pupils per teacher had fallen from 27.1 to 22.0 during the period 1950–72; by the early 1980s, despite the teacher training cut-backs, it was down to 18.6 – remarkably close to the 1972 White Paper target figure. This sustained advance resulted from the earlier expansionist policies and the later tendency of LEAs to respond to falling secondary rolls with curriculum-led staffing arrangements.

In terms of improving the quality of teacher education and training the post-James decade was one of missed opportunity. Some of the developing slack in the system could have been used to lengthen and strengthen initial courses of training and to fully implement the James strategies on induction and in-service development. But the DES' obsession with numbers and costs ensured that there was very little significant progress. Since the 1972 White Paper the majority of BEd students have followed the three-year Ordinary degree route into teaching; yet the Robbins Report (1963) had condemned such a short-cut to an all-graduate profession as one that would involve either a high failure rate or a palpable dilution of degree standards. The misconceived two-year DipHE has simply foundered. Although the government financed two pilot schemes 1974–77 to establish the best means to help new teachers in their induction year, the economic factor has militated against any widespread reform of probationary arrangements. In-service education and training has also received more lip-service than resources; many LEAs have been reluctant to incur much expenditure in this field and even the minimal level of such provision as envisaged by James has not materialised. And since the demise of the ATOs (1975) no new regional bodies for the co-ordination of teacher education and training have been established: this vacuum has deprived the colleges and LEAs of a collective voice and has lent itself to an over-concentration of power at the DES.

However, some improvements have taken place in recent years. In 1973 the void left by the lapsing of the National Advisory Council on the Training and Supply of Teachers was filled by a new Advisory Committee on the

Supply and Training of Teachers; seven years later this body was reconstituted to form the present Advisory Committee on the Supply and Education of Teachers. These two bodies provided the LEAs and the teacher associations with a national forum for the presentation of advice to the Secretary of State. And the declining demand for teachers has enabled the government to raise the standards of entry to the profession. From 1979–80 the non-graduate Certificate qualification was phased out and all applicants for teacher training were required to have 'O' level or equivalent qualifications in English and mathematics. The advance towards an all-graduate profession has gathered momentum; since 1970 the proportion of graduate teachers in maintained schools has risen from 20 per cent to 39 per cent (1982). In part this has been sustained by the growth of full and part-time provision for certificated teachers to undertake special BEd degree courses. And the James critique of the content of the early BEd degree courses has stimulated some reform to give greater weight to professional and practical concerns.

Very recently there have been signs that the DES is switching some of its attentions from the question of numbers to some of the wider and deeper qualitative issues. Sir Keith Joseph's 1983 White Paper on *Teaching Quality* provides the foremost pointer in this direction. In relation to the future of initial and in-service teacher education and training this policy document emphasises the need for:

(i) new criteria for the review and approval of all teacher training courses by the Secretary of State. Such criteria are to be laid down following consultation with the Advisory Committee on the Supply and Education of Teachers. One consideration will be the extent to which courses are closely related to school subjects (especially at secondary level) and to specific age ranges; here the design is to provide a better subject match in secondary schools and to strengthen maths and science teaching in the primary sector. A second consideration will be the extent to which teacher trainers have recent teaching experience in schools; where this may be a weakness teacher-tutor exchanges and secondments are suggested as a means of meeting the situation.

(ii) a more rigorous selection and assessment of trainees during initial training and induction to shake out those unsuitable for the profession. This process is seen to require the much fuller participation of practising teachers than has hitherto been the case.

(iii) a further tightening of entry regulations to check the continued appointment of untrained maths and science graduates to school posts.

(iv) better induction arrangements and more in-service education and training in line with the general thrust of the James Report and subsequent evaluation of the needs and possibilities. This is to include the provision of special management training for heads and other senior staff.

Significantly the White Paper was preceded by a marked increase in the activity of HM Inspectorate in the teacher training field. In 1982 it issued various papers for the attention of the institutions involved and made clear its intention to oversee improvements in the quality of provision. With the UDEs set to become more involved in primary training there was even the suggestion that the Inspectorate should visit them as of right rather than by traditional invitation! Whilst this revived central government interest in the nature of teacher education and training is to be generally welcomed, there are anxieties that it may be misdirected and even unacceptable. Firstly, the Inspectorate's conviction that a top priority is to strengthen subject-education and method-training is seen in some quarters as too restrictive and secondary-oriented. Secondly, a still further accession of power and control to the DES may remove the last vestiges of any real educational partnership in this field. And beyond these concerns is the question of whether the extra resources required to sustain the White Paper's hopes in such areas as the induction year and in-service development can be provided and relied upon.

5   The Teaching Profession in the Post-War Era

Until the 1970s the post-war years were certainly an auspicious period for the teaching profession in England and Wales. This was reflected in three related areas.

(a)   The Demand for Teachers

For over a quarter of a century the post-war demand for teachers remained unsatisfied and sustained an immense expansion of the teaching force. During the period 1950–75 the number of teachers in maintained schools doubled to exceed 450,000. The primary total rose by 55 per cent, its secondary counterpart by no less than 182 per cent. This impressive growth was accompanied by the advance to minimum three-year training courses, a substantial increase in the proportion of graduates, a continuing reduction in untrained graduate entry and the elimination of uncertificated teachers. Unlike the inter-war years this period was one of complete job security for those appointed to teaching posts. Moreover, the expansion of the school system combined with an annual wastage rate of 10 per cent to provide good promotion prospects for career teachers. And to a limited extent there was also a rise in the professional status of teachers, with the enhanced post-war interest in education, the extended duration of training and the relative growth of graduate entry all contributing to this end. But with non-graduates always accounting for at least three-quarters and women some three-fifths of their number the teachers were unable to realise a status position comparable with that of doctors, lawyers and certain other professions.

(b) Conditions of Service

Until very recently the post-war conditions of service were very favourable and would have been unrecognisable to teachers working at the turn of the century. Normal contracts of employment for qualified teachers were for permanent positions and full-time work. The teacher's security of tenure was very strong indeed; only 'gross misconduct' or 'dereliction of duty' (neither clearly defined) provided grounds for dismissal and in both cases the teacher had the right to be heard and represented. And teachers were able to terminate their contracts at two months' notice, except during the summer when a three months' requirement applied. For serious illness the standard entitlement became three months' full pay and three months' half-pay exclusive of holidays. In 1968 the supervision of school meals by assistant teachers became a voluntary matter. When added to generous holidays on full salary such conditions of service aroused envy in some quarters. However, in terms of pay post-war schoolteaching compared unfavourably with many other occupations demanding similar qualifications. The worst effect of this was the perennial shortage of maths and science graduates to meet the growing needs of the secondary schools. But at least the 1944 Act gave statutory authority to the Burnham scales and the regular review of these became accepted practice. And from 1956 a more complex salary structure afforded a growing range of above-basic additions for extra qualifications and certain responsibilities – although secondary teachers gained much more from this than their primary colleagues. Later on the Remuneration of Teachers Act (1965) provided for direct government representation on the Burnham Committee and for arbitration in case of disagreement; whilst this measure was not welcomed by the teachers, their bargaining situation was not critically weakened. Indeed as a public sector occupation the teachers found that the main problem was their vulnerability to government income policies and spending limits, which tended – especially with the onset of inflation – to erode their relative pay position. Happily at the close of this period the grievance received due recognition and the special Houghton inquiry (1974) produced a 27 per cent relativities award for teachers.

(c) Freedom of Teachers

In the inter-war period the professional freedom of teachers had taken firm root in England and Wales and for many years after the Second World War this development was progressively reinforced with the concurrence of all the interested parties. Although the 1944 Act vested responsibility for the school curriculum with the LEAs, the official disinclination to interfere with what was taught and how became a feature of the post-war educational scene. The freedom enjoyed by teachers was associated with and secured by a number of influences and developments.

(i)   Teachers came to exercise a very large measure of freedom in relation to curricula, syllabuses and teaching methods in both primary and secondary schools. This freedom was not seriously restricted by the role of external examining bodies or the Schools Council for the Curriculum and Examinations (1964). Teachers had a choice of examining bodies and different syllabuses whilst the Council's main committees had an in-built teacher majority.

(ii) Teachers were legally secured against any need to teach religious instruction or partake in corporate religious worship and in practice few secondary specialists were called upon to accept much responsibility for unfamiliar subjects.

(iii) Teachers were not subject to any dictatorial oversight of their work. The post-war inspectorate, both local and central, was expected to exercise its influence by persuasion; whilst teachers were constrained to consider inspectorial advice there was no requirement to follow it. Increasingly the traditional pre-war 'full inspections' of individual schools by HM Inspectorate fell in number as this body developed a more diffused and consultative role.

The basic axiom was that teaching is a highly individual and professional matter which admits of no official strait-jacket or inquisitorial monitoring if the best interests of children are to be properly served. This was a view that the teacher associations were always at pains to propagate and defend.

Since the mid-1970s the context in which the teaching profession seeks to advance and protect its interests has altered much for the worse. This followed hard upon a serious loss of public and political confidence in the educational system, the adverse change in the demand for teachers and the financial stringencies of economic recession. The size of the teaching force peaked in 1978–79 and then began to decline; by 1983 there were an estimated 30,000 teachers unemployed and the teacher associations had been forced on to the defensive. In relation to conditions of service new priorities had emerged: to procure curriculum-led staffing policies, to resist the resort to fixed-term contracts, to protect members affected by redeployment or reorganisation, to combat redundancy threats and to secure acceptable early retirement schemes. Meanwhile, despite the special Clegg award (1979) to check the rot, the real value of teachers' pay fell by almost 24 per cent during the years 1974–84. And following Callaghan's Ruskin College speech (1976) the teaching profession was subjected to growing pressure for 'accountability', especially regarding curricula concerns and standards of achievement in schools. The DES pressed the idea of a national curricula framework and the 1983 White Paper stressed the need for incompetent teachers to be dismissed. The LEAs were expected to wield a more positive influence in both directions. Gradually HM Inspectorate assumed a more robust approach and from 1983 its reports on individual schools were made public. In 1978 the Schools Council was reconstituted to end the teacher majorities on its main committees; four years later it was simply scrapped. The two smaller bodies scheduled to replace it, especially the nominated Secondary Examinations Council, will not afford the teaching profession an influence comparable to that exercised within the Schools Council 1964–82. The quest for more accountability also found expression in the Taylor Report (1977) for the reform of school managing and governing bodies; accordingly the 1980 Act provided for the election of parent representatives to the governing bodies of all maintained schools. Finally, despite their determined post-Plowden rearguard action to retain the discretionary use of corporal punishment in schools, the main teacher associations are now close to defeat on this issue. This follows upon its unilateral abolition by a growing minority of LEAs and, decisively, the 1982 European Court decision supporting the legal right of parents to refuse corporal punishment for their children.

Throughout its history the teaching profession has been sectionally divided and weakened by the existence of various separate organisations to represent the interests of teachers (see Chapter 11 for further details). In the post-war years inter-union rivalry helped to subvert the establishment of a Teachers' General Council which might have afforded the benefits of more professional autonomy and internal unity. Given the recent tide of events the continuing fragmentation of the profession has become an even worse handicap. Yet, despite the growing shift towards an all-graduate profession, there seems little or no hope of its being overcome in the foreseeable future.

10 The Development of Educational Administration

The considerable subject matter involved in this particular study, which does much to set the stage for the next chapter, may be conveniently divided into three major parts; the broad perspective, the development of central administration, and the development of local administration.

1 The Broad Perspective

There are a number of basic matters which can be covered at the outset to help place the details of the history of English educational administration into some sort of overall perspective.

(a) The growth of State involvement in educational development in England and Wales has passed through four main historical phases:

(i) the period of *State assistance*, 1833–70: during this phase the central government contented itself with the provision of a growing amount of financial assistance for the voluntary elementary schools and denominational training colleges, although such aid (especially after 1862) was increasingly tied to specific conditions and close inspection.

(ii) the period of *State intervention*, 1870–1900: finally convinced of the inability of the voluntary organisations to provide elementary schooling for the whole nation, the State intervened and through the agency of the School Boards at the local level proceeded directly to fill the gaps with elementary schools provided and maintained by moneys ultimately drawn solely from public sources.

(iii) the period of *State superintendence*, 1900–44: with the establishment of the Board of Education and the new LEAs at the turn of the century, the State's activity in the field of educational development at last became co-ordinated and cohesive and was decisively extended beyond the elementary sector. But the LEAs, established by the 1902 Act, enjoyed too wide a measure of freedom, especially in relation to other than elementary education, and the Board's limited powers of superintendence proved inadequate to ensure reasonably uniform and satisfactory standards of provision throughout the country.

(iv) the period of *State control and direction*, post-1944: the 1944 Act considerably strengthened the powers of the central government at the expense of the LEAs. The latter were categorically placed under the control and direction of the new Ministry of Education, so initiating a centralising process in the field of educational administration which subsequent developments have reflected and reinforced.

(b) The growth of central and local agencies for education formed part of the extension of government activity associated with the widening conception of the role of the State in English society. Before the twentieth century the concept of education as a comprehensive and cohesive service for the nation at large had not emerged; hence the State's involvement in nineteenth-century educational development was both piecemeal and uncoordinated in character.

(c) The foundations of the present administrative system as related to education were laid at the turn of the century by the establishment of the Board of Education and the new LEAs. Since then there has been a great increase in the work of the central and local agencies, together with associated changes in responsibilities and powers; but the essential structure based on the central-local partnership has remained virtually the same.

(d) The system of educational administration in England and Wales has always been primarily concerned with the problem of bringing the necessary financial support to educational development so as to ensure a sufficient supply of schools, teachers and equipment. The annual public expenditure on education has risen from a bare £20,000 in 1833 to a staggering sum of about £12,000 million in 1983; obviously the task of administering such moneys has gradually become a most complicated and onerous one. Critical to local influence on educational development is the percentage of the total cost borne by the local authorities; over most of this century the local rate contribution to the cost of State education has hovered between about one-half and two-fifths, with a long-term tendency to fall somewhat. Thus the proportion has always remained substantial enough to ensure for the LEAs a continuing influence on government educational policy.

(e) The extent to which educational administrators have exercised real influence upon curricula, examinations and teaching methods in schools and colleges has been subject to long-term change. For a whole generation the Revised Code (1862) served as a basis for developing this particular administrative role in very sharp form, but a strong reaction followed which was gradually to secure a remarkable degree of professional freedom for teachers in England and Wales. In the 1890s the 'payment by results' system was finally phased out and a decade later Morant's *Handbook of Suggestions* and revised instructions for the Inspectorate ushered in a new era for the elementary teacher; in the 1920s the Board of Education was prevailed upon to transfer its responsibility for the curriculum and examinations of the training colleges to professional bodies. Meanwhile in 1917, when the School Certificate examinations were launched, the Board delegated responsibility to the semi-independent Secondary School Examinations Council. In the first half of the twentieth century there was a sufficient consensus on what should be taught and how to allow the Board to withdraw its tentacles with confidence, although as a safety-valve the LEAs were empowered to exert control over the school curriculum by the 1944 Act. The disintegration of the former consensus before the advance of modern primary methods and secondary innovation partly explains the setting up within the Ministry of a Curriculum Study Group in 1962; but the professional reaction was hostile and two years later this unit was incorporated into the innocuous Schools Council with its teacher majority arrangements. And although the post-war role of both HM and local inspectors involved the maintenance of educational standards their inclination was to tread warily in face of the now strong tradition of professional freedom.

However, the last decade has seen a major reversal of the earlier twentieth century trend. The new governmental wisdom is that the whole related field of curriculum, examinations and standards is a basic societal concern for which teachers must be held accountable. It was the appearance of the APU (1974) for the monitoring of standards on a national basis which signalled the start of this shift. Then, following the prime-ministerial Ruskin College initiative and the ensuing national debate on education 1976–77, the field of curriculum and examinations became subject to growing central incursion. To re-establish some sort of common framework for five to sixteen primary and secondary schooling the DES produced the new guidelines contained in *The School Curriculum* (1981). Two years later the MSC entered the arena with its centrally-sponsored TVEI for the fourteen to eighteen age-range. Meanwhile the representative Schools Council was abolished, the projected system of sixteen-plus examinations was made conditional upon the formulation of 'national criteria' acceptable to the Secretary of State, and a nominated Secondary Examinations Council was established (1983) to oversee the future development of sixteen to eighteen secondary examinations. In 1984 Sir Keith Joseph launched the new GCSE for sixteen-plus examination purposes and also presented a plan for new AS courses to broaden the academic Sixth Form curriculum. Whilst the outcome of all these developments is unclear as yet, they cannot but adversely affect the professional autonomy of teachers. And, significantly, since the demise of the ATOs (1975), such developments at school level have been matched by the reversion of control over teacher training courses and awards to the central authority, with the 1983 White Paper intent upon establishing clear criteria for the review of existing arrangements by the Secretary of State. Clearly times have changed!

2 The Development of Central Administration

NINETEENTH CENTURY: With effect from 1833 the central government took a varying but growing interest in the different fields of educational development. But the growth was piecemeal and conformed to no overall strategy, resulting in the emergence of several quite distinct central government organs to deal with educational matters. The work of these different bodies is best considered in terms of the main educational fields in which they operated.

Elementary instruction naturally absorbed the overwhelming share of the central government's interest in education during the nineteenth century. The responsibility for shaping and implementing government policy in this field was successively undertaken by two bodies.

(a) The Committee of the Privy Council for Education 1839-56

The establishment of this body in 1839 was the natural outcome of the introduction of annual State building grants for elementary schools six years earlier, grants which, however, had been rather loosely administered by the Treasury on the recommendations of the National Society and the British and Foreign School Society. The purpose of the new Committee was to secure more effective control over the use of the public money provided by Parliament and so justify the growth of State aid to elementary education. The Committee's constitution was somewhat peculiar: established by royal prerogative so as to avoid the religious difficulty, the Committee was not directly responsible to Parliament from whence it received its funds. The Committee was composed of four members (the Lord President, the Lord Privy Seal, the Chancellor of the Exchequer and the Home Secretary) all of whom sat in their capacity as Queen's Privy Councillors. It met only from time to time and its routine work depended very largely upon a full-time Secretary, who was responsible to, but not a member of, the Committee. Inspired by its first Secretary, Dr James Kay (later Kay-Shuttleworth), the Committee was responsible for some outstanding achievements:

(i) the development of a system of specific central grants as an effective administrative means of encouraging and shaping the growth of elementary education. The original building grants were gradually supplemented by various other grants designed to help defray current as distinct from capital costs; the ultimate result of this trend was the introduction of capitation grants in the mid-1850s. The Committee also made the grants available to bodies other than the National and British societies; the Methodist Church and the Catholic Poor School Committee became important beneficiaries. Meanwhile the Parliamentary grant for elementary education rose from £30,000 in 1839 to £369,000 in 1855.

(ii) the application of pressure upon the Anglican Church to accept the operation of a conscience clause in their grant-aided elementary schools. By the 1850s this policy was being made to stick and so presaged one of the important provisions of the 1870 Act.

(iii) the establishment of a central administrative machine capable of coping with the growing responsibilities and work load of the new agency. Kay-Shuttleworth's central office developed steadily so that by 1855 his successor had a staff of forty serving him at Whitehall. Meanwhile the central office had developed a professional arm in the shape of HM Inspectorate; growing from the original pair (one for the Anglican and one for the Nonconformist schools) appointed in 1839, this body was composed of some thirty-odd inspectors by the mid-1850s, thus enabling the Committee to maintain closer contact with the grant-aided schools.

(iv) the introduction of the pupil-teacher system and the associated development of the denominational training colleges. Although the Committee failed to realise the establishment of a State normal school as suggested in its original terms of reference, it did set up and generously subsidise the system which was to provide the country with the great bulk of its elementary teachers down to the end of the century. Through its developing control of college curricula and certification the Committee underpinned the emergence of the first qualified elementary teachers.

(b) The Education Department 1856–1900

The establishment of this body arose out of the mounting Parliamentary criticism of the non-statutory Committee of Council which was not responsible to the House of Commons in spite of its growing demands on the public purse. Accordingly the Committee was reconstituted by statutory means: the post of Vice-President of the Committee of the Privy Council was created, the holder of this post being responsible to Parliament for the work and policy of a newly-formed Education Department. The former Secretary to the Committee now became Permanent Secretary to the new executive Department of State. For the rest of the century the Education Department formulated and implemented State policy in the field of elementary education; although the old Committee of Council continued to accept ultimate responsibility, the critical influence was that wielded by various individuals through the offices of Vice-President and Permanent Secretary.

In considering the work and influence of the Education Department during the period of its existence a number of striking points emerge.

(i) The Department came to exercise close control over the development of elementary education. Before 1856 the Committee had already assumed a position of immense potential power through its development of the specific grant system and its superintendence of the training of teachers. From 1860 the new Education Department gave much sharper expression to central influence and power by the publication of an annual Elementary Code of Regulations which laid down the conditions of the receipt of grant by voluntary and (later) Board schools as well as training colleges. This form of close control, affecting the curriculum, teaching methods and internal organisation of the institutions concerned, reached its height in Robert Lowe's Revised Code (1862) and was only very gradually relaxed during the subsequent 'payment by results' era. As explained in an earlier chapter, the results of such control were extremely double-edged, but on balance probably did more harm than good.

(ii) The 1870 Act greatly increased the importance of the Education Department. Not only was the annual Code given statutory force, but many new functions and powers arose from the appearance of the School Boards. As the new local authorities were untried and without precedent, the balance of power was heavily weighted in favour of the central body. The initial declaration of deficiency and the subsequent establishment of a Board in any school district was the responsibility of the Department. The raising of loans, the compulsory purchase of land for school building and the passage of attendance by-laws by the School Boards were all subject to the approval of the officials of the Education Department. The central body was even given the power to dissolve and replace any School Board which it considered to be failing in its duty and this possibility was taken advantage of on a significant number of occasions.

(iii) The Education Department bore a growing administrative burden, resultant of having to deal directly and separately with over 2,500

School Boards, nearly 800 School Attendance Committees and some 14,000-odd voluntary managing bodies. The passing of the 1870 Act brought a particularly abrupt and large increase in the Department's work load. By the close of the century the permanent staff at Whitehall numbered almost 300, whilst HM Inspectorate had expanded to about 350 members. To increase the efficiency of its operation the Inspectorate had been reorganised on a territorial basis; this was facilitated by the abandonment after 1870 of the inspection of religious instruction so that any inspector could visit both Board and voluntary schools.

(iv) Given the failure of the 1870 Act to define the term 'elementary', the Education Department became party to the development of higher-grade schools and advanced evening classes by the larger School Boards. Liberal governments were happy that the Department should encourage such developments and Sir George Kekewich, its Permanent Secretary 1890–1900, was particularly well-disposed towards them. The introduction of Standard VII in 1882 raised the general level of work in the elementary schools and thus assisted higher-grade experiment; the 1893 Code altered the regulations governing evening classes in a way that facilitated the development of more advanced work by the School Boards. Both these departures were the responsibility of the Education Department and the consequent blurring of the limits of its jurisdiction added to the growing administrative confusion at the centre.

Technical and commercial instruction was another field in which the State interested itself from a fairly early date. The beginnings may be traced back to 1836, but the interest did not assume significant proportions until after the Great Exhibition of 1851. To promote the teaching of science and arts subjects of direct utility to industry and commerce, the Department of Science and Art 1853–1900 was established under the auspices of the Board of Trade. Although placed under the jurisdiction of the Committee of Council and its Vice-President three years later, this new body managed to maintain a virtually independent existence down to the end of the century. Gradually the Department of Science and Art not only emerged as the central authority for technical and commercial education, but as such began to take a growing interest in the secondary field. Any brief consideration of the administrative nature and influence of this Department must include mention of the following noteworthy points.

(a) With effect from 1859 the Department of Science and Art operated a progressively refined 'payment by results' system which dispensed central grants to those institutions, classes and teachers successfully entering candidates for the Department's annual examinations. By the

1890s over 100,000 students were studying for these every year. The annual expenditure of the Department rose from £57,000 to over £770,000, its permanent staff at South Kensington expanded ten-fold and it developed its own branch of HM Inspectorate.

(b) In 1872 the Department introduced a special grant for organised science schools or classes which committed themselves to a three-year scientific and technical course absorbing at least 40 per cent of the available teaching time. By 1897 there were many higher-grade schools and even some endowed grammar schools taking advantage of this financial opportunity.

(c) The Department placed an increasingly wide and liberal interpretation on its initial terms of reference. The range of subjects eligible for examination grants was gradually broadened from six to twenty-five, so that ultimately all secondary school subjects (excepting Classics) were able to benefit from the Department's support. This was another means by which it was rendering some financial assistance to the endowed grammar schools by the close of the century.

(d) Following the Technical Instruction Act (1889), the Department of Science and Art considerably increased its influence as it became responsible for advising the County and County Borough Councils upon the questions of which subjects and institutions were suitable for 'technical' rate-aid. The influence wielded by the Department in this direction was again liberal in character, encouraging county interest in their local endowed grammar schools.

In spite of the considerable achievements of the Science and Art Department, its continued existence was condemned by the Bryce Report (1895); it was seen as a too specialised and independent body which required absorption into a single central authority for education.

Secondary education was a field in relation to which State intervention was threatened rather than realised during the nineteenth century. Following the Taunton Report (1868), the Endowed Schools Commission (1869–73) and the Charity Commission (1874–1900) acted as central government agencies charged with the responsibility of improving secondary provision by the redistribution of endowments and the reform of trust deeds and governing bodies. Although their powers were strictly limited to these pseudo-judicial functions, it seems that the revival of the endowed grammar schools owed much to these government commissioners. But the constitutional position of the Charity Commission was the most anomalous and unsatisfactory of all; it had no political head and its relationship to the other two departments lacked any sort of definition. Worst of all, the Charity Commission had no brief or means to develop secondary education beyond that sector supported by endowments. It was therefore never in a position to realise the ambitious hopes expressed in the Taunton Report or to instrument the prosposals of the Bryce Commission (1895).

TWENTIETH CENTURY: The establishment and development of a single and effective central authority for State activity in all sectors of education is the outstanding achievement of the twentieth century. This historical process centred upon the foundation and work of three bodies.

(a)   The Board of Education 1900–44

Following the Bryce Report, which demanded the rationalisation of central administration, the 1899 Act created the new Board of Education by merging the Education Department, the Science and Art Department and the Charity Commission into a single body. It also established a Consultative Committee to advise the Board on matters referred to it. The President of the Board and his Parliamentary Secretary were to be the political heads of the new government department; unfortunately the President was accorded the salary and status of a junior minister rather than a full Secretary of State. The Board's permanent staff were all to be placed under a single Secretary, of which the first was the able, energetic Robert Morant. Under the Act the Board of Education was given the responsibility for the 'superintendence' of educational matters in England and Wales, but the nature of this particular role and the powers required to exercise it were not clarified. The actual history of the Board of Education not only illuminates the nature of its development but also displays an interesting balance of strengths and weaknesses.

  (i) The Board was always beset by the double disadvantage of the low ministerial status of its President and the extreme vagueness of its superintendence role and powers. Looked upon as a stepping stone to higher office or a retreat for the mediocre, the Presidency was held by no fewer than nineteen politicians in forty-four years; only four of these can be held to have served education with any distinction. Meanwhile the 1902 Act had given the initiative for the development of other than elementary education to the new Part II LEAs. The 1918 Act attempted to bolster the power of the Board by giving it the statutory right to require the submission of development schemes by Part II LEAs, but the post-war economic difficulties and the shelving of so many of the Act's provisions robbed this of its potential significance. Gradually the weakness of the Board's position was recognised as a serious shortcoming in relation to the full implementation of national policy and the realisation of minimal standards of provision across the whole of England and Wales.

(ii) In spite of these handicaps, and inside a single decade, the genius of Morant built the Board into an effective government department capable of shaping national policy and leading the LEAs forward. He realised that, given vigorous leadership and its strong financial influence, the Board could make its presence felt sharply. Internally the Board was organised into elementary, secondary and technological branches; a little later Morant added the medical, legal and finance branches to develop further the specialist structure. In 1907 a separate Welsh Department was created. A year later the Board became a physical entity when the technological branch finally left South Kensington for Whitehall. Meanwhile the forging of the vital partnership between the new central and local authorities for education went rapidly ahead. Whatever its early shortcomings, this was the base upon which the conception and quality of State education was broadened and improved in the period before the Second World War.

(iii) The work of H.A.L. Fisher, President of the Board 1916–22, resulted in the further development of the central machinery and the basis of partnership at the close of the First World War. The 1918 Act introduced the percentage grant system (to replace the previous multiplicity of fixed and separate grants) and the development scheme arrangements which facilitated the growth of a closer and more constructive relationship between the Board and the LEAs. Fisher's establishment of the Burnham Committee and his concern for the status of teachers prepared the way for their recognition as the third vital partner in English education. Within the Board of Education the demands of the new Act necessitated some restructuring of its organisation. The specialist branches were overlaid by a territorial organisational pattern to allow the Board to deal more efficiently with the Part II LEAs whose responsibilities ranged across the whole educational board; somewhat later the organisation of HM Inspectorate, significantly enlarged since 1902, was brought into line with this. The uneasy compromise continued until 1944 when much more thorough-going and unified territorial arrangements were introduced.

(b) The Ministry of Education 1944–64

The 1944 Act strengthened the central authority by replacing the old Board, with its vague superintendence role, by a new Ministry of Education charged with the duty of promoting the education of the people and of controlling and directing the LEAs to that end. The Act provided the Minister

with the means of ensuring that the LEAs met its requirements and contributed effectively to the execution of national policy; it was recognised that
education, though locally administered, is a national concern and consequently the powers of the central agency must be paramount. Section 62
made it the Minister's direct responsibility to secure sufficient facilities for
the training of teachers and the LEAs were required to contribute to that end
at his direction. The clear intention of the Act was to put the new Ministry of
Education firmly in charge of the educational enterprise in England and
Wales. The shift in the balance of power was justified in terms of the serious
pre-war inequalities of educational provision and opportunity between
different areas: in the post-war years the stronger hand of the central
authority helped to reduce the extent of such variations.

Although the tradition of consultation and co-operation between partners,
painstakingly developed by the old Board of Education, certainly held firm
during the life of the Ministry, the centralising potential of Butler's Act
became plain. From the start the Ministry's control of capital spending on
educational buildings was strict and complete. The need for LEAs to submit
development plans for Ministry approval and review provided a routine
basis for the exercise of central influence upon the shape of provision; Conservative governments 1951–64 were able to stifle the rise of comprehensive
secondary schooling without too much difficulty. After the war the Ministry
issued various sets of regulations to clarify the 1944 Act's broad provisions;
such regulations had mandatory force and afforded a means of more detailed
control from the centre. Central government influence was further
strengthened by the 1958 Local Government Act which replaced the specific percentage grant for education by a general fixed grant to cover all
locally administered services. Henceforth central grant aid towards such
recurrent expenditure was to be fixed and determined in advance; local
authorities were required to finance the rest from the rates, thus securing the
Exchequer from the uncertainties of the percentage arrangements that had
ruled for forty years. Although the Ministry of Education was relieved of the
growing financial pressure exerted by its local partners, the new system
weakened its position in certain respects. The Ministry ceased to be the
direct paymaster of the local authorities for educational spending; instead
the authorities received a general grant which it was the task of the Ministry
of Local Government (albeit in consultation with other ministries) to work
out. And the demise of earmarked moneys for various educational purposes
reduced the Ministry's capacity to shape developments by financial means.

Generally speaking, the Ministry of Education was very much content to
abide by the spirit of the 1944 Act and treat the LEAs and the teachers as real
partners. Over twenty years it made use of the Central Advisory Councils,
established new National Advisory Councils and other representative edu-

cational bodies – and even took considerable notice of them. It devolved a great deal of responsibility: to the ATOs for teacher training, to the teachers for the school curriculum, to other bodies for external examinations, and to an unshackled Burnham Committee for teachers' salaries. The fate of the Ministry's Curriculum Study Group 1962–4 was indicative of a central authority still very sensitive to the views of its partners. HM Inspectorate was encouraged to emphasise its advisory and inter-linking roles rather than its traditional function. In all the Ministry's conduct of affairs contributed to a climate in which co-operation, consultation and mutual confidence imbued the workings of the educational partnership and much progress was made at 'ground level'.

(c) The Department of Education and Science 1964

Although successive governments have paid the usual lip-service to the tradition of educational partnership, since 1964 there had been a general drift towards blatant centralisation. This inexorable process, a leading feature of the past decade, has been associated with a number of signal developments:

(i)   the establishment of the DES itself. This new agency assumed the functions of the former Ministry of Education and Ministry of Science and was headed by a Secretary of State enjoying high status. The new super-Ministry was seen as a means of exercising closer supervision of university funding and of ensuring more integration in the field of higher education.

(ii) the rise of the binary system (from 1965) which eroded the influence of the individual LEA upon its post-secondary provision. This became linked (from 1973) with the reorganisation and contraction of teacher training, an operation conducted largely at the dictation of the DES.

(iii) the reorganisation of secondary schooling in response to the comprehensive argument or, more recently, falling rolls. Here the record is one of meddlesome central interference rather than helpful overall direction. Comprehensive secondary reorganisation became a veritable political football as central government issued various alternating Circulars, introduced and then repealed compulsive legislation. And local plans to deal with falling secondary rolls have been bedevilled by DES ambivalence over the Sixth Form/tertiary college solution.

(iv) the revival of direct central government interest in school curricula, examinations and standards of work. Since 1980 the Secretary of State has formulated new guidelines for the five to sixteen school curriculum, has personally intervened in the interminable business of producing a new system of sixteen-plus examining and has now advanced new proposals for the broadening of academic Sixth Form courses. The Schools Council has fallen victim to his unilateral decision to scrap it and a new Secondary Examinations Council nominated by the Secretary of State has been established. Finally, HM Inspectorate has been urged to resume its 'watchdog' role and its reports on individual schools are now made public.

(v) the modification of the Burnham negotiating arrangements (1965) to afford the DES more influence upon teachers' pay settlements. This has inhibited real negotiations over salaries between the LEAs and teachers and has encouraged the teachers to keep the related matter of conditions of service outside of Burnham.

(vi) the passage of the 1980 Local Government Act with its penalties for local authorities which exceed the annual spending limits laid down by the Department of the Environment. This has subjected the LEAs to unprecedented financial control which the even sterner 1984 rate-capping legislation threatens to develop into a veritable strait-jacket. Such measures tend to reduce the LEAs to mere agents of the central authority.

Amidst the developing process of centralisation the DES seems to have lost its way. Even when falling rolls have presented a real opportunity to improve the quality of the educational service the DES has been largely preoccupied with administrative strategies, organisational forms and logistical economies. The growing concentration of power at the centre has not only undermined the long-established partnership in English education but has, paradoxically, weakened thereby the DES' own position in the wider government framework – leaving it vulnerable to the designs of the MSC and other extra-educational interests. And its commitment to the new Rate Support Grant arrangements designed to restrict educational spending is in sharp conflict with its prime responsibility to safeguard the level and quality of provision. Only when the DES returns to the concept and practice of partnership and re-establishes itself as the chief proponent of educational investment and advance will its stature and influence undergo a resurgence. But such an eventuality is in turn dependent upon the degree of commitment and level of priority accorded to the statutory system of education by its political masters.

3 The Development of Local Administration

NINETEENTH CENTURY: Once it became involved, the central government was for many years content to further its growing educational commitment by direct contact with the schools and other institutions receiving State financial assistance. However, the growth of grant-aided elementary and technical education and the urge to expand it further ultimately made it necessary for the central government departments to reduce their administrative burden by the introduction of local agencies for State education. This could have been done by instituting a centralised system along Prussian or French lines, whereby the local agencies would have been run by government officials operating in the provinces. The 1870 Act rejected such a solution in favour of the involvement of local finance and responsibility in educational development in England and Wales. Out of this basic strategy, which for better or for worse has been followed ever since, there arose the first local education authorities.

(a)   The School Boards 1870–1902

These were established under the 1870 Act in those deficiency areas where the voluntary organisations failed to meet the total need for elementary school places. Thus the 2,568 School Boards which gradually came into existence did not cover the whole country, nor were they in any way responsible for the denominational schools existing in their areas. Their job was to fill the gaps with public elementary schools, which they would thereafter administer and help to maintain. The School Boards were *ad hoc* bodies in that their responsibilities were strictly limited to the field of rate-aided elementary education in their own areas. They consisted of from five to fifteen members, varying according to the size of the population of the school district concerned. The School Boards were directly elected by the ratepayers through a cumulative voting system designed to ensure the representation of religious minorities. Under the 1870 Act the School Boards enjoyed a wide range of powers:

(i)   to provide and maintain public elementary schools on the basis of central grants, parental fees and rate-aid. The latter could be obtained on annual demand from the local rating authorities which were initially the municipal borough corporations and the civil parishes; thus the School Boards used rate moneys without having the onerous responsibility of raising them.

(ii)   to make attendance compulsory between five and thirteen years through the by-laws, but subject to requirements laid down by the Education Department. The detailed nature of this power changed as a result of later legislation but was retained in substance. In areas where no School Board existed, School Attendance Committees were established for the purpose of framing and enforcing appropriate by-laws.

(iii) to decide for or against religious worship and instruction in the Board
       schools, though subject to the Cowper-Temple and conscience clauses
       of the Act. Whilst it was usual for a School Board to opt for undenomi-
       national religious worship and instruction, a very tiny minority chose
       the purely secular alternative.
(iv) to remit the fees of necessitous children attending either Board or deno-
      minational schools in the area concerned. The power of remission in
      relation to poor children attending church schools was lost in 1876 and
      fifteen years later the Boards were in any case required to provide free
      elementary education on demand.
(v) to appoint their own full-time salaried officials and to delegate powers
     of control over individual schools to a body of managers. Clerk to the
     School Board was a normal appointment and from this office is des-
     cended the Chief Education Officer of today. But some of the larger
     Boards appointed local inspectors as well. Only London and Liverpool
     seem to have taken much advantage of the power to set up managing
     bodies.

Within the confused framework of local educational administration the
School Boards aroused opposition and criticism. The denominational
interests disliked them as the source of rate-aided competition. The
endowed grammar school governing bodies objected to the development of
the higher-grade elementary schools. Some of the new Technical Instruction
Committees did not take too kindly to the provision of advanced evening
work by certain Boards. Ratepayers were only too ready to accuse the more
progressive Boards of extravagance and irresponsibility in the use of public
money. Many of the small rural School Boards were palpably inefficient.
Because their use of the rates to develop higher-grade and advanced studies
was always questionable in law, the School Boards became increasingly
vulnerable and were finally toppled by their enemies at the turn of the
century. But meanwhile they had made universal elementary education a
reality and the larger, more progressive Boards had set an example of dedicated public service which could not be lost upon the new LEAs.

(b)   The Technical Instruction Committees 1889–1902

Following the Local Government Act of 1888, which introduced the
modern system of multi-purpose local authorities, these committees
emerged as a result of two additional measures. Firstly, the 1889 Technical
Instruction Act empowered the new County and County Borough Councils
to raise a 1d rate to provide or support technical education. The councils
were allowed to establish Technical Instruction Committees, wholly or

partly drawn from council members, to undertake the responsibility. Secondly, the 1890 Local Taxation (Customs and Excise) Act made the proceeds of an increased duty on beer and spirits available to the councils, with the recommendation that it be used to promote technical education. Thus the Technical Instruction Committees were able to utilise the so-called 'whisky money' for developing their work.

Although this legislation was only permissive, the majority of County and County Borough Councils established Technical Instruction Committees and by 1900 they were dispensing almost £1 million in aid of technical education. In any study of the short history of these committees a number of points are particularly noteworthy.

(i)   There were wide variations in the degree of autonomy enjoyed by the Technical Instruction Committees and their full-time Directors or Secretaries. Some councils (e.g. London) gave them almost a free hand, whilst others (e.g. Manchester) limited their role to a strictly advisory one; overall the arrangements approximated to the latter rather than the former position.

(ii) At first many Technical Instruction Committees placed a narrow interpretation upon technical education and focused their energies on the provision of instruction which met the needs of local industry and business. Later a much wider interpretation emerged, once experience had shown a sound secondary education to be the necessary foundation for advanced technical instruction. Such a development was encouraged by the policy and example of the central Department of Science and Art. Many Technical Instruction Committees granted aid to local secondary schools, obtaining representation on their governing bodies and even the right of inspection, and thereby began to influence their curricula, examinations and the like. The generous assistance received by a large number of endowed grammar schools from the London Technical Education Board was tied to the reciprocal provision of many scholarship places open to talent. Thus by 1900 many County and County Borough Councils had in practice become authorities for secondary as well as technical education.

(iii) The Technical Instruction Committees were of great potential significance because they were the offspring of the multi-purpose councils, which were thus able to prove themselves in the field of local educational administration, albeit in what seemed a narrow sector. But the widening of their role by the committees went far towards anticipating the Part II LEAs of the 1902 Act.

By the close of the nineteenth century the administrative framework at the local level was even more confused than at the centre. The School Boards, the School Attendance Committees, the Technical Instruction Committees, the voluntary school managers and the governing bodies of the endowed grammar schools ploughed their supposedly separate but over-lapping furrows, with conflict and disharmony the order of the day. In 1895 the Bryce Report made it clear that the proper development of secondary education was contingent upon the rationalisation of local educational administration.

TWENTIETH CENTURY: The development of a single type of local authority for all fields of State education is the outstanding achievement of this period. It has been associated with an increasing official concern to concentrate local responsibility for education in the hands of fewer and larger authorities. This historical process has taken place as a result of and within the framework of certain outstanding legislative enactments.

(a)   The 1902 Education Act

As the main architect of this measure, Morant aimed at a unified structure of local educational administration based on the multi-purpose authorities established in 1888, dismissing the *ad hoc* approach to rationalisation as an inferior alternative. As already shown to some extent in Chapter 5, the 1902 Act included many far-reaching administrative provisions.

(i)   The existing local agencies were replaced by three hundred and eighteen new LEAs. The majority of these were Part III LEAs (i.e. populous municipal boroughs and urban districts) charged with responsibility in their areas for elementary education only. The rest were Part II LEAs which were also given powers for the development of 'other than elementary' education in their areas; these were the County and County Borough Councils which had previously given rise to the Technical Instruction Committees. Both types of authority were to delegate all except their financial powers to local education committees, the majority of members to be drawn from or nominated by the parent council; but the Act also required the co-option of professional people such as were representative of the various sectors of education. It was made possible for these committees to operate through a system of sub-committees and the Part II LEAs in particular took full advantage of this.

(ii)   The new LEAs were given many administrative responsibilities. They were charged with the financial support and development of the former Board and voluntary elementary schools; the latter now received rate-aid in respect of their current costs, but were incorporated into the unified administrative framework with one-third of their managers being appointed by the LEA. The Part II LEAs were required (as far as they thought desirable) to develop secondary education, technical education and teacher training facilities and to take responsibility for the co-ordination of all forms of education. Subsequent legislation provided for the development of the School Medical Service by all the LEAs and empowered them to introduce school meals.

(iii) The 1902 Act did not require the existence of a managing or governing body for all schools within the statutory system. Naturally the voluntary schools had managers, with a denominational majority to safeguard their special position, details of which have already been described. Non-provided secondary schools receiving financial support from the Part II LEAs all had their governing bodies on which the benefactor was suitably represented. But the establishment of managing or governing bodies for the provided schools was very largely a matter for the discretion of the local education committees; generally speaking the county grammar schools were so privileged whereas the provided elementary schools were not.

Although the 1902 Act completed the foundations of a national system of educational administration, the subsequent history of the new LEAs showed the arrangements to suffer from certain serious weaknesses.

(i) The LEAs were left with too much discretion, especially in relation to the permissive nature of their powers in respect of other than elementary education. The result was considerable variation in the attitudes and performances of the LEAs on such matters as secondary development, Hadow re-organisation, teacher training, technical and adult education, and teachers' pay.

(ii) The existence of so many Part III LEAs made for greater expense and produced a serious administrative dichotomy in the county areas, which consequently included numerous enclaves where elementary education was beyond the jurisdiction of the County (Part II) LEA. This arrangement, born of political expediency rather than administrative logic, gave rise to a number of difficulties. The organisation and co-ordination of scholarship examinations for the transfer of Part III elementary pupils to Part II grammar schools was not easy from the outset; later on the development of selective central schools by some Part III LEAs tended to exacerbate the situation. The execution of Hadow re-organisation and the aspiration towards parity of esteem for the various secondary schools were not helped by the distinction between the two types of LEA. Nor did the organisation and development of evening class work benefit; such work was the financial and administrative responsibility of the Part II LEAs, but very often the buildings and the teachers were supplied by the Part III LEAs with their separate accounts. Such problems affected, to a greater or lesser extent, over two-thirds of the county areas. The County Borough LEAs (Part II) were, of course, quite unaffected, controlling both elementary and other than elementary education throughout their respective areas.

(b) The 1944 Education Act

This did much to increase the importance and improve the effectiveness of local educational administration, though at the price of some shift in the balance of power towards the central government. As the most important provisions affecting the LEAs have already been dealt with at length in Chapter 7, a short recapitulation must suffice. The Part III LEAs were abolished, leaving the County and County Borough Councils with sole local responsibility for education. Their actual responsibilities were both extended and more strictly defined and they were required to organise provision in consecutive primary, secondary and further stages. They were to ensure that each and every school under their control had a properly constituted managing or governing body. The modification of the dual system (in terms of the arrangements for the controlled, aided and special agreement categories) required the LEAs to extend increased financial aid to, and to readjust their relationship with, the voluntary schools. They were made responsible for ensuring the provision of compulsory religious worship and instruction in their schools. They were required to contribute to the development of teacher training facilities and to pay the Burnham salary scales. The Fisher percentage grant system was retained, but the exact formula was revised in favour of the LEAs. They were empowered to make grants for further study beyond the school-leaving age. The Act also provided for the establishment of local education committees through which the LEAs were to discharge all their non-financial educational functions; the continuance of work through sub-committees was allowed for as well. A new departure was the requirement that all LEAs must appoint a Chief Education Officer, the actual appointment made being subject to the approval of the Ministry.

During the period 1944–71 there were a number of developments which affected the nature and growth of post-war local educational administration.

(i) The immediate post-war years witnessed the establishment of a large number of divisional executives. In order to relate educational development to local circumstances in the large county areas, the 1944 Act allowed for (at the Minister's discretion) schemes of divisional administration. The schemes, drawn up by the County LEA and approved by the Minister, were to divide the county area into smaller administrative units and equip each of them with a divisional executive for the delegation of functions in respect of primary and secondary education. These executives were not directly elected bodies, being composed of County representatives, the nominees of the urban and rural district councils and other co-opted members. They were graced by their own divisional education officers. Under such schemes large municipal boroughs or urban districts (i.e. those with over 60,000 people or 7,000 pupils in 1939) could qualify for the status of excepted districts. Subject to consultation with the County LEA and the Minister's approval, such towns could make their own schemes which might include the additional delegation of functions related to further education. In their case the local elected council became the divisional executive. Altogether some two hundred divisional executives were set up, including over forty excepted districts, to complicate the structure of local educational administration. Whilst they served as sources of local influence upon educational development, the divisional executives tended to raise the cost and reduce the pace of administration in the county areas.

(ii) The Local Government Act of 1958 introduced the Rate Support Grant arrangement by which the central government gave a general fixed grant to each local authority towards the annual cost of all its services. The abandonment of earmarked percentage grants for education had two significant effects. It inevitably weakened the position of the local education committees, faced as they were with a new need to argue for their fair share of the Rate Support Grant. And, as far as it can be estimated, it seems that during the 1960s the new system resulted in a significant rise in the proportion of the total educational bill borne by the LEAs.

(iii) The London Government Act of 1963 changed the face of local educational administration in the greater metropolitan area. The measure abolished the London and Middlesex County Councils and introduced a two-tier system of local government consisting of the Greater London Council and the councils of the various inner and outer metropolitan boroughs. The outcome for educational administration was interesting as well as significant. The twenty outer London boroughs were given full status as LEAs. But to maintain the continuity of educational development in central London, a special committee of the Greater London Council was given responsibility for education throughout that area. The *ad hoc* Inner London Education Authority, serving a population of almost four millions, was the result. In consequence of these new arrangements the total number of LEAs in England and Wales rose to one hundred and sixty-four.

Given the post-war shift in the balance of power it was important that the LEAs should be able to speak with one voice in the national forum and so maximise their influence upon policy and events. This need was more than amply met by the Association of Education Committees (AEC). In 1945, with forty years of experience behind it, this body finally came to include all the local education committees of England and Wales thus traversing the separate County Councils' Association and Association of Municipal Corporations which represented the parent bodies. Whilst the AEC held annual and other general meetings, the major working responsibility fell upon the Executive Committee and its permanent staff in London. Appointing Sir William Alexander as its full-time Secretary in 1945 the AEC found a man of real calibre and commitment to education who was to lead it successfully for over a quarter of a century. By such means the AEC undertook a number of important functions: it consulted with the Ministry, provided for representation on various national bodies (e.g. Burnham and the Schools Council), submitted evidence in response to important inquiries (e.g. Plowden and James) and provided an advisory service for individual LEAs. It also encouraged its member committees to adopt national standards in regard to discretionary awards and allowances, capitation grants, ancillary assistance and other matters. There is no doubt that the AEC wielded a very considerable and wholesome influence within the prevailing framework of educational partnership 1944–72.

(c)   The 1972 Local Government Act

By the 1960s it was increasingly felt that the organisational structure and geographical pattern of English local government needed to be radically reformed if it was to satisfy current and future needs. In the field of education there emerged a strong body of opinion that condemned the existence of so many different and small LEAs and of the divisional administration arrangements in county areas. It was argued that 'bigger and better' LEAs were the answer to the problem of promoting greater administrative and educational efficiency, especially in the special and post-secondary sectors. Both the DES and HM Inspectorate presented such a viewpoint to the Redcliffe-Maud Commission when it reported (1969) to the government on the whole subject of local government reform. In revised form the recommendations of the Maud Report served as the basis for actual legislation three years later. The provisions of the 1972 Local Government Act were of far-reaching significance for local educational administration.

(i) Outside Greater London (which was unaffected) the total number of English and Welsh LEAs was reduced from one hundred and forty-three to eighty-three. A few of the old county authorities (e.g. Rutland, Westmorland and Huntingdonshire) were absorbed into larger local government units. Almost fifty of the existing county boroughs lost their former control of education as the result of absorption. The divisional executives and excepted districts were swept away. The total result was markedly to increase the average size of LEAs and to abandon the requirement that they should delegate some of their functions in certain areas to minor representative bodies.

(ii) In the great conurbations (West Midlands, Greater Manchester, Merseyside, West Yorkshire, South Yorkshire and Tyneside) a two-tier system of six metropolitan areas divided into thirty-six metropolitan districts was introduced. Local responsibility for education was devolved upon the latter rather than the former, although many critics insisted that some of the metropolitan districts were too small to develop satisfactorily the full range of educational services.

(iii) The rest of the country was covered by a two-tier system of forty-seven counties divided into approaching three hundred districts. But responsibility for education was lodged with the large county authorities although for administrative convenience and to offset the danger of remoteness they were allowed to operate through area offices.

(iv) The new LEAs still had to discharge all their non-financial educational functions through the established mechanism of statutory local education committees, but they could now appoint Chief Education Officers without reference to the central Department. The existing Rate Support Grant system for the financing of local educational expenditure remained unchanged.

As the arrangements took effect (1974) it was claimed that they would contribute to an improvement in the range and quality of local educational provision. It is difficult to substantiate that this has been the case and from some quarters there is a call for a reversion to smaller local government units. Certainly there is the view that many of the old County Boroughs displayed a greater commitment to education than some of the larger County authorities which absorbed them. And in response to the Bains report (1972) many of the new authorities turned to the corporate management of their wide-ranging responsibilities; the result has been to weaken the position of the local education committees and Chief Education Officers subjected to such caucus control. Another unhappy result of reorganisation was the demise of the AEC which gave way to the Council of Local Education Authorities (CLEA). This Council, based on equal representation from the new Association of County Councils and Association of Metropolitan Authorities, was subject to its decisions receiving the approval of its parent bodies; as such it was not well designed to provide the LEAs with the single and united voice so badly needed in subsequent years.

In the wake of reorganisation an official inquiry was mounted into the management and government of maintained primary and secondary schools. The resultant Taylor Report (1977), *A New Partnership for Our Schools*, was critical of the existing arrangements and made radical proposals for reform. Its leading recommendations were that each school should have its own governing body composed of equal numbers of representatives of the LEA, the school staff, the parents of school pupils and the local community at large; that real power be delegated to governing bodies so that the whole range of school activity (including curriculum and finance) would be open to their influence; that governors undergo a course of training provided by each LEA. Inevitably the report was regarded as a threat by the LEAs whilst the NUT saw it as a busybodies' charter. But strong support from parental interests determined the government to proceed – albeit with caution. The 1980 Education Act gave muted expression to some of the Taylor proposals: all schools were to have their own individual governing bodies (except that two primary schools could have one in common) and each governing body was to include elected parent and teacher governors with the headteacher as an *ex officio* member. But the powers of governing bodies and their basic relation to the LEA as established by the 1944 Act remained unchanged. Thus the total outcome has been less than weighty. Whilst the interest of many governing bodies in their schools has been reactivated, their powers are no greater and the majority of governors are still political nominees.

(d)   The Local Government Planning and Land Act 1980

From 1975 central government policies induced a decline in real educational expenditure and a rise in the share borne by the local rates. This Act introduced a new Rate Support Grant formula designed to predetermine how much a local authority should spend on its various services. To exceed the annual total amount 'allowed' by the Department of the Environment incurs penalties in respect of the succeeding allocation. With educational spending accounting for two-thirds of their expenditure this measure subjected the LEAs to unprecedented constraints and further reduced the resources available for the schools and the rest of the statutory system. In 1982 the deteriorating situation was substantiated by a report of HM Inspectorate covering the ninety-six English LEAs; it assessed their individual levels of provision in respect of teaching staff, non-teaching personnel, in-service training, induction, advisory services, premises and capitation allowances to find that in only five cases was the provision 'satisfactory or better' under *all* the major resource headings. And 'satisfactory' was defined in terms of the duty laid upon LEAs by Section 8 of the 1944 Act, with the possible implication that in some areas provision might have fallen below legal requirements. Reference to the widespread incidence of parental help for the purchase of such basic school items as books and materials gave further grounds for alarm. Not surprisingly the Inspectorate also found that the differential gaps in the level of provision between individual LEAs was widening. But to the dismay of most local education committees the Secretary of State's response was simply to deny that there is any marked relationship between spending and standards.

In the quarter century following the 1944 Act the LEAs played a dual role. Their basic function or 'static' role was to provide and administer the essential resources (human and material) vital to the everyday functioning of their schools and other educational institutions. But beyond this they developed a 'dynamic' role which helped to 'change the shape of things' in education. For example, the rise of 'open-plan' schools, the development of middle schools and other comprehensive alternatives, the emergence of polytechnics, new departures in provision for handicapped pupils and the growth of teachers' centres owed much to the initiative and vision of progressive LEAs. Alas, recent developments – culminating in the 1984 rate-capping legislation – have not only inhibited their dynamic role but also pose a serious threat to their capacity to fulfil satisfactorily their basic function.

11 The Present Structure of the English Educational System

1 The General Framework

A broad understanding of the contemporary English educational system may be promoted by initial reference to its unique features and its inter-related layers of operation.

(a) Unique Features

The educational system in England and Wales is distinguished from arrangements operating in many other countries by a number of character-istic features:

(i) the distribution of power and responsibility within the State system. The development and continuance of a complicated mechanism of checks and balances means that the system of education in England and Wales depends upon the co-operative and complementary efforts of the central government, the local authorities, the teaching profession, the churches and other voluntary bodies. Despite the encroachments of post-war centralisation, especially in more recent years, education remains a national service which is locally provided and administered. Over two-fifths of local authority spending is rate-supported and edu-cation is the major item of such expenditure; although central govern-ment exerts strong influence upon the total sums expended, the details of educational spending are locally determined.

(ii) the marked degree of professional freedom enjoyed by teachers in the schools. After 1902 the central and local education authorities were increasingly content to leave such matters as the curriculum, teaching methods, internal organisation and discipline in schools to the profes-sional judgement of teachers. Seventy years later teachers had come to exercise much influence upon the conduct of external examinations and boasted a degree of professional freedom that was the envy of their fellows in most other countries. Although the centrally orchestrated demand for a shift from autonomy to accountability over the past decade has questioned their position, teachers have retained a decisive influence upon what goes on in schools. The outcome of the 1977–81 central government attempt to produce a clear and firm national framework for the five to sixteen school curriculum was less than prescriptive and leaves headteachers and their staffs with much room for manoeuvre within the very broad guidelines laid down.

(iii) the major contribution of voluntary organisations to the statutory system of education. The dual arrangements established in 1870 continue to operate in modified form; over one-fifth of primary and secondary pupils at present attend church schools, and the religious (primarily Anglican and Roman Catholic) organisations still hold an important place in teacher training and have recently secured a foothold in the wider field of higher education. And, to a small extent, various voluntary bodies also contribute to the total provision made by the LEAs for special and further education.

(iv) the existence of the private sector alongside the State system. Centred upon the prestigious and expensive public boarding schools, this sector has maintained the real substance of its independence from State control and continues to have an importance out of all proportion to the number of fee-paying pupils it serves.

In different ways these features reflect a traditional and rooted objection to the centralised State control of education in this country (cf. France). Thus our system allows for the exercise of considerable local discretion and supports a surprising diversity of educational provision; the wide variations in pattern and practice between individual LEAs continues to give particularly sharp expression to this.

(b) Layers of Operation

In contemporary educational administration three layers of operation may be distinguished at both central and local levels (see diagram overleaf).

(i) *Political Layer*

This is concerned with decision-making in education and has ultimate responsibility for the development of policy and provision. The Secretary of State for Education and Science, on behalf of central government, makes the major decisions in accordance with party political attitudes and professional advice. A team of junior Ministers assists the Secretary of State in the dis-

The Basic Structure of Contemporary Educational Administration

Layers of Operation	CENTRAL structure	LOCAL structure
Political	DES	Local Education Committee
Concerned with policy and decision-making; carries final public responsibility for educational matters	Secretary of State (general policy, science and research, allocation of resources and other sensitive areas)	Consists of Chairman & Vice-Chairman, majority of Council members and a minority of co-opted members
Personnel involved subject to political change both central and local	Junior Ministers (with various responsibilities related to higher and further education, schools and other matters) All political figures	Undertakes the duties and exercises the powers of the multi-purpose local authority in the field of education. It operates a sub-committee structure and delegates some powers to the governing bodies of schools and other educational institutions
Administrative Concerned with the provision of advice and information to the political layer and with the execution of decisions and the day to day working of the educational system	Permanent Civil Service staff serving DES at Whitehall Permanent Secretary Deputy Secretary (3) Branch Under Secretaries (assisted by many other staff of lower grades)	Permanent Local Government Officers, administrative and clerical staff serving the local authority in the field of education Director of Education Deputy Other Education Officers (variable division of responsibilities)
Personnel involved give continuity and stability to educational system		
Advisory Links the administrative and political layers with the staff and institutions operating in the field and provides a means through which advice and information can be established and communicated	Her Majesty's Inspectorate Standing Committees (e.g. ACSET, SEC) Special Committees (e.g. James, Taylor and Warnock) DES consultation with other interested parties	Local Inspectorate (includes Advisers/ Organisers) *ad hoc* sub-committees of the Local Education Committee Consultation with teachers, churches and other interested parties But Director of Education acts as both main filter and power-house for passage of advice and information to Local Education Committee

ACSET = Advisory Committee on Supply and Education of Teachers
SEC = Secondary Examinations Council

charge of his or her responsibilities. The local education committees, on behalf of their parent County or Metropolitan District Councils, make important decisions affecting their own areas and shaped by local government politics, local needs and local professional advice. Here political responsibility is vested in the elected councillors who form the majority of the local education committee and finally in the parent Council itself.

(ii) *Administrative Layer*

This is concerned with the provision of advice and information for the making of decisions and with the execution of those decisions and the day to day running of the system. Because the DES Ministers and the local education committees usually take serious notice of the advice rendered by their leading administrators, the latter can often wield a critical influence upon the process of decision-making. Thus Sir James Hamilton, Permanent Secretary to the DES 1976–83, did much to inspire and sustain the recent shift towards more centralist intervention and control in education. The executive functions of the DES range from the routine administration of teachers' superannuation to effecting the contraction and reorganisation of teacher training. At the local level the creative power behind dynamic development has generally been that of the Director of Education (or Chief Education Officer); the records of Sir Alec Clegg in the West Riding of Yorkshire and of many others testify to this. On the executive side some of the administrative tasks are purely routine and recurring (e.g. the maintenance of adequate provision, the allocation of funds and the payment of teachers' salaries), whilst others involve the implementation of new policy or schemes related to such matters as comprehensive reorganisation, curriculum innovation, 'special educational needs' or (for some) the new technical and vocational education initiative. And, since the mid-1970s, the educational, organisational and financial implications of falling rolls have confronted local administrators with extra problems.

(iii) *Advisory Layer*

This is encompassed by and works through the administrative layer but can be separately distinguished. At both central and local levels there are advisory staff concerned with maintaining contact between the administrative layer and the actual institutions and practitioners in the field. Such contact enables them to accumulate the sort of knowledge and experience which can be drawn upon for various purposes by the administrators who render advice or execute policy. The DES is helped in this respect by the enduring and wide-ranging work of HM Inspectorate; but where there is a need for ongoing advice upon or an intensive inquiry into some particular educational area or concern, the DES can turn to certain standing committees (such as the Advisory Committee on the Supply and Education of Teachers or the Secondary Examinations Council) and to special *ad hoc* bodies which may be set up to report on a specific matter (e.g. James, Taylor and Warnock Committees). The LEAs employ their own advisers or inspectors as a means of strengthening contact between the office and their schools and other institutions, although the Director of Education and his senior colleagues also undertake visits to supplement or reinforce the efforts of their advisory staffs. *Ad hoc* sub-committees of the local education committee also provide a means of inquiring into and reporting upon any particular matter of local educational concern.

Thus the English educational system involves, both at the central and local levels, an odd combination of amateurs and professionals, with the latter advising and executing whilst the former are hesponsible for actually making the major decisions. But because these decisions are often determined by the advice give , the professional administrators enjoy much more power than it might at first appear.

2 The Department of Education and Science

Its direct line of descent is the Committee of Council for Education 1839–56; the Education Department 1856–1900; the Board of Education 1900–44; the Ministry of Education 1944–64.

(a) Powers and Responsibilities

These were considerably increased by the 1944 Act, under which the central authority has the duty 'to promote the education of the people of England and Wales' and 'to secure the effective execution by local authorities, under (its) control and direction, of the national policy' (Part I, Section 1). National policy is legally the policy which finds expression in the 1944 Act, subsequent amending legislation and the regulations which the DES issues with Parliamentary approval to fill in the details related to the broad legislative requirements. The actual power of the central authority to control and direct is not easy to pin down in terms of either its exact source or extent, but it may be said to consist in a number of mutually reinforcing elements.

(i) The 1944 Act emphasised the mandatory duties (rather than permissive powers) of the LEAs. Under Section 99 the Minister assumed the right to declare any LEA in default of its obligations, to issue appropriate directions and to enforce them, if necessary by legal action (writ of mandamus). The Minister was armed with similar powers in respect of managing and governing bodies.

(ii) Under the 1944 Act's enigmatic Section 68 the Minister was empowered to decide that an LEA is acting unreasonably, or proposes to do so, in a respect not directly covered by statute or regulation, and to intervene to give such directions as he thinks expedient. Again, such powers were to cover managing and governing bodies as well. The exact legal implications of Section 68 remain unclear. For many years it never underwent testing in the courts as the threat of taking it that far proved enough (e.g. in the Durham dispute of 1952 when the County LEA attempted to enforce trade union membership on all its staff). On the face of it Section 68 gives the Minister powers which are only limited by his interpretation of 'reasonable' and 'expedient'. The power seems so wide and unaccountable that Section 68 caused much concern and debate in 1944 and only Butler's persuasive arguments secured its passage. Yet in 1976 when the Secretary of State took legal action to prevent the incoming Tameside Conservative Council from suddenly reversing the comprehensive reorganisation plans of its Labour predecessor the central authority lost the case on appeal. Although this experience questioned the 'trump-card' value of Section 68, it still remains an important potential source of central power.

(iii) Under the 1980 Act (Sections 12/13) the Secretary of State has powers related to the opening, closure or reorganisation of individual schools, particularly where the proposals for change involve voluntary schools or attract objection from ten or more local electors. Once involved the Secretary of State may approve, reject or modify the proposals, although modification is contingent upon consultation with the LEA concerned. Thus, on occasion, he can wield direct influence upon the process of school reorganisation.

(iv) Under Sections 100/111 of the 1944 Act, which authorises the central authority to clarify its broad legislative provisions by means of issuing Standing Rules and Orders, the Minister has the power to control by regulation. Such regulations relate to schools, further education, teacher training, special educational needs, student awards and various other matters. But the threat of bureaucratic rule by regulation is met by the requirement that such Standing Rules and Orders be subject to consultation and the final approval of Parliament. But once issued they enjoy the force of law.

(v) Traditionally the central authority has wielded substantial power through its financial influence. The capital expenditure of LEAs is subject to the annual approval of the DES which also sets standards for the design of school premises. Recurrent expenditure by local authorities on education is heavily dependent upon central financial support. Under the old specific percentage grant system based on earmarked funds for education, central financial influence could be directly exerted by the Ministry. Since 1958 the operation of the general Rate Support Grant arrangements has blunted this instrument of central power. But the annual negotiations over the financing of all locally administered services presented the central government with the means of exerting an influence upon the level of local expenditure on education. Recently, any tendency for local authorities to overspend on education (beyond agreed estimates) has been checked by the 1980 Local Government Act's provision for consequent financial penalties. And now further Conservative legislation (1984 Rates Act) has provided the central government with more extensive powers to control high spending authorities and even a reserve power to limit rate increases in respect of every local authority. However, whilst the central government is tightening its control over the total expenditure of local authorities, the capacity of the DES to finely shape educational development by financial means remains very limited. The allocation of Rate Support Grant moneys to particular educational items is determined by the local authority; thus, for example, in-service training may not receive the national funding meant for it because of diversion elsewhere. In 1978–79 Shirley Williams as Secretary of State unsuccessfully pressed the case for specific grants being made a substantial element in education funding. The present government has instituted a modest change; under the 1984 Education (Grants and Awards) Act specific grants are to form one-half per cent of LEA spending (amounting to some £50 million for 1985–86) to enable the DES to promote certain developments in the direct fashion of the Manpower Services Commission. But the tiny fraction of moneys involved is hardly going to produce major change.

Further central influence is projected through the medium of circulars, memoranda and pamphlets, and is also exerted through HM Inspectorate. But these means depend on the co-operative response of the LEAs, the teachers and other parties concerned; for example, a DES Circular can only acquaint LEAs with the wishes of the central authority and has no statutory force, even though it is no light matter to ignore one.

The responsibilities of the DES are numerous and critical. Apart from the general duty to promote the education of the people and to develop policies calculated to achieve that end, the DES has a number of specific functions:

(i) to set minimum standards of provision and ensure that these are being met by the LEAs and others involved. Given the adverse effects of educational expenditure cuts, substantiated by reports of HM Inspectorate and other surveys, the DES has been accused recently of not fulfilling this function properly.

(ii) to control the rate, distribution, nature and cost of educational building within the national context of available resources for capital expenditure. And the DES must consult with the local authority associations to agree upon the annual level of recurrent educational expenditure.

(iii) to determine the requirements for recognition as a qualified teacher and to provide for and control the training and supply of such personnel. The DES is further responsible for the implementation of the Burnham salary negotiating procedures and scales and for the running of the teachers' superannuation scheme.

(iv) to support financially by direct grants certain institutions and activities that do not come under the jurisdiction of the LEAs. Voluntary colleges, some non-provided special schools and the assisted places scheme fall into this category, and educational research is also directly financed by making central grants available for this purpose to university departments and other reputable bodies.

(v) to settle any serious disputes between any of the other elements which make up the educational system. Thus children are safeguarded against the effects of LEAs, governing bodies, teachers' organisations, church bodies and parents failing to agree on any important matter.

However, in relation to the exercise of control and direction and the fulfilment of its accepted responsibilities, it is also important to appreciate what the DES does not do and what it may be seeking to do. In contrast to the central agency in many other countries, it does not provide or run schools or any other educational institutions, it does not engage or employ teaching staff and it does not select or publish educational textbooks. Despite recent developments the legal responsibility for the school curriculum lies with the LEAs; the central Department's *School Curriculum* (1981) publication seeks to provide guidelines for the exercise of that responsibility. Although the exact legal position has never been clear the DES now seeks to dominate the field of external examinations for schools. The establishment of the directly nominated Secondary Examinations Council (1983) constitutes an important new departure aimed at securing greater central control of secondary examinations and associated curricula.

(b) Internal Organisation of the Department of Education and Science

Basically one must distinguish between three groups of people with differing roles:

(i) *Ministers*

The Secretary of State for Education and Science and his junior Ministers are political appointees, subject to sudden change following elections or ministerial reshuffles. They are responsible to the government and to Parliament for the policy and the conduct of their department, and are usually politicians with real interest in, if not direct experience of, the field of education. They formulate national policy, initiate any necessary legislation and are expected to press the claims of education within the government's total programme. The division of work amongst these political heads is a flexible one, although the Secretary of State deals with the most politically sensitive areas (e.g. general policy and allocation of resources). In the years 1981–3 there were three junior Ministers dealing with the schools, higher education and further education plus youth respectively. Ultimate political responsibility for the DES resides of course with the Secretary of State; rather disconcertingly this office has been held by no less than eleven different politicians over the past twenty years.

(ii) *Civil Service Personnel*

The DES is served by some three thousand Civil Service staff, headed by a Permanent Secretary and his three Deputy Secretaries. The latter cover the following composite areas: schools and educational building; post-school education and civil science; teachers, planning and statistics. Beyond this the DES is further divided into particular Branches each headed by an Under Secretary. Three of these report directly to the Permanent Secretary; most important is the Finance Branch which consults with the Treasury and the Department of the Environment in connection with the annual Rate Support Grant settlement. The other Branches concerned with various aspects of schools provision, further and higher education, teachers and so forth report to one of the Deputy Secretaries. Most Branches then break down into constituent divisions in the usual Civil Service manner. The Permanent Secretary and his staff undertake responsibilities according to grade, ranging from the direct provision of advice to the political heads to the maintenance of routine contact with the LEAs and other bodies; they carry out the executive functions of the Department, communicating national policy and exercising control. As the Civil Service staff are outside the political arena, they contribute a measure of continuity and stability to central administration. And, at the top levels, they can certainly influence its flavour and direction.

(iii) *Her Majesty's Inspectorate*

This body is the professional arm of the DES and is composed of some five hundred officers organised on a general, specialist and territorial basis. It is headed by a Senior Chief Inspector with direct access to the Secretary of State and the Permanent Secretary. Six Chief Inspectors co-ordinate its work in different educational fields; territorially the Inspectorate is organised in seven geographical divisions with a Divisional Inspector in charge of each. About sixty Staff Inspectors undertake national responsibility for various subjects, phases or aspects of education. The Inspectorate serves as a professional link with the LEAs and their schools, other educational institutions and bodies. In the post-war period its role became increasingly advisory and consultative; its essential functions were to help maintain satisfactory standards, to spread new and sound educational developments throughout the system by personal contact and the organisation of conferences and courses, and to render professional advice to the Department. But recent developments, borne by the demand for greater educational accountability, have seen a change of emphasis. The DES has urged the Inspectorate to reassert its 'watchdog' role; its reports on individual schools have been made public since 1983 and such areas as teacher training have come under closer scrutiny. Whilst the Inspectorate has asserted its authority more strongly and overtly, its traditional independence secures it from becoming the central authority's lackey. Significantly its report on *The Effects of Local Authority Expenditure Policies on the Education Services of England* (1981) showed that financial cuts were leading to a decline in standards of provision and clearly implied that central government must bear some responsibility.

Special arrangements exist for the central administration of education in Wales. Whilst political responsibility for the universities and civil science is retained by the Secretary of State for Education and Science, such responsibility for schools and other non-university education in the Principality lies with the Secretary of State for Wales. This transfer of powers, begun in 1970, has given rise to the Education Department of the Welsh Office in Cardiff, with its own Permanent Secretary and small Inspectorate. A distinctive function of the Department is to sustain the teaching and use of the Welsh language.

(c) Vital Relationships for the Department of Education and Science

As a major government department the DES is involved in a number of crucial relationships. It is of course responsible to the Secretary of State for national educational policy and its implementation; this responsibility includes such matters as educational legislation and regulations, the financial estimates and the handling of Parliamentary questions and debates on education. At central level the DES also has important relations with the Department of the Environment, the Treasury and the MSC because their roles directly affect the education service. The most vital link is that between the DES and the LEAs; the former shapes national policy and lays down minimal requirements whilst the latter work within the broad framework so provided. Finally, it is both traditional and desirable for the DES to consult and develop sound working relations with such bodies as the teachers' organisations and the churches.

3 Local Education Authorities

The direct line of descent is the School Boards 1870–1902; the Technical Instruction Committees 1889–1902; Part II County/County Borough and Part III Municipal Borough/Urban District LEAs 1902–44; County and County Borough LEAs 1944–74.

(a) Structural Framework

Since 1 April 1974, from which date the 1972 Local Government Act took effect, LEAs have operated within a framework distinguished by a number of structural features.

(i) Within the new two-tier system of local government covering England and Wales educational responsibility is exercised by a total of 105 elected councils operating as LEAs. Outside Greater London the country is divided into two forms of county – Metropolitan and non-Metropolitan – for local government purposes; each county is then divided into district council areas and local government functions are shared between the two tiers. In the six densely-populated Metropolitan Areas (West Midlands, Greater Manchester, Merseyside, West Yorkshire, South Yorkshire and Tyneside) educational responsibility is lodged at the lower level where a total of 36 Metropolitan District Councils serve as LEAs. Thus in Greater Manchester, for example, the Metropolitan Area Council deals with such matters as police, highways and transport whilst the Wigan, Bolton, Salford, Trafford, Bury, Manchester, Rochdale, Oldham, Tameside and Stockport Metropolitan District Councils (ten in all) are responsible for education. In the less urbanised non-Metropolitan or Shire Counties educational responsibility resides at the higher level and is discharged by the 40 English and 8 Welsh County Councils. In the Greater London area (reorganised in 1963) the responsibility rests with the 20 Outer

London Boroughs and the *ad hoc* Inner London Education Authority. However, the present (1984) Conservative government now intends to abolish the Greater London Council and the Metropolitan Area authorities. In the educational arena the main significance of this is the prospective demise of the Inner London Education Authority, created in 1963 as a special committee of the Greater London Council. For many years the Inner London Education Authority has been the highest per capita spender on education in the country and has won a reputation for financial extravagance amongst Conservative politicians. It is likely to be replaced by a directly-elected Inner London Education Authority rather reminiscent of the old London School Board; this would at least ensure the continuance of Inner London as a single administrative unit for education.

(ii) Each LEA is required to establish a local education committee. A majority of its members must be drawn from the parent council, the remainder being co-optees with experience in education and acquaintance with educational conditions in the local area. The elected majority provides for accountability and the co-options allow for church, teacher, university or other representation on the committee. The parent council must consult its local education committee before exercising its educational functions and may delegate all of its responsibilities and powers to the committee, excepting the borrowing of money and the raising of rates. Although the degree of such delegation does vary, most committees are left to make the decisions, with the council usually content to give them its formal approval. However, since 1974 many local authorities have adopted Bains-type corporate management arrangements. Here the policy and proposals of the local education committee, principally where cost factors attract attention, are subject to the scrutiny of a key Policy and Resources Committee composed of various committee chairmen and assisted by a team of chief officers headed by the authority's Chief Executive. Financial exigencies have encouraged the resort to corporate management and the establishment of such super-Committees in local government.

(iii) The local education committee is empowered to work through a system of sub-committees in order to cope with its wide-ranging business. Originally the tendency was for local education committees, especially those serving large authorities, to establish a considerable number of standing sub-committees to deal with such matters as primary education, secondary education, further education, special services, sites and buildings, youth employment and finance and general purposes. But subsequently the trend has been for most authorities to adopt a reduced sub-committee structure involving less specialisation. The function of such sub-committees varies between different authorties. In some authorities their role is restricted to making recommendations; in other authorities they enjoy substantial power to act in their areas of responsibility.

(iv) The local education committee is supported by an Education Department headed by a Director of Education or Chief Education Officer. The Director of Education is expected to identify the issues and marshal the business requiring the attention of the local education committee and to accept executive responsibility for developing local provision. He is the committee's major source of professional advice and often leaves the imprint of his own personal influence upon local policy and development. However, in some forms of corporate management the Director's power can be restricted and as one of the team of chief officers assisting the Policy and Resources Committee he may have to spend more time on corporate business than educational matters. It is a statutory requirement that each LEA appoint a Director of Education; both he and his professional staff are recruited originally from the ranks of qualified and serving teachers. The Director of Education is backed by a Deputy and a number of subordinate Education Officers (arranged in tiers according to seniority and the size of the LEA) whose overall pattern of responsibility varies and is subject to change. Additionally, for the administration of specified areas in non-Metropolitan Counties, the LEA may appoint Area Education Officers. Quite distinct are the local inspectors, advisers and organisers who compose the Director's advisory staff. As well as providing the main link with the schools and assisting the classroom teacher with specialist advice, they are concerned with the development of teacher centres and the mounting of local courses for teachers. Behind the Director and his professional team are a large number of local government staff dealing with the various levels of administrative and clerical work at the education offices. Finally, where appropriate the expertise of other principal officers (e.g. the Treasurer or Chief Architect) and their assistants is made available to the local education committee and its Education Department.

(b) Duties and Powers

The basic responsibility of the LEAs is set out in Section 7 of the 1944 Act. This is 'to contribute towards the spiritual, moral, mental and physical development of the community' by securing the provision of efficient primary, secondary and further education in the area for which they are responsible. Particular duties and powers, with more emphasis on the former than the latter, are spelled out by other provisions of the Act and subsequent amending legislation. The duties include:

(i) making adequate and satisfactory provision of primary and secondary schooling suited to pupils' different ages, abilities and aptitudes;

(ii) having regard to the need for securing special educational provision for pupils with special educational needs and ensuring, as far as is practicable, that such pupils are educated in an ordinary school;

(iii) meeting adequately and efficiently the local need for further education in its various forms;

(iv) establishing, maintaining or otherwise assisting institutions for the training of teachers as directed by the central authority;

(v) ensuring that the premises and accommodation of all their schools and other educational establishments conform to minimum standards;

(vi) following set procedures regarding the opening, closure or reorganisation of individual schools (Sections 12/13 of 1980 Act);

(vii) making arrangements, as far as compatible with the efficient use of resources, for the exercise of parental choice on school admissions;

(viii) seeing that parents fulfil their duty to ensure that children of compulsory school age receive efficient full-time education;

(ix) drawing up instruments and articles of government for maintained schools and other educational institutions and providing for suitable governing bodies to exercise the responsibilities laid down;

(x) ensuring the implementation of compulsory collective worship and religious instruction in all its maintained schools;

(xi) contributing substantially, according to an agreed formula, to the total cost of maintaining and developing the statutory system of education in its own area;

(xii) making mandatory awards to students from its area who are pursuing first degree or comparable post-school couhses;

(xiii) establishing its own local education committee and appointing a Director of Education;

(xiv) providing a Careers Service for its schools and other educational institutions and appointing a Careers Officer to run it.

Under Section 43 of the 1944 Act the LEAs were required to provide, after a date to be specified, a system of county colleges for compulsory part-time education for all young persons up to eighteen years not in full-time schooling. But with other developments always enjoying higher priority this important provision has remained in limbo for some forty years. Had it been implemented the education service would have been well placed to respond to the growth of youth unemployment in recent years. Instead it is the MSC, working from outside the educational system, which has assumed responsibility for meeting the problem. The powers vested in the LEAs include:

(i) the compulsory purchase of land for the exercise of their functions.

(ii) the opening, closing or reorganisation of individual schools, albeit subject to Section 12/13 procedure.

(iii) the control of secular education in the schools they maintain. Since 1944 this power has afforded the means by which LEAs might shape the school curriculum. Until recently it has lain dormant but LEAs are now expected to fully exercise such power within the 1981 guidelines provided by the central authority.

(iv) the control of teacher appointments, though with reservations in respect of voluntary aided schools.

(v) the inspection of any educational institution they maintain, either directly or (on request) through HM Inspectorate.

(vi) the making of discretionary awards to students on full or part-time courses of further or higher education not eligible for mandatory awards.

(vii) the provision for pupils at maintained schools of milk, meals or other refreshment at such charges as they think fit. But it is a duty to provide suitable facilities for pupils bringing their own mid-day refreshment to school and to make free meals available to those pupils entitled to them.

(viii) to assist pupils at maintained schools, as deemed appropriate, with travelling, clothing and maintenance payments.

(c) System of Finance

The bulk of public expenditure on education is undertaken by the LEAs. Over half of the sums involved is provided by central government through the Rate Support Grant and the rest is supplied from local rates. The Rate Support Grant is paid yearly to help cover the cost of local services as a whole and there are no earmarked moneys for education. The system is designed to provide an equitable pattern of Treasury support, with adjustments for variations in local needs and resources between individual authorities. The annual Rate Support Grant settlement is the outcome of detailed negotiations between the central government and local authority associations; conducted under the auspices of the Department of the Environment this long process decides the relevant level of local authority expenditure, the proportion to be met by the Treasury and the exact distribution of the central grant among the local authorities. Educational spending is worked into the process after prior consultations between the DES and local authority associations, but once the Rate Support Grant is finalised each authority determines the budgetary allocations between its various local services. Under these arrangements central influence upon local authority expenditure hinges upon fixing the Rate Support Grant; beyond that the local authority's control of its own rate contribution allows for a lot of flexibility in the size of the total budget. However, since 1980 central government has sought to exert much more control over the total expenditure of local authorities. It now sets an annual level of local authority expenditure beyond which financial penalties operate to discourage overspending; and following the 1984 Rates Act even stricter controls are to hand, including a reserve power enabling the government to directly limit rate rises in every authority. Such developments must seriously reduce the capacity of LEAs to provide for local educational needs to the extent and in ways they might feel desirable.

As the most important of their various services education accounts for about two-thirds of the annual expenditure of LEAs. Yet the Rate Support Grant arrangements leave education to secure its proper share of resources and consequently there is a continuing need to safeguard the service from other competing demands. This has led the Society of Education Officers to call for a return to separate funding for education. Nor, with so much expenditure pre-empted, is there much room for manoeuvre with the local authority's education budget. On average about one-half is accounted for by teachers' salaries. And other salaries, buildings and fixed plant, student grants and related payments absorb another one-third. Capitation allowances, paid to individual schools for the purchase of equipment, books, stationery and other materials, must compete with other items for what remains – hence the recent tendency for some schools to accept or even seek financial help from parents to safeguard such provision.

With teachers' salaries such a large cost item the Burnham arrangements for their negotiation assume major importance. These operate under the Remuneration of Teachers Act (1965) which confines the exercise to salary scales, affords the Secretary of State representation on the management panels and provides for arbitration in case of disagreement. Long dissatisfied with this situation the LEAs would like the arrangements to be changed. They favour the combined negotiation of salaries and conditions of service, the abandonment of arbitration and, possibly, an end to central representation on the management panels. But such changes require legislation and are not likely to eventuate in the near future.

(d) School Governance

School governing bodies form an intermediate tier in the administrative structure. They have delegated responsibility for the general direction of their particular schools and are one of the means of affording each school an individual identity. Such bodies are constituted under instruments of government which are now subject to the provisions of the 1980 Education Act. Thereby the governing bodies of all maintained schools must include persons appointed by the LEA concerned; in the case of county schools the majority of governors may be political appointees and some may have little interest in education. Further, all county and voluntary controlled schools must include at least two elected parent and two elected teacher governors, although for small schools one teacher governor is deemed sufficient. Foundation trustees hold a special position on the governing bodies of voluntary schools; they must constitute at least one-fifth of the governors of controlled schools and have a clear majority in the case of aided and special agreement schools. In all maintained schools headteachers, unless they decide otherwise, are governors *ex officio*. And, basically, all maintained schools are to have their own individual governing bodies; but two primary schools may be grouped under one such body and the Secretary of State can make other exceptions. The LEAs were required to apply the terms of the new Act to all maintained schools in England and Wales by September 1985.

Once constituted, school governing bodies operate under articles of government designed to define their functions and powers. But in practice they still lack a clear and positive role. Although they are made responsible for the general direction of their school, governing bodies usually occupy a sort of 'no-man's land' between the LEA and the headteacher. Whilst school governors may have nominal charge of their school's finance, buildings and staffing, the real arbiter in these areas is the LEA. And whilst they may have similar responsibility for the conduct and curriculum of the school, there is a strong tradition of headteacher autonomy in this field. Moreover, the fact that they usually meet so infrequently also militates against school governors establishing a leading role for themselves. Thus, except in the case of voluntary-aided and special agreement schools, there is a tendency for school governors to be mere figureheads who are called upon to grace speech day proceedings and 'sit in' on various staff appointments. Of course, with thousands of schools in the maintained system, there are wide variations in the nature and extent of governors' influence. A minority of governing bodies have shown a capacity for actively representing the interests of their school, especially in the face of reorganisation plans that might affect its fortunes. In the wake of the Taylor Report (1977) and the 1980 Act, the current trend is towards school governing bodies showing more interest and exercising more influence. Significantly governing bodies are expected to ensure that their schools conform to the new 5–16 curriculum guidelines (1981) provided by the central authority. And now the present government, with its devotion to increasing consumer influence upon State education, seems set on making further important changes in the way county and voluntary controlled schools are governed. The 1984 consultative Green Paper on *Parental Influence at School – a new framework for school government in England and Wales* contains proposals for giving parents a built-in majority on governing bodies, clarifying the functions of such bodies and firmly enhancing their role in school life. However, as they are disliked by both the LEAs and the teacher associations and require legislation to implement them, the future of these government proposals must be regarded as uncertain.

4 National Associations

The English educational system, although centred upon the DES, depends for its effective working upon consultation and co-operation on a continuing basis, so that national policy and practice in education becomes as far as possible the expression of a consensus distilled from various sources within the system. In this regard certain bodies are especially important.

(a) Associations Representing the Local Education Authorities

Until 1974 the County Councils' Association and the Association of Municipal Corporations represented the multi-purpose interests of the local authorities. Although they always showed a strong interest in post-war educational developments, it was through the separate Association of Education Committees (AEC) that local authorities spoke with a single voice in the field of education. All three associations enjoyed substantial representation on the management panel of the Burnham Committee, but their leading spokesman in negotiations was the Secretary of the AEC. Such arrangements acknowledged education's special place as local government's most important service and did much to strengthen the hand of the LEAs in their dealings with central government and the teachers.

Since 1974 different arrangements have prevailed and weakened the voice of LEAs in the national forum. The multi-purpose interests of local government are now represented by the Association of County Councils and the Association of Metropolitan Authorities. Not only are these two bodies often at loggerheads, but there is no real counterpart to the former AEC. Instead the Council of Local Education Authorities (CLEA) provides a limited bridge between the two Associations in respect of educational concerns. This Council consists of an equal number of members from each Association but cannot make unilateral decisions on their behalf. Whilst the Council makes policy recommendations, considers any matters referred to it and provides general information and advisory services, it is not responsible for major educational policy decisions, ministerial consultations, parliamentary contacts or the Burnham negotiations. From the outset the two parent Associations determined to treat education as part of the totality of local government services and not as a separate entity. Thus they have reserved the real power for themselves and often operate through their own Education Committees rather than the joint Council. Consequently the latter is but a pale shadow of the old AEC and the LEAs lack their former cohesion.

However, on behalf of the LEAs, the two Associations and the joint Council undertake, as best they may, a number of functions:

  (i)   to negotiate and consult with the central authority in regard to proposed legislation, regulations, circulars and other memoranda for policy development and routine working.
 (ii)   to submit evidence and present the viewpoint of the LEAs to various bodies undertaking inquiries directly or indirectly concerned with education (e.g. Taylor Committee).
(iii)   to advise and represent particular LEAs when at issue with the central authority, the teachers' organisations or any other interested party.
 (iv)   to represent the LEAs on various national bodies concerned with education (e.g. Advisory Committee on the Supply and Education of Teachers).
  (v)   to negotiate with the teachers' organisations on terms of employment. Whilst the parent Associations represent the LEAs on the Burnham Committees for salary negotiation, the joint Council has led the continuing attempt to secure some sort of national agreement on the still separate matter of teachers' conditions of service.

(b) Associations Representing the Teachers

There are various, and certainly too many, bodies concerned with promoting the interests of serving teachers. This fragmentation is a reflection of the sectional divisions traditionally associated with the teaching occupation and a crucial factor in limiting the professional influence and status of teachers. For many years the teachers' organisations have recognised the need for a Teachers' General Council to control entry to the profession, to secure probationary standards and to discipline cases of serious misconduct or dereliction of duty. But they have failed to agree between themselves and with the central authority upon how such a Council should be set up, who should compose it and what exact powers it should have. Despite its potential for also providing a focal point for professional co-operation and unity on a wider front there seems to be little hope of the impasse being overcome.

Teaching is an occupation in which there is no closed shop; nevertheless teachers are highly organised with the great majority of them subscribing to some union or association. Collectively such organisations have a membership of some 400,000 serving primary and secondary teachers, with three main and rival bodies dominating the scene.

(i) *National Union of Teachers*

Since 1870 this body has been, and still remains, the most powerful of the teachers' organisations. Drawing its members from all sections of the profession, the NUT accounts for about 51 per cent of teachers in maintained schools. Although its main strength lies in the primary sector and amongst women teachers, this union claims to stand for the common interest of all teachers and its sheer size gives it a leading position in educational politics. Affiliated to the Trades Union Congress since 1970, its Secretary is a member of the General Council. On the Burnham teachers' panel for salary negotiations the NUT enjoys a bare majority of the available places. Its close alliance with the National Association of Teachers in Further and Higher Education extends its influence into the field of post-school education. In recent years the NUT has led the resistance to educational cuts and centralist policies. But its image and influence have suffered from the internal activity of left-wing elements and involvement in non-educational issues like unilateral disarmament. And, as the need for professional unity has become more urgent, the teachers' largest union has not provided a decisive lead towards it. In particular, its attitude in relation to the establishment of a Teachers' General Council has been seen as less than constructive.

(ii) *National Association of Schoolmasters/Union of Women Teachers*

The National Association of Schoolmasters (NAS) originated in 1922 following a breakaway from the NUT and for over thirty years applied much of its energies to opposing equal pay for women teachers. The Union of Women Teachers (UWT) began as a separate entity in 1965 by which time equal pay had been realised. With both organisations championing the interests of career teachers they merged in 1976 to form the NAS/UWT which presently accounts for some 25 per cent of teachers in maintained schools. Two-thirds of the members are male and three-quarters are secondary teachers; there are more male secondary teachers in the NAS/UWT than any other body. As its membership rose the merged union finally secured (1981) commensurate representation on the Burnham teachers' panel where it now holds six of the thirty-one places. It has also developed a reputation for militancy on salaries and conditions of service and for a traditional stance on corporal punishment and other professional concerns. This seems to have recommended it to many non-graduate career teachers especially. Although affiliated to the Trades Union Congress since 1968, the NAS/UWT has concentrated its attentions on those matters which relate directly to the interests of working teachers. But its long-standing and sometimes bitter rivalry with the NUT has been and still is a major source of division within the profession.

(iii)   *Assistant Masters and Mistresses Association (AMMA)*

This body was formed in 1978 through the amalgamation of the Assistant Masters' Association and the Association of Assistant Mistresses. For many years the two parent foundations had served the interests of graduate teachers in selective schools; from the late 1960s the comprehensive tide and the move towards an all-graduate profession combined to broaden and strengthen their position. At present the AMMA represents some 14 per cent of teachers in maintained schools although the bulk of them are from the secondary sector. It has four places on the Burnham teachers' panel and significant representation on many other educational bodies. The AMMA also operates in the private sector with one in six members working in independent schools. It has the reputation of being the least militant and most professional of the major teachers' organisations, but has taken a hard line recently over educational cuts which threaten additional burdens for its members. Not affiliated to the Trades Union Congress, it seeks to avoid political postures and always confines its activity to purely educational concerns. Typically the AMMA regrets the failure to establish a Teachers' General Council which it regards as a leading priority.

Four other teachers' organisations deserve notice. The Professional Association of Teachers was formed in 1970 for those teachers opposed to any sort of strike action and it has grown to include over 4 per cent of serving teachers. The National Association of Headteachers serves the interests of some 20,000 heads of whom three-quarters are drawn from the primary sector. The Secondary Heads Association has about 3,000 members including a few from independent schools. All three organisations are represented on the Burnham teachers' panel. The National Association of Teachers in Further and Higher Education covers the post-school public sector of education and embraces teacher training staff. Its large membership looks to it for the negotiation of salaries through the separate Burnham Further Education Committee. Unlike the three preceding bodies it is affiliated to the Trades Union Congress.

The teachers' organisations exert their influence through certain established channels. At the national level they maintain contact with the DES and with the CLEA; they also work through such nationally representative bodies as the Burnham Committees and the Advisory Committee on the Supply and Education of Teachers. At the local level the unions are in continuing consultation with the LEAs and teacher representatives serve as co-opted members on local education committees.

The teachers' organisations have two major roles to play and these sometimes come into conflict. Firstly, they operate as labour associations undertaking the role of ordinary trade unions, involving in some cases affiliation to the Trades Union Congress. Secondly, they operate as professional bodies, looking upon themselves as repositories of pedagogic knowledge and expertise and as responsible sources of professional advice for the central authority and other interested parties. Given this dual role the various organisations attempt to perform a number of functions:

(i)   to negotiate and consult with the central authority in regard to proposed legislation, regulations, circulars and other memoranda for policy development and routine working.

(ii) to submit evidence and present the teachers' viewpoint to various inquiry bodies (e.g. James Committee) and to undertake their own investigations and formulate policy recommendations with the aim of influencing government and public opinion; in the latter respect sponsored Parliamentary spokesmen, annual conferences and odd reports help to publicise and press union views.

(iii) to provide individual members with a wide range of services which include legal advice and assistance, professional journals, insurance arrangements, benevolent schemes and even building society facilities.

(iv) to represent teachers on various national bodies concerned with education such as the Advisory Committee on the Supply and Education of Teachers, the Schools Curriculum Development Committee, the National Foundation for Educational Research and the School Broadcasting Council.

(v)   to negotiate teachers' salaries through the Burnham machinery and to consult with the CLEA and individual LEAs in respect of conditions of service and contractual arrangements.

(c)   Associations Representing Other Interested Parties

There are also national bodies or organisations to look after the interests and to present the views of the various churches, local education officers, local inspectors and advisers, school governors and parents. The emergence of parents as an educational pressure group is a relatively recent development which the National Confederation of Parent-Teacher Associations and the Confederation for the Advancement of State Education have done much to promote. The former embraces over 2,500 member associations representing more than a million parents and the latter led the campaign to secure parental places on school governing bodies, local education committees and the late Schools Council.

5   The Organisational and Institutional Pattern of Educational Provision

The diagram on page 244 shows the basic organisational and institutional pattern of educational provision now existing in England and Wales. It may be amplified as follows:

(a) Some 94 per cent of children receive their full-time education in maintained schools. Whilst most of them leave at sixteen, almost one in ten stay on until the age of eighteen. Although the maintained system includes nursery and special schools, the great mass of pupils are found in primary, middle and secondary schools as the following figures show:

England and Wales (1984)	Number of Schools	Number of Pupils
Primary	21,155	3,838,545
Middle	1,334	439,390
Secondary	4,032	3,623,598
Sum total	26,521	7,901,533

The maintained school population is at present declining from the 1977 peak of 9.0 million to an estimated size of less than 7.2 million by the late 1980s. By that time the number of primary pupils should begin to rise somewhat but the secondary total will decline until the early 1990s. In response to the developing problem of falling rolls it is planned to remove progressively over one million places from the maintained school system by 1986–87. This ongoing process involves the closure of individual schools, limited reorganisation schemes involving a particular stage of schooling or more radical changes affecting the overall pattern of provision in a given locality.

(b) The period of compulsory schooling begins at the age of five with entry into the primary or 'first' stage of education. But the maintained system includes over 600 nursery schools (two to four years) and many nursery classes (three to four years) attached to infant schools or departments. In 1981 they provided some 240,000 children with full or part-time

nursery schooling, with 40 per cent of three- and four-year-olds benefiting. And, despite the current pressure on educational budgets, some
LEAs allow children to begin their primary schooling before the statutory age of admission. At five years most children enter infant (five to
seven) or primary (five to eleven) schools, although a minority join
'first' schools which generally cover the five to eight or five to nine age
groups. The five to seven infant schools transfer their pupils to seven to
eleven junior schools and many five to eleven primary schools are sub-
divided into infant and junior departments. Most 'first' schools link up
with eight to twelve or nine to thirteen middle schools.

(c) The immediate post-war pattern of provision was much simpler than
the existing one. To provide secondary education for all the 1944 Act
enforced a rigid division at eleven-plus and the great majority of
LEAs chose to organise their secondary education along tripartite
(grammar/technical/modern) or bipartite (grammar/modern) lines.
Since the early 1960s the comprehensive tide has produced a more
complex pattern with selective and comprehensive arrangements (each
with their own sub-variations) still co-existing in a quarter of LEA
areas. And the middle school comprehensive alternative, authorised by
the 1964 Education Act, has dismantled the established eleven-plus
dividing line and blurred the distinction between primary and secondary schooling in some areas.

(d) The reorganisation of secondary education proceeded very largely on
the basis of the four main comprehensive alternatives presented in
Circular 10/65. These are the all-through eleven to eighteen comprehensive school, the two-tier system with complete transfer from a junior
to a senior comprehensive at thirteen or fourteen, the eleven to sixteen
comprehensive plus Sixth Form (or tertiary) college arrangement and
the middle school pattern involving transfer at twelve or thirteen to
senior comprehensives. Each of these variants has its strengths and
weaknesses, but the most important single factor determining choice
has been the nature of the existing school buildings and the cost of adap-
tation. All-through eleven to eighteen comprehensives (sometimes
having a split-site basis) currently account for about one-half of secondary pupils. Meanwhile, falling rolls are encouraging LEAs to switch to
Sixth Form (or tertiary) college arrangements and to abandon either
middle school or two-tier patterns of provision.

(e) The diagram on page 244 encompasses most schools and other institutions composing the statutory system of education as well as the universities. But it ignores the independent schools which account for half a
million pupils and about 6 per cent of the total school population; nor
does it show the assisted places scheme, a sort of tiny bridge between the

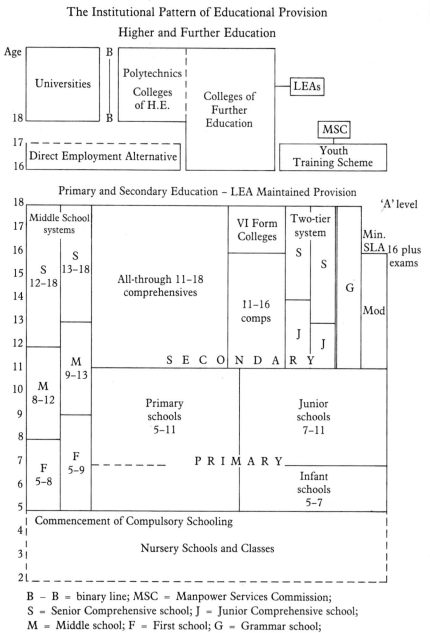

The Institutional Pattern of Educational Provision

Higher and Further Education

Primary and Secondary Education – LEA Maintained Provision

B – B = binary line; MSC = Manpower Services Commission;
S = Senior Comprehensive school; J = Junior Comprehensive school;
M = Middle school; F = First school; G = Grammar school;
Mod = Modern school; Min. SLA = minimum school leaving age

maintained system and the private sector, which is likely to involve over 30,000 pupils by 1986–87. Also absent from the basic picture are nearly 1,700 special schools with some 130,000 pupils; over nine-tenths of this provision lies within the maintained system. However, as the new approach to special educational needs develops the importance of this hitherto separate sector will decline. Finally, the diagram does not distinguish between county and voluntary schools or between co-educational and single-sex schools. More than one-fifth of primary and secondary pupils attend voluntary schools, mainly Anglican or Roman Catholic. All nursery and infant schools are co-educational, and single-sex schools are now few and far between at the junior and secondary levels.

(f) The minimum school-leaving age is sixteen years. At that juncture secondary pupils may proceed to Sixth Form studies, to further education or into direct employment. However, given the recent sharp growth of youth unemployment, many early school-leavers now enter the Youth Training Scheme (YTS) designed to provide sixteen- to seventeen-year-olds with the sort of training and work experience which may better equip them to take a job if and when available. The YTS, launched in 1983–4 and aimed initially at 450,000 school-leavers, is under the control of the MSC; although Colleges of Further Education will contribute to the overall provision there is no place for the secondary schools in the new project.

(g) Until the 1970s teacher training institutions, latterly named Colleges of Education, constituted a separate and distinct sector of the statutory system. But the last decade has seen their enforced integration into the public sector of further and higher education. Here teacher education and training is now based in fifty-odd polytechnics and Colleges of Higher Education (including some twenty voluntary colleges) where it takes place alongside a range of other degree options. On the other side of the binary line about thirty UDEs provide one-year professional training for postgraduate students.

Postscript

Since the early 1970s the State system of education in England and Wales has been passing through the most difficult and dispiriting period of its post-war development. Over the last decade or so the maintained schools have had to contend with or accommodate to a whole range of changes and problems. These include the raising of the school leaving age to sixteen; the major restructuring of local government; the crucial phase of comprehensive reorganisation; the disruption of the teacher training system; the contraction of school rolls with all its attendant difficulties; the populist censure of progressive pedagogy and school standards; the spate of initiatives aimed at curricular and examination reform; the reversion of HM Inspectorate to a more inquisitorial role; the reform of school government and accession of parental influence; the progressive delimitation of corporal punishment in schools; the deteriorating economic situation with its untoward effects upon educational finance; the diminution of teachers' salaries and career prospects; the unhappy demotion of education in the political scale of priorities; and the sharp reinforcement of the post-war centralising process and consequent erosion of the traditional system of partnership, co-operation and consultation in English education. For those involved at or near to the 'chalk-face' in the provision of our children's schooling, to suffer such unrelieved pressure and instability is depressing enough; but worse still is the ultimate discouragement that there seems little hope of any early improvement in the situation.

Any consideration of current concerns and future prospects in relation to the State system of schooling presents a rather gloomy picture, mainly because the overall context in which educational development takes place has become the most restrictive and unfavourable since the 1944 Act. In particular, changes in the political, economic, administrative and demographic contexts have produced a new environment which is distinctly hostile to the Butler conception of State educational provision and advance.

For some time now the maintained system has faced an increasingly unfavourable tide of political change. In the mid-1970s widespread dissatisfaction with its failure to 'deliver the goods' led to the demotion of education on the scale of national priorities by all political parties. Consequently, in the last two parliamentary elections education did not figure very prominently despite the efforts by teacher associations to make it an issue. In 1979 the electorate returned the most right-wing Conservative government of the post-war era, ending the long period of consensus politics which had prevailed and proved so favourable to education since 1945. A new political ideology and thrust quickly emerged which is not sympathetically disposed to the welfare state in general or State education in particular. Economic deeds must now take precedence over social needs and various public services are under seige. Better value for money is demanded of the maintained schools and to that end various strategies have developed. To some extent, owing to enhanced parental rights and privatisation (e.g. of school meals and cleaning), 'market forces' are being brought to bear upon State provision. Competition from the independent sector has been strengthened through the assisted places scheme. But the main strategy is to increase the degree of central control over the maintained system in the hope that closer regulation will improve quality without extra public expense. School curriculum and examinations and the training, appointment and management of teachers are subject to growing central influence, albeit exerted through normal channels. But associated with this is the greater emphasis being given to instrumental studies and training in the role of schools and colleges, with the centrally directed MSC now projected into traditional LEA territory to ensure the desired shift is made. And, given the resounding Conservative electoral victory of 1983, these policies will continue for the immediate future. Any prospect of a change of policies more acceptable to those involved in manning and running the State system depends upon a change of government. Currently, with the Labour party still divided and hamstrung by its strong left-wing elements and the new Liberal-Social Democratic Alliance having lost its initial momentum and appeal, there is a real possibility of Tory rule continuing into the early 1990s.

The advent of Thatcherite Conservatism may have been partly the result of a growing recognition that the post-war British economy needed urgent revitalisation and a lessening of the burden of public expenditure which the welfare state required it to bear. The deepening economic recession which beset the country from the close of the 1970s simply reinforced the case for a new strategy. Thus, over the last five years, the Thatcher government has been more determined to limit public expenditure than any previous post-war administration. Worse still for education is the government's 1983 electoral undertaking that priority for restricted public moneys would be accorded to defence, law and order, the health service and retirement pensions. In 1980–1 education spending constituted 11.7% of total public expenditure; by 1985–6 it is scheduled to fall to 10.1% at a time when public expenditure itself is taking a declining share of the gross national product.

The prime target for government attention is local authority spending within which educational expenditure is the major item. Initially the tactic was to tighten the reins by means of the government's Rate Support Grant and associated penalties for over-spending beyond total expenditure targets credited to each authority. Now the penalties have been sharply increased and rate-capping legislation has been passed to enable the government to deal directly with over-spending authorities, or even to place a general limit upon rate rises across the board. No longer will individual LEAs be able to respond to central government parsimony by recourse to the rates. In this context the recent White Paper on *Public Expenditure Plans 1984-5 to 1986-7* assumes added significance for education. In money terms local authority educational spending is to rise by 4% for 1984-5 and by 8½% for the three year period 1984-7. The government claimed that the 1984-5 increase would 'allow broadly for the maintenance of current policies' provided that teacher's pay and inflation rose by very little. Apart from the presumptous provisos, the claim is palpably misleading because of the false baseline used for the scheduled 'increases'. In 1983-4 local educational expenditure exceeded the set target by some 7%. Thus to use the 1983-4 spending target rather than the actual amount spent as the baseline for future increases in reality demands serious cuts – with the difference that the requisite powers are now available to ensure acquiescence. Many more teachers' jobs will go and compulsory redundancies may result under the growing pressures. Marginal concerns such as school meals, pre-schooling and the youth service will be hit hard. In many schools the situation is likely to worsen in respect of maintenance and repairs, books and equipment and the breadth of curricula provision. Given the warnings already made by HM Inspectorate about deteriorating provision consequent upon shortage of resources, the prospect is now one of really serious damage to the State system. In *Education Observed* (1984), a review of reports published by HM Inspectors in the first half of 1983, it is shown that primary schools 'do not have any spare resources' and that in secondary schools 'resources are fully or even overstretched (with) the overall picture (being) one of gradual deterioration with a few bright but many black spots'. Significantly, on the inside cover of this DES publication there appears the bald declaration: 'Nothing said in this report is to be construed as implying government commitment to the provision of additional resources.'

The political and economic changes already considered have had a major and largely untoward impact upon the administrative context in which post-war State educational provision has developed. Traditionally the framework for the administration of State education has been one geared to partnership, consultation and co-operation between the central authority, the LEAs and the teachers. Recently this long-established framework has been rent by serious conflict, usually resultant of the government's determination to increase its own power and even to act without adequate or any consultation.

The developing situation is one which increasingly suffers the worst of two worlds – a *de jure* system basically decentralised and founded on partnership which still engenders certain expectations, alongside a *de facto* system of growing centralisation and Whitehall control which provokes conflict and bitterness. Thus relations between the government and the local authorities have reached an all-time low since the 1983 election. The rate-capping legislation is seen by its victims as a deadly blow at the very basis of local democracy, restricting the time-honoured capacity of elected councils to decide the level of provision in their own areas – both for education and other services. They also object to the new education support grants which enable the central authority to siphon off one-half per cent of the Rate Support Grant for centrally determined purposes; here a principle is at stake, especially as the initial trifling percentage could be the thin edge of the wedge for the subsequent expansion of DES specific grants at the expense of locally determined spending. And special anger has been aroused amongst the LEAs by the government inspired MSC incursion into their operational territory – first through the TVEI (1983) and now through the projected MSC take-over of some 25% of non-advanced further education. Meanwhile, the Tory government has not gone out of its way to engage the friendship of the teacher associations either. Apart from presiding over a serious erosion of teachers' salaries and subjecting the profession to consumer accountability, it has abolished the Schools Council with its in-built teacher representation and replaced it with new bodies whose members are nominated by the Secretary of State. Consultation with the teacher associations is no longer accorded its prior importance and the NUT wields less influence upon national education policy than at any time since 1945.

The demographic factor, which inspired the savaging of the post-war system of teacher training in the 1970s, has increased the difficulties of the schools in recent years and continues to do so. It is estimated that by the close of the 1980s the school population of England and Wales will have declined by about one-fifth from the 1977 peak of nine million. Such falling rolls require the parallel contraction and redeployment of the teaching force, the reorganisation or closure of schools to maintain viable units and take some 40% of surplus places out of the system, and a conscious effort to safeguard the breadth and balance of the school curriculum. They also afford a prime justification for according education a lower priority than other claims upon public moneys. And, although it is acknowledged that falling rolls require the adoption of curriculum-led staffing policies by responsible LEAs, the government has not allowed for this in educational spending targets. Throughout the 1980s the demographic problem will act as an adverse influence upon job, pay and promotion prospects in both the schools and the teacher training sector.

Arising out of the depressing overall context is the most potentially damaging feature of all for the future of maintained schooling in England

and Wales. Teachers' morale has now reached such a low ebb that it poses a threat to professional commitment and performance. The expenditure White Paper proposes a further loss of some 20,000 teaching posts 1984–7 and, meanwhile, the whole profession continues to suffer a progressive erosion of its living standards. Ten years after the Houghton relativity award the teachers needed a 31% salary rise to recover the real income levels established in 1974. Initially offered a 3% increase they resorted to industrial action before having to accept a demoralising 5.1% arbitration award (1984); consequently they have slipped even further down the league table of pay for comparable occupations. And promotion opportunities are now so restricted that about 25% of teachers are trapped at the top of their pay scales. A further source of discouragement is their public image which has never really recovered from the bad press received in the mid-1970s; despite assurances from HM Inspectorate and other reliable sources, there is still the widespread belief that standards in many schools are unsatisfactory and must be improved. This helps to sustain the demand for more professional accountability and parental influence, for closer supervision of the school curriculum and examinations and for more stringency in the recruitment and promotion of staff. The insistent demand is for better teaching quality at no extra public expense. Yet effective teaching is often undermined by serious disciplinary problems fed by parental indifference, administrative compromise or muddle (e.g. over corporal punishment) and the disaffection of adolescent pupils faced by youth unemployment. And good teaching remains undervalued by a school system in which 'to get on is to get out' (of the classroom) into middle or senior school management, higher education, the LEA advisory service or educational administration.

However, to be fair, the situation is not altogether one of unrelieved gloom. In recent years there have been a number of positive developments and there are a few encouraging signs for the future. So far teaching posts have not been reduced in line with falling rolls and consequently the pupil-teacher ratio has improved to a record level of 18:1 (1984). Additionally there has been a marked improvement in the qualifications and calibre of entrants to teacher training, whilst the proportion of teachers with degrees continues to rise and currently exceeds two-fifths. Over 90% of eleven-plus pupils are now in comprehensive schools and a higher proportion of the relevant age group is passing external examinations at all levels than ever before; as interest in a return to eleven-plus selection seems to have waned (even amongst Conservative ranks) there may be a chance for consolidation without the distraction of a continuing controversy over secondary organisation. And within the comprehensive framework the gradual advance of the 11–16/Sixth Form or tertiary college pattern makes for greater economy and organisational sense. Meanwhile, on a widening front, there has been a sustained and on-going attempt to bring more order, relevance and efficiency to the State system of schooling; centred on the reform of school curricula and examinations and the raising of standards of teaching and learning in schools, this may bear some worthwhile educational fruit in the years ahead.

By the mid-1970s the child-centred rationale, the professional autonomy of teachers and the subject-based GCE and CSE examinations had combined to produce a diverse and confused curriculum which in many schools was insufficiently broad, balanced, relevant or differentiated. Whilst the primary curriculum was devoid of any agreed framework, the 11–16 secondary curriculum provided traditional liberal fare for all pupils by means of a developing system of wide-ranging subject options. Five years' work on the problem produced *The School Curriculum* (1981) which espoused a basically common curriculum throughout the years of compulsory schooling and engaged the LEAs to exercise control in accordance with the new guidelines. But beyond this, as if recognising that the need for relevance and motivation required more to be done, the government has made various other initiatives. The TVEI, now extended to involve over half of the LEAs, aims to provide 14–18 year old pupils with a wider range of alternative courses. And within the normal curriculum, especially at secondary level, the schools have been encouraged to give an important place to craft, design and technology (CDT) and to computer studies. Since 1980 the DES Microelectronics Education Programme has been developed 'to help schools prepare children for life in a society in which devices and systems based on microelectronics are commonplace and pervasive'; and the parallel Department of Industry's Micros in Schools scheme has now provided a micro-computer for three out of every four maintained schools. The Low Achievers Programme, a pilot scheme launched in 1982 and presently involving thirteen LEAs, is aimed at the bottom 40% of 11–16 secondary ability with a view to generating more interest and success for such pupils albeit on a narrower curricular front. The new CPVE and AS courses hold out the prospect of some belated change in the curricular fare offered to both less able and academic Sixth Formers. Although it is too early to assess or speculate upon the results of these various developments, they do constitute a real attempt to provide a more organised, functional and stimulating school curriculum.

In the field of secondary examinations the Thatcher government inherited a situation of considerable confusion and inertia. At least the last five years have seen some positive steps in a number of directions. In 1980 the common sixteen-plus examination idea was endorsed subject to the formulation of acceptable criteria for subject syllabuses and assessment procedures. This painstaking exercise for securing GCE 'O' level standards in any new arrangements was duly completed and now the Secretary of State has given his approval to the new GCSE. For less able pupils staying on at school the insufficiently functional CEE has been replaced by the new CPVE which is being developed by the City and Guilds of London Institute and the

Business and Technical Education Council for examinations at seventeen plus. There is even the longer-term prospect of the CPVE arrangements being further developed to provide a basis for a new functional curriculum and system of certification encompassing the TVEI and YTS courses as well. And, finally, for academic Sixth Formers the projected AS examinations offer the best hope yet of making real inroads upon the narrow tradition of specialised study in the Arts or Sciences.

Recently, and especially since Sir Keith Joseph became Secretary of State, the question of school standards has become a priority concern and the DES has mounted a wide-ranging and thorough tightening-up process aimed at their improvement. Clearly the reform of school curricula and examinations will play a major role in this process; indeed with the new sixteen-plus examination an attempt is to be made to shift away from relative towards absolute standards of assessment by means of more explicit grade descriptions. But many other initiatives are also being brought to bear. The 1980 Act committed the LEAs to a new school admissions procedures for strengthening parental choice and required all schools to publish information on matters such as their curriculum, internal organisation and examination results. From 1983 HM Inspectorate's reports on individual schools were openly published by the DES – another calculated move to keep schools on their toes. Recognising that external examinations afford only a narrow measure of a pupil's worth, the DES is encouraging the development of graded tests in core subjects and more broadly conceived records of achievement (including non-academic) for all pupils. Pilot LEA schemes for the shaping of a national system of pupil records of achievement are being initiated and funded by the DES from 1985. The White Paper on *Teaching Quality* (1983) also sought to raise school standards through improving the performance of teachers. All existing teacher training courses were to be reviewed against new criteria and modified as necessary. Such criteria covering the selection of trainees, the quality of academic content the professional aspects of training and final assessment procedures were quickly agreed by the DES and the Advisory Committee on the Supply and Education of Teachers; in 1984 a new nominated Council for the Accreditation of Teacher Education was formed to undertake the actual review over the next two to four years. Prospective outcomes include the strengthening of the academic side of many BEd courses, the extension of postgraduate training courses by six weeks and the much fuller involvement of practising teachers in trainee selection and teaching practice supervision. Additionally, the White Paper looked for a major improvement in the management of the teaching force. The LEAs were enjoined to tighten their arrangements for the appointment, probation, re-deployment and promotion of staff and to invoke dismissal procedures to deal with the small minority of incompetent teachers. Significantly, negotiations are under way for a major restructuring of teachers' salary scales, which the DES and LEAs hope will provide for an extended probationary period and a new professional grade involving teacher assessments to identify both those teachers deserving extra reward and those needing help or a way out. Finally, given the vital importance of good leadership to high standards in schools, inevitably the position of head-teachers has become subject to growing scrutiny and suggestion. Sir Keith Joseph has proposed that all first-time heads should face a two-year period of probation followed by regular LEA assessment throughout their subsequent career.

Whether the centrally-directed attempt to improve school curricula and examinations, teacher performance and educational standards will prove successful or beneficial is debateable. The central government needs to secure the full support of both the LEAs and the teachers for such designs; but it will not do so if their pursuance is associated with palpably inadequate funding and a cavalier attitude to educational partnership. If overdone, the promotion of a tight managerial regime based on written criteria, rules and regulations at the expense of long-standing informal working practices and professional freedoms is a double-edged strategy; it may produce too much subservience and can hardly inspire the sort of enthusiasm and initiative so crucial to good teaching. Whilst the phasing-out of the separate GCE 'O' level and CSE examinations will be generally welcomed, their tight-knit GCSE replacement will intensify the perennial danger of sixteen-plus examination demands dominating both the curriculum and pedagogy of the secondary schools. Whether the protection of academic standards is worth such a price will remain a matter of dispute – especially to those who argue in favour of freeing the schools completely from the thraldom of sixteen-plus examinations. Moreover, out of the on-going curricula and examination reforms there could emerge a new tertiary tripartism based upon sharply differentiated academic ('A' and 'AS') courses, TVEI courses and CPVE/YTS courses; such a development would have seriously restrictive implications for both educational and occupational opportunity. And too many reformist measures and initiatives, following hard one upon another, can have a most unsettling effect upon the schools and further deny them the stability and continuity they sorely need. The prospective attempt to assess the performance of teachers and heads for pay and promotion purposes or for weeding-out the incompetent also faces a veritable minefield of diffi-culties and dangers; even if some workable formula can be found and agreed, the financial carrot required to persuade the teacher associations to swallow this nasty pill would have to be singularly enticing. Appropriately this would confront the Conservative government with the fundamental question it prefers to brush aside – whether it is sufficiently concerned about the State system of schooling to provide the extra finances necessary for improvements to be made.

All things considered it would be unrealistic to view the immediate future of the State system of schooling with much optimism. Whilst there is a good case for central government trying to infuse the system with more order, relevance and efficiency, much more than this is required to ensure its future well-being. Firstly, the maintained system must be more generously funded to restore teachers' salaries to proper professional levels and to afford all State schools sufficient resources for their developing needs. Secondly, there must be a return to something approaching the real educational partnership between the central authority, the LEAs and the teachers which provided the basis for advance throughout the thirty years following the 1944 Act. To this mutually beneficial end the DES should moderate its centralist predilections, the LEAs should scrap their ineffectual joint Council (CLEA) in favour of a more potent collective mouthpiece and the teachers' associations should urgently seek to strengthen their professional voice by devising some permanent means of inter-union co-operation and understanding. Thirdly, there is a need for the sort of leadership — reminiscent of H.A.L. Fisher or R.A. Butler in calibre and spirit – which would unite and inspire the State educational service in the current quest for improvement; such leadership can only be provided by a Secretary of State who is perceived to have the interests of the service and its staff really at heart and who, when it comes to the crunch, is prepared stoutly to defend and champion its cause both within government circles and on the wider public stage. Unhappily these needs are not being fulfilled at the present time and there seems little hope of them being met in the foreseeable future.

Appendix – Education Ministers in their Political Context

Since the 1856 Act ministers responsible to central government and Parliament for grant-aided education in England and Wales have served under a number of different titles:

1856–1900   Vice-President of the Committee of Council for Education (i.e. government Head of Education Department)
1900–44   President of the Board of Education
1944–64   Minister of Education
1964–84   Secretary of State for Education and Science

Period	Prime Minister	Government	Education Minister	Period
1855–8	Lord Palmerston	Whig	W F Cowper	1857–8
1858–9	Lord Derby	Conservative	C B Adderley	1858–9
1859–65	Lord Palmerston	Whig	R Lowe	1859–64
1865–6	Lord Russell	Whig	H A Bruce	1864–6
1866–8	Lord Derby	Conservative	T L Corry	1866–7
1868	B Disraeli	Conservative	Lord Montagu	1867–8
1868–74	W Gladstone	Liberal	W E Forster	1868–74
1874–80	B Disraeli	Conservative	Viscount Sandon	1874–8
			Lord Hamilton	1878–80
1880–85	W Gladstone	Liberal	A J Mundella	1880–85
1885–6	Lord Salisbury	Conservative	E Stanhope	1885
			Sir H Holland	1885–6
1886	W Gladstone	Liberal	Sir L Playfair	1886
1886–92	Lord Salisbury	Conservative	Sir H Holland	1886–7
			Sir W Hart Dyke	1887–92
1892–4	W Gladstone	Liberal	A H Acland	1892–5
1894–5	Lord Rosebery	Liberal		
1895–1902	Lord Salisbury	Conservative	Sir J E Gorst	1895–1900
			Duke of Devonshire	1900–2
1902–05	A Balfour	Conservative	Marquess of Londonderry	1902–5

1906–8	Sir H Campbell-Bannermann	Liberal	A Birrell	1906–7
			R McKenna	1907–8
1908–15	H Asquith	Liberal	W Runciman	1908–11
			J A Pease	1911–15
1915–16	H Asquith	Coalition (L)	A Henderson	1915–16
			Lord Crewe	1916
1916–18	D Lloyd George	Coalition (L)	H A L Fisher	1916–22
1918–22	D Lloyd George	Coalition (C)		
1922–3	A Bonar Law	Conservative	E F Wood*	1922–4
1923–4	S Baldwin	Conservative		
1924	R MacDonald	Labour	C P Trevelyan	1924
1924–9	S Baldwin	Conservative	Lord Percy	1924–9
1929–31	R MacDonald	Labour	Sir C P Trevelyan	1929–31
			H B Lees-Smith	1931
1931–5	R MacDonald	National (C)	Sir D Maclean	1931–2
			Lord Irwin*	1932–5
1935–7	S Baldwin	Conservative	O Stanley	1935–7
1937–40	N Chamberlain	Conservative	Earl Stanhope	1937–8
			Earl de la Warr	1938–40
1940–45	W Churchill	Coalition (C)	H Ramsbotham	1940–41
			R A Butler	1941–5
			R Law	1945
1945–51	C Attlee	Labour	Ellen Wilkinson	1945–7
			G Tomlinson	1947–51
1951–5	W Churchill	Conservative	Florence Horsbrugh	1951–4
1955–7	Sir A Eden	Conservative	Sir D Eccles	1954–7
1957–63	H Macmillan	Conservative	Viscount Hailsham	1957
			G Lloyd	1957–9
			Sir D Eccles	1959–62
1963–4	Sir A Douglas-Home	Conservative	Sir E Boyle	1962–4
			Viscount Hailsham	1964
1964–70	H Wilson	Labour	M Stewart	1964–5
			A Crosland	1965–7
			P Gordon-Walker	1967–8
			E Short	1968–70
1970–74	E Heath	Conservative	Margaret Thatcher	1970–74
1974–6	H Wilson	Labour	R Prentice	1974–5
			F Mulley	1975–6
1976–9	J Callaghan	Labour	Shirley Williams	1976–9
1979–84	Margaret Thatcher	Conservative	M Carlisle	1979–81
			Sir K Joseph	1981–4

(L) = Liberal dominated Coalition   (C) = Conservative dominated Coalition
* became Viscount Halifax in 1933

Summary of Balance of Political Power at Westminster 1868–1984
(a) 1868–1915 (47 years)
      Conservative or Conservative-dominated government = 23 years
      Liberal or Liberal-dominated government = 24 years
(b) 1915–45 (30 years)
      Conservative or Conservative-dominated government = 24 years
      Liberal or Liberal-dominated government = 3 years
      Labour or Labour-dominated government = 3 years
(c) 1945–84 (39 years)
      Conservative or Conservative-dominated government = 22 years
      Labour or Labour-dominated government = 17 years

Bibliography

General Texts

BARKER, R. (1972) *Education and Politics: a study of the Labour Party.* Oxford: Clarendon Press.

BARNARD, H.C. (1961) *A History of English Education from 1760.* London: University of London Press Ltd.

CRUICKSHANK, M. (1963) *Church and State in English Education: 1870 to the Present Day.* London: Macmillan.

CURTIS, S.J. (1967) *History of Education in Great Britain.* (7th edn) London: University Tutorial Press.

DENT, H.C. (1970) *1870–1970 Century of Growth in English Education.* London: Longman.

EAGLESHAM, E.J.R. (1967) *The Foundations of Twentieth-Century Education in England.* London: Routledge and Kegan Paul.

LAWSON, J. and SILVER, H. (1973) *A Social History of Education in England.* London: Methuen.

LOWNDES, G.A.N. (1969) *The Silent Social Revolution.* (2nd edn) London: Oxford University Press.

MURPHY, J. (1971) *Church, State and Schools in Britain, 1800–1970.* London: Routledge and Kegan Paul.

MUSGRAVE, P.W. (1968) *Society and Education in England since 1800.* London: Methuen.

RICHMOND, W.K. (1978) *Education in Britain since 1944: a personal retrospect.* London: Methuen.

SIMON, B. (1960) *The Two Nations and the Educational Structure 1780–1870;* (1965) *Education and the Labour Movement 1870–1918;* (1974) *The Politics of Educational Reform 1920–1940.* London: Lawrence and Wishart trilogy.

SIMON, B. and TAYLOR, W. (eds) (1981) *Education in the Eighties – The Central Issues.* London: Batsford.

WARDLE, D. (1970) *English Popular Education 1780–1970*. London: Cambridge University Press.

DES (1970) *Trends in Education* (1870 Centenary Issue). London: HMSO.

Texts Supplying Documentary and Contemporary Sources

GOSDEN, P.H.J.H. (1969) *How They Were Taught*. Oxford: Blackwell.

HYNDMAN, M. (1978) *Schools and Schooling in England and Wales: A Documentary History*. London: Harper and Row.

MACLURE, J.S. (1979) *Educational Documents: England and Wales 1816 to the Present Day*. London: Methuen.

VAN DER EYKEN, W. (1973) *Education, the Child and Society*. Harmondsworth: Penguin.

Elementary and Primary Education

BENNETT, N. et al. (1976) *Teaching Styles and Pupil Progress*. London: Open Books.

BIRCHENOUGH, C. (1938) *History of Elementary Education in England and Wales from 1800 to the Present Day*. (3rd edn) London: University Tutorial Press.

BURGESS, H.J. (1958) *Enterprise in Education: the work of the Established Church in the education of the people prior to 1870*. London: SPCK.

HORN, P. (1978) *Education in Rural England 1800–1914*. Dublin: Gill and Macmillan.

HURT, J. (1971) *Education in Evolution: Church, State, Society and Popular Education 1800–1870*. London: Hart-Davis.

HURT, J. (1979) *Elementary Schooling and the Working Classes, 1860–1918*. London: Routledge and Kegan Paul.

McCANN, P. (ed) (1977) *Popular Education and Socialization in the Nineteenth Century*. London: Methuen.

PLUCKROSE, H. (1979) *Children in their Primary Schools*. Harmondsworth: Penguin.

SELLECK, R.J.W. (1972) *English Primary Education and the Progressives 1914–1939*. London: Routledge and Kegan Paul.

SMITH, F. (1931) *A History of English Elementary Education 1760–1902*. London: University of London Press Ltd.

STURT, M. (1967) *The Education of the People*. London: Routledge and Kegan Paul.

SUTHERLAND, G. (1971) *Elementary Education in the Nineteenth Century*.

London: Historical Association.

SYLVESTER, D.W. (1974) *Robert Lowe and Education.* London: Cambridge University Press.

WHITBREAD, N. (1972) *The Evolution of the Nursery-Infant School.* London: Routledge and Kegan Paul.

Secondary Education

ARCHER, R.L. (1966) *Secondary Education in the Nineteenth Century.* (2nd edn) London: Cass.

BAMFORD, T.W. (1967) *The Rise of the Public Schools.* London: Nelson.

BANKS, O. (1955) *Parity and Prestige in English Secondary Education.* London: Routledge and Kegan Paul.

BERNBAUM, G. (1967) *Social Change and the Schools 1918-1944.* London: Routledge and Kegan Paul.

DAVIS, R. (1967) *The Grammar School.* Harmondsworth: Penguin.

EDWARDS, A.D. (1970) *The Changing Sixth Form in the Twentieth Century.* London: Routledge and Kegan Paul.

EDWARDS, R. (1960) *The Secondary Technical School.* London: University of London Press Ltd.

FENWICK, I.G.K. (1976) *The Comprehensive School 1944-1970.* London: Methuen.

GRIFFITHS, A. (1971) *Secondary School Reorganisation in England and Wales.* London: Routledge and Kegan Paul.

KAZAMIAS, A.M. (1966) *Politics, Society and Secondary Education in England.* Philadelphia: University of Pennsylvania Press.

PARKINSON, M. (1970) *The Labour Party and the Organisation of Secondary Education 1918-65.* London: Routledge and Kegan Paul.

PEDLEY, R. (1978) *The Comprehensive School.* (3rd edn) Harmondsworth: Penguin.

RUBINSTEIN, D. and SIMON, B. (1969) *The Evolution of the Comprehensive School 1926-66.* London: Routledge and Kegan Paul.

TAWNEY, R.H. (1922) *Secondary Education for All.* London: Labour Party; Allen and Unwin.

TAYLOR, W. (1963) *The Secondary Modern School.* London: Faber and Faber.

Schools' Curricula and Examinations

GORDON, P. and LAWTON, D. (1978) *Curriculum Change in the Nineteenth and Twentieth Centuries.* London: Hodder and Stoughton.

JEFFREY, C.B. (1958) *External Examinations in Secondary Schools*. London: Harrap.

KELLY, A.V. and BLENKIN, G. (1981) *The Primary Curriculum*. London: Harper and Row.

LAWTON, D. (1973) *Social Change, Educational Theory and Curriculum Planning*. London: University of London Press Ltd.

MONTGOMERY, R.J. (1965) *Examinations: an account of their evolution as administrative devices in England*. London: Longman.

PEARCE, J. (1972) *School Examinations*. London: Collier-Macmillan.

SCHOOLS COUNCIL (1975) *The First Ten Years 1964–74*. Bath: Mendip Press.

Special Education and Welfare Services

CLARK, F. LE G. (1948) *Social History of the School Meals Service* London: National Council of Social Service.

HENDERSON, P. (1975) *The School Health Service 1908–74*. London: DES.

JACKSON, S. (1966) *Special Education in England and Wales*. London: Oxford University Press.

LEFF, S. and V. (1959) *The School Health Service*. London: H.K. Lewis.

PRITCHARD, D.G. (1963) *Education of the Handicapped 1760–1960*. London: Routledge and Kegan Paul.

Teacher Training and the Teaching Profession

BROWNE, J.D. (1979) *Teachers of Teachers: a history of the Association of Teachers in Colleges and Departments of Education*. London: Hodder and Stoughton.

DENT, H.C. (1977) *The Training of Teachers in England and Wales 1800–1975*. London: Hodder and Stoughton.

HENCKE, D. (1978) *Colleges in Crisis: the Reorganisation of Teacher Training 1971–77*. Harmondsworth: Penguin.

GOSDEN, P.H.J.H. (1972) *The Evolution of a Profession*. Oxford: Blackwell.

NIBLETT, W.R., HUMPHREYS, D.W., and FAIRHURST, J.R. (1975) *The University Connection 1923–73*. London: NFER.

RICH, R.W. (1933) *The Training of Teachers in England and Wales during the Nineteenth Century*. London: Cambridge University Press.

TROPP, A. (1957) *The School Teachers*. London: Heinemann.

Educational System, Government and Administration

BARRELL, G.R. (1979) *Teachers and the Law*. (5th edn) London: Methuen.

BIRLEY, D. (1970) *The Education Officer and his World*. London: Routledge and Kegan Paul.

BISHOP, A.S. (1971) *The Rise of a Central Authority for English Education*. London: Cambridge University Press.

BLACKIE, J. (1970) *Inspecting and the Inspectorate*. London: Routledge and Kegan Paul.

BROOKSBANK, K. and ACKSTINE, A.E. (eds) (1984) *Educational Administration*. (2nd edn) Harlow: Longman.

DENT, H.C. (1977) *Education in England and Wales*. (2nd edn) London: Hodder and Stoughton.

FENWICK, K. and McBRIDE, P. (1981) *The Government of Education*. Oxford: Robertson.

GOSDEN, P.H.J.H. (1966) *The Development of Educational Administration in England and Wales*. Oxford: Blackwell.

KOGAN, M. and PACKWOOD, T. (1974) *Advisory Councils and Committees in Education*. London: Routledge and Kegan Paul.

LAWRENCE, B. (1972) *The Administration of Education in Britain*. London: Batsford.

PILE, Sir WILLIAM. (1979) *The Department of Education and Science*. London: Allen and Unwin.

REGAN, D.E. (1977) *Local Government and Education*. London: Allen and Unwin.

Other Texts

ALLEN, B.M. (1934) *Sir Robert Morant*. London: Macmillan.

BRYANT, M. (1979) *The Unexpected Regolution. A Study in the History of thi Ecucation of Women and Girls in the Nineteenth Century*. London: University of London Institute of Education.

CORBETT, A. (1978) *Much to do about Education*. (4th edn) London: Council for Educational Advance/Macmillan.

JUDGES, A.V. (1952) *Pioneers of English Education*. London: Faber and Faber.

KAMM, J. (1965) *Hope Deferred: Girls' Education in English History*. London: Methuen.

LEESE, J. (1950) *Personalities and Power in English Education*. Leeds: Arnold.

ROGERS, R. (1980) *Crowther to Warnock*. London: Heinemann.

SMITH, F. (1923) *The Life and Work of Sir James Kay-Shuttleworth*. London: Murray.

Official Sources

BOARD OF EDUCATION publications. London: HMSO.

(1925) Report of (Burnham) Departmental Committee on *The Training of Teachers for Public Elementary Schools.*

(1926) Report of (Hadow) Consultative Committee on *The Education of the Adolescent.*

(1931) Report of (Hadow) Consultative Committee on *The Primary School.*

(1933) Report of (Hadow) Consultative Committee on *Infant and Nursery Schools.*

(1938) Report of (Spens) Consultative Committee on *Secondary Education with special reference to Grammar Schools and Technical High Schools.*

(1943) Report of (Norwood) Committee of Secondary School Examinations Council on *Curricula and Examinations in Secondary Schools.*

(1944) Report of (McNair) Departmental Committee on *Teachers and Youth Leaders.*

MINISTRY OF EDUCATION publications. London: HMSO.

(1959) Report of (Crowther) Central Advisory Council on *15 to 18*

(1960) Report of (Beloe) Committee of Secondary School Examinations Council on *Secondary School Examinations other than GCE.*

(1963) Report of (Newsom) Central Advisory Council on *Half Our Future.*

DEPARTMENT OF EDUCATION AND SCIENCE publications. London: HMSO.

(1965) Circular 10/65 on *The Organisation of Secondary Education.*

(1967) Report of (Plowden) Central Advisory Council on *Children and their Primary Schools.*

(1972) Report of (James) Committee on *Teacher Education and Training.*

(1972) White Paper on *Education: A Framework for Expansion.*

(1973) Circular 7/73 on *The Development of Higher Education in the Non-University Sector.*

(1975) Report of (Bullock) Committee on *A Language for Life.*

(1977) Report of (Taylor) Committee on *A New Partnership for our Schools.*

(1978) Report of (Warnock) Committee on *Special Educational Needs.*

(1978* Report of (Waddell) Committee on *School Examinations.*

(1982) Report of (Cockcroft) Committee on *Mathematics Counts.*

(1983) White Paper on *Teaching Quality.*

DES Booklets/Pamphlets

   (1983) *The educational system in England and Wales.*
   (1983) *The Department of Education and Science – a brief guide.*
   (1983) *The Work of HM Inspectorate in England and Wales.*
   (1983) *HM Inspectors today: Standards in Education.*

DES Reports on Education. Issued at frequent but irregular intervals, these are very concise and highly instructive. Strongly recommended are the following:

   No. 16 *Health at School* (November 1964)
      23 *Special Education Today* (July 1965)
      29 *The Schools Council* (February 1966)
      31 *The Local Education Authorities* (October 1966)
      37 *Her Majesty's Inspectorate* (June 1967)
      47 *The Certificate of Secondary Education* (June 1968)
      49 *Colleges of Education* (October 1968)
      61 *Health at School* (February 1970)
      72 *Raising the School Leaving Age* (September 1971)
      77 *Special Education: A Fresh Look* (April 1973)
      81 *Nursery Education* (January 1975)
      87 *The Growth of Comprehensive Education* (March 1977)
      92 *School Population in the 1980s* (June 1978)
      98 *Teacher Numbers – Looking Ahead to 1995* (March 1983)

DES *Statistics on Education:* published annually, they cover England and Wales *combined* until 1977 and England and Wales *separately* thereafter.

   (1963) Report of special Robbins Committee on *Higher Education*. London: HMSO.

Index